Ethics in Youth Sport

The influence of professional, adult sport on youth sport is now a global concern. Children are involved in high-stakes competitive sport at national and international levels at an increasingly young age. In addition, the use of sport as a medium for positive youth development by governments and within the community has fuelled ambitious targets for young people's participation in sport at all levels. In this important study of ethical issues in and around youth sport, leading international experts argue for the development of strong ethical codes for the conduct of youth sport, and for effective policy and pedagogical applications to ensure that the positive benefits of sport are optimized and the negative aspects diminished.

At the heart of the discussion are the prevailing standards and expectations of youth sport in developed societies, typically consisting of the development of motor competence, the development of a safe and healthy lifestyle and competitive style, and the development of a positive self-image and good relationship skills. The book examines the recommendations emerging from the Panathlon Declaration and the debates that have followed, and covers a wide range of key ethical issues, including:

- emotional and physical abuse
- aggression and violence
- doping and cheating
- values and norms
- teaching and coaching
- integrity management.

Ethics in Youth Sport is focused on the application of ethical policy and pedagogies and is grounded in practice. It assumes no prior ethical training on the part of the reader and is essential reading for all students, researchers, policy makers and professionals working with children and young people in sport across school, community and professional settings.

Stephen Harvey is Senior Lecturer in Physical Education and Sport Studies at the University of Bedfordshire, UK.

Richard L. Light is Professorial Research Fellow in the School of Health Sciences at the University of Ballarat, Australia.

Routledge studies in physical education and youth sport
Series Editor: David Kirk, University of Bedfordshire, UK

The *Routledge Studies in Physical Education and Youth Sport* series is a forum for the discussion of the latest and most important ideas and issues in physical education, sport and active leisure for young people across school, club and recreational settings. The series presents the work of the best well-established and emerging scholars from around the world, offering a truly international perspective on policy and practice. It aims to enhance our understanding of key challenges, to inform academic debate, and to have a high impact on both policy and practice, and is thus an essential resource for all serious students of physical education and youth sport.

Also available in this series

Ethics in Youth Sport

Policy and pedagogical applications

**Edited by
Stephen Harvey and
Richard L. Light**

Routledge
Taylor & Francis Group

LONDON AND NEW YORK

First published 2013
by Routledge
2 Park Square, Milton Park, Abingdon, Oxon OX14 4RN

Simultaneously published in the USA and Canada
by Routledge
711 Third Avenue, New York, NY 10017

Routledge is an imprint of the Taylor & Francis Group, an informa business

British Library Cataloguing in Publication Data
A catalogue record for this book is available from the British Library

Library of Congress Cataloging in Publication Data
Ethics in youth sport : policy and pedagogical applications / edited by
Stephen Harvey and Richard Light.
p. cm. -- (Routledge studies in physical education and youth sport)
Includes bibliographical references and index.
1. Sports for children--Moral and ethical aspects. 2. Sports--Moral and
ethical aspects. I. Harvey, Stephen, 1973- II. Light, Richard, 1951-
GV709.2.E85 2012
796.083--dc23
2012007402

ISBN: 978-0-415-67903-9 (hbk)
ISBN: 978-0-203-80692-0 (ebk)

Typeset in Times
by Taylor & Francis Books

Contents

Illustrations

Figures

Tables

Contributors

Dean M. Barker is a senior lecturer at the Institute of Food and Nutrition, and Health Sciences at the University of Gothenburg, Sweden. He is interested in many pedagogical facets of physical education and has examined the topics of socio-moral teaching and learning, and cultural difference.

Natalie Barker-Ruchti is a senior lecturer at the Institute of Food and Nutrition, and Health Sciences at the University of Gothenburg. She has focused on various aspects of sports coaching using post-structural and feminist theory. She is currently examining learning in elite athletic settings with Olympic athletes from different sports.

Michael D. Burroughs is a PhD candidate in the Department of Philosophy at the University of Memphis, USA. Michael is a dedicated teacher and co-founder of Philosophical Horizons, a philosophy for children program in Memphis. His philosophical interests include ethics, social/political philosophy and social ontology.

Tania Cassidy is a senior lecturer in pedagogy in the School of Physical Education at the University of Otago, Dunedin, New Zealand. She is the lead author of *Understanding Sports Coaching* (Routledge) and is on the editorial board of six international journals that publish research in sports coaching.

Steve Cobley (CPsychol) is a senior lecturer in skill acquisition and sport psychology within the Faculty of Health Sciences at the University of Sydney (Australia). His research interests examine developmental factors that constrain learning and performance. Steve lectures across undergraduate and postgraduate provision associated with sports science, coaching and physical education.

Joke De Bouw is a researcher at the Faculty of Physical Education and Physiotherapy, Vrije Universiteit Brussel (VUB, Belgium). Joke is also a teacher at secondary school and is engaged as an athlete and youth coach in volleyball. In 2011 she carried out a research project to test and compare two teaching methods (deductive and inductive) in a course on fair play and integrity in sport in the educational programme of youth sport coaches.

Hayley Fitzgerald is a senior lecturer at Leeds Metropolitan University, UK. Prior to this she was a researcher at Loughborough University and managed a range of projects supporting young disabled people in physical education and youth sport. Hayley has also worked for a number of disability sport organizations in England.

Stephen Harvey is a senior lecturer in physical education and sport at the University of Bedfordshire, England. Prior to working in higher education, Stephen worked as a physical education teacher and as a further education lecturer. He has extensive experience of pedagogical models via his work as a teacher, sports coach and academic researcher.

Jeanne Adèle Kentel has taught in primary, secondary and teacher education programmes in Canada and England. She completed her doctorate in curriculum studies at the University of Alberta, Canada. Her research covers a broad spectrum of areas of critical pedagogy including gender, marginalization in sport and education, culturally relevant physical education, ontological and technological relationships, ecological education, movement literacy and bodily ways of knowing. Jeanne is a singer and songwriter and has a passion for dance.

Gretchen Kerr is a professor and associate dean in the Faculty of Physical Education and Kinesiology at the University of Toronto. Gretchen serves as a harassment officer for Gymnastics Ontario and Gymnastics Canada, and has a wealth of teaching and research experience in child development and athlete-centred sport.

David Kirk is the Alexander Chair in physical education and sport at the University of Bedfordshire, England. He has published widely in physical education and curriculum change, and on youth sport. His interests lie in the social construction of physical education and sustainable curriculum renewal in physical education through models-based practice.

Richard L. Light is professorial research fellow at the University of Ballarat, Australia and was previously director of the Carnegie Research Institute in the UK. His programme of research focuses on the socio-cultural dimensions of sport and physical education pedagogy and he is widely published in this area. He is author of the book, *Game Sense: Pedagogy for Performance, Participation and Enjoyment*, published by Routledge in 2012.

Steffie Lucidarme is a doctoral researcher and assistant in the Department of Movement and Sport Sciences at Ghent University, Belgium. Her research interests include sports policy, performance management and inter-organizational relationships. She has also experience as a sports administrator and sports coach.

Jeroen Maesschalck studied public administration and philosophy at the University of Ghent (Belgium), the London School of Economics (UK) and the Katholieke Universiteit Leuven (Belgium). He is currently associate professor at the Katholieke Universiteit Leuven, where he is the director of the Leuven Institute of Criminology. He is also research fellow at the Free University of Amsterdam.

Kristine De Martelaer is an assistant professor at the Faculty of Physical Education and Physiotherapy, Vrije Universiteit Brussel (VUB, Belgium) where she is head of the Department of Movement Education and Sports Training. She currently teaches sport history and philosophy, didactics, curriculum PE and basic life support. Her research is situated within pedagogy: experiences and expectations of children and teachers/coaches with PE, youth sport and play, job profile and competences of PE teachers and PE/youth coaches and ethics in (youth) sport. She is president of the International Centre for Ethics in Sport (ICES).

Paul Miller is currently a PhD student within the Carnegie Faculty at Leeds Metropolitan University (UK). Prior to this, Paul worked as an HR manager and has returned to academia to examine issues related to the social construction of talent within sport and education.

Jim McKenna is professor of physical activity and health in the Carnegie Faculty at Leeds Metropolitan University, England. His background in research emphasizes community interventions to encourage physical activity. Jim also has extensive experience of theoretical frameworks through his work as a teacher, academic mentor and sports coach.

Toni M. O'Donovan is a senior lecturer with the University of Bedfordshire, England. Her research interests are in the area of pedagogy in physical education, focusing particularly on models-based practice.

Jim Parry is former head of the Philosophy Department and head of the School of Humanities at the University of Leeds. He is now visiting professor of philosophy at the Faculty of Physical Education and Sport, Charles University in Prague, and Visiting Professor of Olympic Studies 2012, Gresham College, London.

Uwe Pühse is head of the Institute of Exercise and Health Sciences at Basel University, Switzerland. He has published extensively on the topic of social learning in sport and physical education, and has led international comparison projects. Recently he has turned his attention to health benefits of participation in sport.

Ashley Stirling completed her PhD at the University of Toronto. She has conducted several research projects on maltreatment in sport and strategies for athlete protection. In 2007, Ashley received the AASP Thesis Award, and in 2009 was awarded the ECSS Young Investigator Award.

Katrien Struyven is an assistant professor at the Vrije Universiteit Brussel (VUB, Belgium) at the Educational Sciences Department. She teaches different courses in the domain of learning and instruction in the Masters of educational science and the academic teacher training programme. Starting her career as a PhD student in 2001, she successfully completed her doctoral degree on the topic of 'the effects of student-activating teaching/learning environments on student teachers' learning' in May 2005. Her research interests lie within the field of learning, instruction and assessment in higher and teacher education.

Kevin Till is an associate researcher with the Carnegie Faculty at Leeds Metropolitan University (UK). Kevin's research interests focus upon talent identification, selection and development. Kevin is also a strength and conditioning coach within professional Rugby League.

Deborah P. Tollefsen is an associate professor and chair of the Philosophy Department at the University of Memphis, USA. Her research and teaching interests include social and feminist epistemology, philosophy of mind and psychology, and philosophy of education. Deborah teaches in Philosophical Horizons, a philosophy for children program in Memphis.

Yves Vanden Auweele is professor (Em.) of sport psychology at the Katholieke Universiteit Leuven (Belgium). He was coordinator of the European Masters Programme for exercise and sport psychology and member of the managing council of the European Federation of Sport Psychology. He was senior author of the Panathlon Declaration on Ethics in Youth Sport.

Nicolette Schipper-Van Veldhoven is programme manager of research at the Netherlands Olympic Committee*Netherlands Sports Confederation (NOC*NSF). Prior to this, Nicolette worked as a physical education teacher and associate professor. She is a research adviser on sexual harassment and abuse and sports pedagogy. She has extensive experience of physical exercise programmes for children with special needs.

Paul M. Wright is an associate professor in the Department of Kinesiology and Physical Education at Northern Illinois University, USA. Paul has worked extensively in designing, delivering and evaluating physical activity programs for underserved youth. The primary focus of his scholarship is the Teaching Personal and Social Responsibility model.

Introduction

Richard L. Light and Stephen Harvey

Sport as we know it today finds its origins in nineteenth-century schools of the middle classes of England, where it was explicitly articulated as a medium for the socio-moral development of the future leaders of society (Mangan 1981). Despite massive social and economic changes since then, the idea of using sport as a means of developing 'character' and other positive social learning, such as learning to work in a team, has formed an enduring justification for the provision of sport for young people in schools and in sports clubs, in both western and non-western settings (see, for example, Sherington 1983; Light 2000). Despite a more recent and popular view of sport as a useful means of combating lifestyle diseases such as obesity (see, for example, Gard and Wright 2009), and growing awareness of how children's and youth sport can be corrupted by the influence of elite-level professional sport, assumptions about positive socio-moral learning occurring for young people through playing sport have proven to be remarkably resilient (see, for example, Holt 2009).

Over the past two decades there has been rapid development in the provision of sport for children as young as 5 years of age in most economically developed countries, but not without concern about the influence this has on their moral, social and physical development. First noted in the United States (Martens 1982), the influence of professional, adult sport on youth sport is now widely recognized as a global problem. In addition to the growth of adult-organized grassroots programmes in youth sport across a wide range of sports, high-stakes competitive youth sport played at national and international levels is now an increasingly frequent occurrence. This is evidenced, most dramatically, by the staging of the inaugural Youth Olympic Games (YOG) in Singapore in 2010, with 3500 athletes aged between 14 and 18, from 205 countries competing in the same 26 sports that are on the programme for the 2012 London Olympics. In 2012 the winter version will be staged, with both summer and winter YOGs to be conducted on four-year cycles, as is done with the Olympic Games.

McIntyre's concept of sport having internal and external 'goods' is useful here for identifying how elite-level, professional sport can impinge upon the social, moral and ethical learning that can result from young people's engagement in sport and the problems that can arise from high-stakes versions of youth sport. As Harvey, Kirk and O'Donovan explain in Chapter 7,

McIntyre sees internal goods as being unique to the practice of sport, and can only be gained through 'wholehearted' participation. Using basketball as an example, this means that to acquire internal goods such as not only the skills and tactics learnt, but also the understandings of etiquette, and of the rules and traditions of basketball such as respect for opponents, a player must be immersed in its practice. A professional basketball player can also gain external goods such as money, fame and prestige from the sport but these external goods are not unique to basketball in the way that the skills, strategies, knowledge of traditions and cultural knowledge of it are.

As Harvey *et al.* point out in Chapter 7, the pursuit of external goods is most obvious in professional sport, but becomes a problem when the desire for external goods outweighs the pursuit of internal goods. When this happens, sport as an ethical practice is invariably corrupted through practices such as cheating and the use of illegal drugs as a means of gaining a performance advantage in the quest for external goods. If the pursuit of external goods becomes paramount over the internal goods of a sport, Harvey *et al.* suggest, in the long run sport can become unsustainable as a practice. The emphasis on external goods in professional sport, as represented in the media, and the media's role in actually creating them or enhancing their value, impacts upon the practice of youth sport, where internal goods should be emphasized in the pursuit of realizing sport's capacity to engender a range of positive and lasting learning and development.

Moreover, governments seeking to combat a range of perceived social ills, such as alienation and delinquency among young people, have identified sport as a mechanism for promoting and fostering positive youth development. In the UK, for example, the nurturing of good citizens is one of three major goals of the Physical Education and Sport Strategy for Young People, funded by millions of pounds of public money, with the other two goals being the production of successful international sports teams and the erasure of obesity. Such government interest in youth sport has fuelled ambitious targets for young people's participation in sport at all levels in the UK and many other countries. All of these developments suggest that, in the early twenty-first century, sport is becoming an increasingly important aspect of youth culture (Green *et al.* 2005). They also suggest that the meanings made of sport, and the influence it has on the development of young people as they move into the adult world, is far more complex and full of tensions and contradictions than it was in the late nineteenth-century schools of England.

Drawing on the concept of a social field used by French sociologist, Pierre Bourdieu (see, for example, Bourdieu 1986), the field of sport with its emphasis on playing for the sake of the game and the use of sport for young people as a medium for positive social learning is now profoundly changed by the influence of the field of commercial, commodified sport that has emerged from the intrusion of the business field into the field of sport, with its very different values (Webb *et al.* 2002). These developments suggest that there is a significant threat to the enduring ideals of sport as a medium for positive moral and social development and the capacity for children's and youth sport to deliver this learning. There is also concern with an associated range of worrying ethical issues such as physical abuse (including overtraining), emotional and sexual abuse (see for example Stirling and Kerr 2007), practices that are harmful to young people's immediate and long-term health, gender inequity and inequality of opportunity to participate or compete fairly due to disability or unfair age groupings, all of which are dealt with in this book. Within this context we suggest that there is a *prima facie* case for the development of strong ethical codes for the conduct of youth sport, and for policy and pedagogical applications of these codes to ensure that the positive moral, social and physical benefits of participation in sport for young people are optimized and the negative influences diminished.

We recognize the challenges involved with this task due to the deeply situated nature of sport and the ways in which it is influenced by larger and very powerful economic and social forces shaping how, and what, young people learn in and through engagement in sport as both participants in sport and consumers of it. As Cook and Cole (2001) remind us, the impact of children's participation in sport does not end with the referee's whistle and nor is it neatly bounded by the sidelines of the playing field. The 'play frame' within which youth sport is practised is permeable and extends well beyond the players, the game and the community built around it (Cook and Cole 2001: 227). Commercial, professional and highly competitive sport can, and does, therefore, impact powerfully on children's behaviour, and their moral and social development. This occurs in both explicit and easily identifiable ways and in implicit ways that are often difficult to identify yet so significant *because* they are implicit. For example, while children may criticize violence in sport within the media they can unknowingly enact the very same behaviour that they condemn in their own games (Light 2008).

There is, however, much that those involved in sport – from policy makers, National Governing Bodies and the International Olympic Committee (IOC) to coaches, teachers and parents – can do. Indeed, there is a pressing need for these concerns to be addressed but, apart from the initiative of the Panathlon organization, there is little evidence of any systematic, organized activity in this area of significant need. On its website Panathlon describes itself as a non-government, non-profit-making, non-political association, of all Panathlon Clubs, juridically recognized by the Italian Government and by the IOC, and a member of the General Association of International Sports Federations (GAISF) and of the International Committee for Fair Play (CIFP). The word Panathlon is of Greek origin with *pan* meaning all and *athlon* meaning sport; all sports. In November 2008, Panathlon ran a conference in Ghent, Belgium, to consider expert opinion on how the Panathlon Declaration on Ethics in Youth Sport, written and approved in September 2004 and subsequently endorsed by the IOC and many other sports and public organizations, might best be implemented. Some of the presentations made at the Ghent 2008 conference, further elaborated by their authors, form the basis of this book, centred on approaches to ethics in youth sport and policy applications. They are supplemented by additional chapters, particularly on the pedagogical applications of ethical approaches to youth sport, from scholars across the globe, to provide an international perspective on a profoundly important issue for youth sport.

The book

Ethics in Youth Sport: Policy and Pedagogical Applications highlights particular applications of policy and pedagogies associated with youth sport ethics, grounded in practice. It identifies and engages in debate on ethical issues in youth sport, aimed at assisting with optimizing the positive benefits of participation on sport for youth while contributing toward diminishing the negative aspects. The policies and pedagogies elaborated on and discussed in this book have a wide-ranging application to many sports and to both school and community sport contexts. The focus of the book on policy and pedagogical applications is action-oriented (philosophy-in-action) and aimed at readers interested in, or working with sport and leisure from an applied perspective. Following on from the Panathlon Declaration (2004) and the ensuing conference in Ghent (in 2008), this book draws on contributions from researchers in Europe, the UK, North America, Australia and New Zealand to debate and take forward the ideas and spirit of the Panathlon Declaration as applied to the practice of youth sport. In doing so we aim to sustain and develop approaches to organizing and managing the practice of youth sport in school and community settings across the globe.

In Chapter 1 Maesschalck and Vanden Auweele draw from public administration and business ethics to propose recommendations on how to avoid the 'implementation deficit' in youth sport, in reference to the fact that, despite there being many good intentions and plans in place, none seem to make a difference on the ground. They focus on 'integrity management', arguing that to be effective in youth sport it needs to consist of three pillars. These are: (1) instruments that, together, perform the four functions of integrity management, which are determining and defining, guiding, monitoring and enforcing; (2) processes to keep those instruments alive; and (3) structures to ensure that the work is actually done by focusing on both managers and 'integrity actors'.

Kerr and Stirling follow on from discussions on policy and implementation strategies to examine the ways in which young athletes' talents and interests may be nurtured in a developmentally appropriate manner. They begin by providing a review of the historical changes in society's views of children and child development. Their review of the sport science research then provides evidence to suggest several positive outcomes of children's participation in sport, while also identifying the potential for negative outcomes when sport programmes are not delivered in a developmentally appropriate manner. Using Erikson's psychosocial theory of child development they propose considerations for the design and delivery of a developmentally appropriate child-centred sport model.

The staging of the inaugural Youth Olympic Games in Singapore in 2010 has significant implications for youth sport and raises a host of ethical issues due to the overlapping of values associated with sport's role in the development of children and young people and elite-level, commodified sport. In Chapter 3, Parry and Lucidarme take a look at the YOG to outline some of the principles underlying them, and some of the practical challenges faced in implementing them. They outline some innovative ideas that were implemented in the youth version of the Olympic Games, many of which address ethical issues, but warn that many of the issues covered simply highlight already existing challenges for the Olympic movement, in a novel form.

In Chapter 4 de Martelaer, de Bouw and Struyven look at two means of initiating a pro-active approach for developing values and norms in sport and physical education. One is the use of international and national documents designed to help youth coaches and teachers reflect and work on values and norms in sport and physical education. The other approach involves using instructional possibilities starting from the pedagogical unit of Objective–Teaching behaviour–Learning behaviour–Outcomes (see, for example, Mosston and Ashworth 2002). The author argues that it is more important to focus on *behaviour* than on *subject matter* when working on values and norms in sport. The chapter provides illustrations of 'golden moments' and reflection in youth sport and physical education situations, beginning with approaches such as those based on Theory of Constructs for Education (TOCfE). It then offers insight into the importance and actions of coaches and physical education teachers as role models for social behaviour, closing with advice for teacher training and coach education.

Focused on Relative Age Effects (RAE), Cobley, Miller, Till and McKenna consider evidence of participation inequalities, exclusion and subtle forms of indirect discrimination that dominate popular youth sports. They illustrate how a preoccupation with talent identification and development is impacting upon and changing local-level youth sport participation on a day-to-day basis and transgressing the Panathlon Declaration (2004). Focused on RAE-based discrimination and talent development inefficiencies in youth sport, they provide macro-to-micro recommendations for 'positive action' that they argue must make the needs of youth the central concern in the face of the imposition of adult values systems and goals. Recent work on RAE has highlighted the subtle yet very significant ways in which age grouping can discriminate against many young people's fair participation in sport and the opportunities made available to them to reach their full athletic potential (see, for example, Cobley *et al.* 2008). Likewise, coaching pedagogy can have a powerful ethical influence on youth participation in sport and the equality of opportunity provided for young people to experience enjoyment, satisfaction and developing ability in sport. Chapters 6 and 7 examine the ethical dimensions of two pedagogical models for teaching/coaching sport that have had a significant influence upon physical education teaching and sport coaching: Game Sense and Sport Education.

In Chapter 6, Light considers Game Sense pedagogy from an applied ethics perspective to explore the ethical nature of particular features of it and the influence that these features can have on the socio-moral development of young people. He identifies and examines three core ethical features of Game Sense pedagogy. These are (1) the provision of inclusive learning experiences; (2) the use of dialogue and the ways in which this redresses unequal power relationships; and (3) the provision of a supportive socio-moral environment. Maintaining the focus on pedagogical models, in Chapter 7 Harvey, Kirk and O'Donovan examine the ways in which a young person can become a literate sports person and develop ethical conduct through engagement in the Sport Education Model. A review of the Sport Education research literature provides evidence to suggest that although notions such as inclusion and personal and social development are part of the architecture of this model, rather than simply being caught, ethical conduct must be taught. The authors then present four pedagogical applications of Sport Education for the promotion of ethical development: (1) an 'ethical contract', (2) sports panels, (3) modified games, (4) awards.

Reinforcing the message from Harvey, Kirk and O'Donovan, but focused on Dutch sports clubs, Van Veldhoven reminds us in Chapter 8 that the benefits arising from young people's participation in sport are not automatic outcomes. She suggests that they are, instead, dependent upon the context within which sport is played, with the key to achieving positive outcomes in youth sport being the relationship between the educator and the educated. Echoing Light's emphasis on dialogue and a supportive environment, she suggests that establishing this relationship requires the educator being sensitive to the wishes and needs of the educated, and establishing dialogue based upon mutual understanding and respect. She argues that this should be underpinned by a commitment on the part of the educator and all involved in sports clubs to act in the best interests of young athletes and stand up for their interests. In the following chapter Kentel examines the gender inequities prevailing in youth sport despite human rights legislation. She confronts what she describes as the mythical nature of efforts such as Title IX and Olympic gender equality targets. Through critical analysis of three narrative accounts, she examines the *ideal* of gender equity in sport using vignettes drawn from the media and personal life stories. She suggests that a merger of critical media and non-genderist pedagogies might provoke the young to engage in transforming what remains an equity myth. Drawing on Martin Heidegger's philosophy of discourse as uncovering, and Paulo Freire's liberatory practice of freedom, she provides a theoretical framework for moving the gender conversation forward. She argues that this needs to involve engaging young people in critical discourse about the difficulties of equity as a way of making bare (in German, *bloss*) the complex nature of being a young person in sport.

Coaches clearly play a central role in shaping the ethical dimensions of youth sport but the coaching literature suggests that their beliefs about coaching are well established prior to attending any coach education programme (see, for example, Cassidy *et al.* 2004). This suggests that university sport coaching courses may offer valuable opportunities for encouraging ethical practices in coaching. In Chapter 10 Cassidy pursues this idea by documenting and exploring her own explorations and reflections as a coach educator introducing undergraduate students to sport ethics. The initial discussion focuses on how practices, informed by the work of well-established scholars in sport ethics, are challenged by the question: 'How should one conduct and practice an ethical life without recourse to a universal set of ethical guidelines?' (Markula and Pringle 2006: 21). The second part of the chapter documents the explorations and the subsequent reflections that occurred as a consequence of accepting the challenge posed by the above question.

In Chapter 11 Barker, Barker-Ruchti and Pühse aim to illustrate how 'moral thinking' is connected to practice and to introduce an alternative approach to ethical pedagogies. They present three interaction episodes from three physical education lessons in Switzerland, after which they outline a social constructionist perspective. They then examine the episodes through a constructionist lens, thinking about how constructionist understandings might inform future pedagogies to make several suggestions. They suggest that sport and physical education practitioners should: (1) avoid universal understandings of ethics; (2) consider pupils as members of communities that are held together by shared practices; and (3) account for context when evaluating pupils' actions.

In Chapter 12, Wright, Burroughs and Tollefsen report on the delivery of outreach programmes that teach philosophy to children in urban schools in the United States of America. The approach used in these programmes is grounded in the philosophical literature on ethics, the development of virtue, philosophy for children, critical pedagogy and positive youth development through sport. The outreach programmes teach life skills and values through sport and physical activity in urban environments using a range of pedagogical strategies; examples of these are provided and suggestions for implementing them are offered.

Internationally, with an increasing acknowledgement of diversity in schools and other community contexts has come greater recognition for the need to work towards inclusive practice. Inclusion has steadily permeated youth sport and we continue to be bombarded with an assortment of messages reminding us to be inclusive. Within this context Hayley Fitzgerald in Chapter 13 interrogates the mantra of inclusion by focusing on issues concerning disability. She offers a number of short interview extracts generated from young disabled people that focus on their reflections of (inclusive) physical education. Drawing on these extracts and the ten criteria outlined by Fernández-Balboa (2011), she discusses the utility of rethinking inclusion through the lens of ethical education. In concluding, she argues that practising in ways that promote an ethical education will help practitioners to work in a more meaningful way with (disabled) young people that will enable the latter to have positive and fulfilling experiences of youth sport.

References

Bourdieu, P. (1986) *Distinction: A Social Critique of the Judgment of Taste.* London: Routledge.

Cassidy, T., Jones, R. L. and Potrac, P. (2004) *Understanding Sports Coaching: The Social, Cultural and Pedagogical Foundations of Coaching Practice.* London: Routledge.

Cobley, S., Abraham, C. and Baker, J. (2008) 'Relative age effects on physical education attainment and school sport representation', *Physical Education & Sport Pedagogy*, 13: 267–76.

Cook, D. T. and Cole, C. L. (2001) 'Kids and sport', *Journal of Sport and Social Issues*, 25(3): 227–8.

Fernández-Balboa, J. (2011) 'Sailing towards "Happycity": Ethics plus education', in J. A. Kentel (ed.) *Educating the Young: The Ethics of Care.* Oxford: Peter Lang, pp. 39–60.

Gard, M. and Wright, J. (2009) *The Obesity Epidemic: Science, Morality and Ideology.* London: Routledge.

Green, K., Smith, A. and Roberts, K. (2005) 'Young people and lifelong participation in sport and physical activity: A sociological perspective on contemporary physical education programmes in England and Wales', *Leisure Studies*, 24(1): 27–43.

Holt, N. (ed.) (2009) *Positive Youth Development Through Sport.* London: Routledge.

Light, R. L. (2000) 'A century of Japanese rugby and masculinity: Continuity and change', *Sporting Traditions*, 16(2): 87–104.

Light, R. L. (2008) *Sport in the Lives of Young Australians.* Sydney: Sydney University Press.

Mangan, J. A. (1981) *Athleticism in the Victorian and Edwardian Public School: The Emergence and Consolidation of an Educational Ideology.* Cambridge: Cambridge University Press.

Markula, P. and Pringle, R. (2006) *Foucault, Sport and Exercise: Power, Knowledge and Transforming the Self.* London: Routledge

Martens, R. (ed.) (1982) *Joy and Sadness in Children's Sport.* Champaign, IL: Human Kinetics.

Mosston, M. and Ashworth, S. (2002) *Teaching Physical Education* (5th edn). New York: Benjamin Cummings.

Panathlon International (2004) *Declaration on Ethics in Youth Sport.* Ghent: Panathlon International.

Sherington, G. (1983) 'Athleticism in the antipodes: The AAGPS of New South Wales', *History of Education Review*, 12: 16–18.

Stirling, A. and Kerr, G. (2007) 'Elite female swimmers' experiences of emotional abuse across time', *Journal of Emotional Abuse*, 7(4): 89–113.

Webb, J., Shirato, T. and Danaher, G. (2002) *Understanding Bourdieu.* Sydney: Allen and Unwin.

1 Managing ethics in youth sport

An application of the integrity management framework

Jeroen Maesschalck and Yves Vanden Auweele

Introduction[1]

There seem to be two pressing problems in youth sport. First, there is evidence of serious ethical transgressions that involve severe forms of child abuse and which require both unambiguous condemnation and appropriate policy reactions (e.g. Walsh and Giulianotti 2001; DeSensi and Rosenberg 2003; Boocock 2004; David 2004; Panathlon Flanders 2004; Vanden Auweele 2004; Brackenridge 2006; Donnelly and Petherick 2006; Vanden Auweele *et al.* 2008; UNICEF 2010). Second, there is also a host of more subtle dilemmas where it is not always obvious what appropriate behaviour should be and where those dealing with the dilemma are often left in the dark by their colleagues and managers. Ethical dilemmas can be defined as 'situations where values and norms are at stake and where a choice has to be made between several alternatives, while good reasons can be given for each of these alternatives' (translated and adapted from Karssing 2001: 93). In other words, whatever one does, there will be a moral cost, such as certain values, norms or interests not being respected. Two examples in Box 1 illustrate this (Maesschalck and Vanden Auweele 2008).

Box 1 Examples of ethical dilemmas in youth sports

You are a trainer of a youth team playing at international level. One of your players has serious problems at home, including being beaten seriously by his father. This may have a negative impact upon his performance in the game. You are approaching an important match and you have a good replacement for this player. Yet, you know that if you do not let the boy play the game, his already low self-esteem will deteriorate even further. Moreover, it is very likely that his father will use this as an excuse to abuse him even more. What will you do?

You are a manager. One of your young athletes has been caught doping. He will be severely punished. You know that the medical doctor of your team has provided him with the products. The controlling institutions are not aware of this because the athlete refuses to tell them where he obtained the illegal products. The medical doctor is an otherwise very loyal and professional doctor and this

---

behaviour was probably exceptional. What will you do? Will you remain silent? Will you give him a warning? Will you punish the doctor internally? Will you report his involvement in the case to the lawyer of the athlete and/or to the controlling institutions and claim there is a shared responsibility? Perhaps you will do something else?

The dilemmas described in Box 1 are not straightforward situations where the rules will unambiguously tell the actor what to do. Often, individual organizational members are facing these issues by themselves. They do not know who to turn to for advice and, even when they ask for advice, they might be left in the dark about what an appropriate solution would be. However, a deeper analysis of these two problems is not the aim of this chapter. For our purposes we limit ourselves to the observation that there is at least a perceived moral deficit in youth sport that deserves attention, and that there are a number of risks of integrity violations that should be managed.

We first recognize a valuable step in the right direction in the recent issuing and endorsement of declarations, such as the Panathlon Declaration on Ethics in Youth Sport (Panathlon International 2004), charters such as the Council of Europe's European Sport Charter (2001), and standards containing impressive lists of noble and important ethical aspirations (see, for example, EUPEA 2002; Boocock 2004: 166). The adoption by many organizations worldwide of such declarations, charters and/or standards suggests that the content of these is widely shared. However, reported instances of child abuse, and the fact that these declarations, charters and/or standards do not provide obvious solutions to many of the ethical dilemmas faced by individuals involved in youth sport, suggest that this policy response to our two ethical dilemmas outlined in Box 1 has not yet been satisfactory. It seems that this area faces what could be called an implementation deficit. There are many good intentions and plans but these do not seem to make a difference on the ground as they are not implemented in practice.

In looking for a more effective policy response, we will turn to the experience in businesses (business ethics) and public sector organizations (administrative ethics) that have faced similar problems. Specifically, we will introduce a framework that was developed by the senior author for the Organisation for Economic Co-operation and Development (OECD; Maesschalck and Bertok 2008). This Ethics Management Framework was developed to be used by public sector organizations but this chapter will argue that, with adaptations, it can also be used as a model for designing ethics management systems in youth sport.

The chapter starts with a discussion of two approaches to integrity management that will underpin the remainder of the discussion. It then introduces the integrity management framework and subsequently discusses its three 'pillars': instruments, processes and structures. These are briefly introduced and then applied to integrity management in youth sport.

Two approaches to integrity management

Before turning to the actual framework, it is useful to introduce a basic recommendation that underpins not only the framework introduced here, but also most of the prescriptive literature on integrity management. The recommendation is to always look for an appropriate balance between two fundamental approaches to integrity management (see, for example, Lewis 1991; Paine 1994; Maesschalck 2004–5) that we will here refer to as 'rules-based' and 'values-based', but are known under other labels as well.

The rules-based approach to integrity management emphasizes the importance of external controls on the behaviour of the members of an organization. It prefers formal and detailed rules and procedures as means to reduce, or ideally prevent, integrity violations. The values-based approach, on the other hand, focuses on guidance and 'internal' control (for example, control exercised by organizational members on themselves). Thus, rather than being about controlling, this approach is about supporting and stimulating. It aims to stimulate understanding and daily application of values as well as improve ethical decision-making skills through activities such as interactive training sessions, workshops, ambitious codes of values and individual coaching.

A modern integrity management framework has two goals: (1) preventing serious integrity violations on the one hand, and (2) promoting integrity through stimulating understanding, commitment and capacity for ethical decision-making on the other. Consequently, a modern integrity management framework judiciously combines both the rules-based and values-based approaches and ensures the coherent balance of their components within one integrity framework. Indeed, each of the two approaches has its weaknesses and should therefore not be applied wholesale. This echoes Morgan's (2006) recommendation that sport's ethical problems should be dealt with using a balanced approach, excluding being hypercritical and cynical on the one hand and being too romantic with regard to the power of the positive potentials of sport on the other. In such a balanced approach, the rules-based component will constitute the elementary legal framework and will provide the teeth of the system, ensuring a minimal level of ethical behaviour. The values-based approach adds value to this rules-based approach, ensuring that one is ethically more ambitious than this minimum of simply avoiding integrity violations.

Introducing the integrity management framework

In this chapter the term 'integrity' denotes the application of generally accepted values and norms in daily practice. Integrity management, then, specifies the activities undertaken to determine, stimulate and enforce integrity and prevent integrity violations within a particular organization. The integrity management framework refers to the whole of those instruments within that organization, as well as the processes and the structures that bring those instruments to life.

Specifically, the integrity management framework consists of three main pillars (Maesschalck and Bertok 2008). The primary pillar is that of the instruments of integrity management, which is organized according to the four functions that it performs: (1) determining and defining integrity; (2) guiding towards integrity; (3) monitoring integrity; and (4) enforcing integrity. Instruments only have an impact when they are brought to life and kept healthy through the other two pillars of the framework: those of processes and structures. One indeed needs a continuous development process through which the framework can be developed and maintained within the organization. By 'structures', we refer to the organizational aspect of integrity management: Who is responsible for what in integrity management? And how are the initiatives of the many actors whose activities have an impact upon the organizational members' integrity coordinated?

This framework is designed as a general framework that can be applied in organizations of all varieties, from a local sport club, to national and international federations, and global sports organizations. Of course, the level of development and the size of the elements will differ, but the hypothesis is that organizations at all these levels will need to perform the four functions of integrity management and establish one or several processes, and some degree of institutionalization (e.g. by appointing an ethics officer), if they want to stimulate ethical decision-making and prevent integrity violations.

The framework follows a 'systemic approach', which implies two important choices First, it implies that the focus will not only be on individual instruments, but also on the integrity management framework as a whole, as system of interdependent components. The underlying assumption is that the effectiveness of integrity management depends as much on the synergies between the instruments as on the effects of the individual instruments separately. An ethics code by itself will not have much impact, an integrity training session will not really make a difference, and one inspection will probably not leave a lasting impression. It is the combination of such measures that will have a significant effect, a joint effect that is much larger than the mere sum of the effects of the individual instruments. Therefore, instruments should always be assessed together, with particular attention to their synergies.

Second, the integrity management framework will not be considered a closed system but, instead, as an *open system* that is embedded in a wider 'integrity context'. This means that integrity management instruments should not only be coordinated with each other, they should also be coordinated with other, related actors and factors that might have an impact upon the organizational members' integrity.

Instruments

This section will address the four instruments of integrity management that are commonly used in public and private sector organizations, ones that might be useful in the context of (youth) sports organizations. Many integrity management instruments have been developed in recent years and they have been classified in many different ways. This chapter proposes to organize these instruments according to four functions that should be fulfilled in a sound integrity management framework: (1) determining and defining integrity; (2) guiding towards integrity; (3) monitoring integrity; and (4) enforcing integrity. For each of these functions, some instruments that have been developed to fulfil the four functions and that might be useful in the sport sector will be discussed.

Function 1: Determining and defining integrity in youth sport

The first function of an integrity management framework is to determine the expectations of behaviour: which values are important for the organization, which rules should be obeyed? There are various instruments that can be used in different combinations to determine and define integrity and the actual mix of instruments will depend on local circumstances. We offer some examples that have relevance for the sport sector.

Risk analysis

One increasingly popular way to determine integrity is by focusing on the risks to integrity. In a process of risk analysis one would map sensitive processes and sensitive functions and identify the points where there is a significant vulnerability for integrity violations. This analysis would then be the basis for recommendations to the organization on how to increase the organization's resilience towards these vulnerabilities. In the context of youth sport, one important area of risk is that of safeguarding and protecting children. A risk analysis would thus map sensitive processes, such as recruitment of volunteers and coaches, travelling to international competitions with children, initiation rituals or nutrition and weight-loss regimes, and sensitive functions such as caretaking or coaching, and identify the points where there is a significant vulnerability for integrity violations. This would then be a basis for recommendations on how to reduce these risks, typically by structural measures.

Analysis of ethical dilemmas

There are similarities between a dilemma analysis and a risk analysis but there is an important difference in overall philosophy. Dilemma analyses tend to have a bias towards the values-based approach to integrity management and that will be reflected in the analysis itself as well as in the recommendations that are drawn from it. Two differences are particularly notable. First, while risk analysis focuses on problematic situations (risks) that should be reduced, dilemma analysis starts from the assumption that dilemmas are inevitable and that it is not always desirable to try and avoid dilemmas. Sometimes it is better to accept that there are areas where dilemmas might occur and to trust and support staff in dealing with them. Second, like all rules-based instruments of integrity management, risk analysis shows some distrust in the organizational members. The organization has to be protected from members who might abuse weaknesses in its risk-resistance. Dilemma analysis, on the other hand, tends to be more trustful. The organization should know what the dilemmas are, so as to better support its members in dealing with those dilemmas (DeSensi and Rosenberg 2003).

Code of conduct or code of ethics

Integrity codes are probably the best-known instruments of integrity management. When looking at youth sport, there are already various standards (see, for example, Boocock 2004), embedded in various charters (see, for example, the charter of the Council of Europe 2001) and declarations (see, for example, the Panathlon Declaration on Ethics in Youth Sport 2004). These documents contain important principles and guidelines, but typically do not present themselves as codes of conduct for sports federations and clubs. This is more an advantage than a disadvantage, because it provides an excellent opportunity for sports organizations to translate these declarations, charters and/or standards into codes that are specific for their own members and that can be used in daily practice.

When drafting codes for youth sport, one might keep in mind a typical distinction that is often made in business ethics between a code of conduct and a code of ethics. This distinction usually refers to both the contents of the code and the way in which it is enforced. The code of conduct is a typical instrument used in a rules-based approach to integrity management. It starts from the assumption that people are essentially self-interested and that they will only behave with integrity when this coincides with their self-interest. Hence, a preferably detailed code of conduct will describe as specifically and unambiguously as possible what behaviour is expected. Such a code of conduct will also establish strict procedures to enforce the code: systematic monitoring and strict punishment of those who break the rules through a particular sport's disciplinary procedures covering complaints, grievances, appeals, suspensions and reinstatement. A code of ethics, on the other hand, is rooted in the values-based approach. It focuses on general values rather than on specific guidelines for behaviour, thus putting more trust in the organizational members' capacities for independent moral reasoning. As for the choice between the two types of codes, the recommendation is to situate this in the broader question about the balance between the rules-based and the values-based approaches.

Structural measures

This subsection refers to specific measures that add rules or make other changes to the structure of the organization such as handling social pressure and tensions, conflict of interest policy, gift and gratuity policy, and separating and rotating functions.

HANDLING SOCIAL PRESSURE AND TENSIONS

Social pressure on young athletes, whether it comes from the parents, trainer or federation, must be dealt with by forms of consultation in appropriate structures and channels of communication. In particular, the questions and expectations of the parents should not be left unaddressed. Parents are too often kept out of the training programme with the justification being that their participation is inconvenient. Trainers and federations should channel parents' enthusiasm and energy. This would allow them to temper excessive demands and expectations from the parents. Conversely, this would also allow the parents to keep an eye on the training programme and its possible risks. Thus, communication between the trainer and the parents and the legitimate involvement of the parents in supervision offers a possibility of corrective action in both directions.

CONFLICT OF INTEREST POLICY

It is important for federations and clubs to be aware of possible situations of conflict of interest and think of ways to avoid these. For example, some parents coach their own children. It is important to be aware of these risks and to take preventive measures to avoid such problems by, for example, ensuring that parents are not involved in decision-making concerning their own child.

GIFTS AND GRATUITIES POLICY

The general principle of gifts and gratuities policy is that managers, trainers, referees and other actors are expected not to ask for or accept gifts or gratuities from individuals (such as parents) or organizations (such as sponsors) that may influence their impartiality. Yet, in practice it is not always realistic and sometimes not even desirable to strictly prohibit all types of gifts and gratuities. One could imagine situations where a parent would be deeply insulted when he/she offers something of limited value as a token/signal of his/her appreciation for the trainer's or coach's efforts. Moreover, by strictly prohibiting such small gifts, one runs the risk of trivializing integrity management, and even bringing it into ridicule. Thus, a more nuanced policy will be needed.

SEPARATING FUNCTIONS

Particularly vulnerable areas (for example, advising and giving nutrition supplements and substances to young athletes; selecting athletes for an important international competition; contracting a sponsor for youth sports) could be split up into several sub-tasks that will be performed by different staff members, thus increasing the number of people that would need to be involved if one wanted to commit an integrity violation. It is expected that this will increase oversight and control, thus reducing the risk of integrity violations.

ROTATING FUNCTIONS

If staff members perform the same vulnerable task for a long time, the risk will increase that they will develop undesirable routines and relations with young athletes, providers or other stakeholders, which might in turn increase the risk for integrity violations. It could be appropriate, therefore, to systematically rotate those trainers, directors, administrators, referees, etc. between different specialties or functions. At the same time, one should also attempt to ensure knowledge management and maintain appropriate capacity in key functions.

A review of the instruments supporting management areas

Supporting management areas, such as personnel management, financial management or information management, involves many instruments that perhaps do not have integrity as their main goal, yet can nevertheless play a crucial role in stimulating integrity or preventing integrity violations. To illustrate this, we provide three examples from within personnel management, but this is just one element of a potentially very long list of possible interventions. For some further illustration of these examples, see Maesschalck and Bertok (2008: 44–8). As for personnel management, we briefly address recruitment, promotion and training.

First, in regard to the recruitment of trainers, managers or caretaking staff, one can imagine many interventions. One could, for example, double-check the statements made by the candidate coach, administrator or volunteer in his/her curriculum vitae (for example, checking references, asking for original degree certificates, former volunteer jobs, etc.) to prevent unsuitable people from working on activities that involve children. One could also check the candidate's background, particularly looking for previous incidents of relevant misconduct and, in particular, child abuse convictions or dismissals because of abuse. Such screening schemes could be criticized as being intrusive (particularly when volunteers are under consideration), expensive and selective, because only those who have been apprehended and convicted are listed, but they can successfully exclude dangerous individuals from children's sport (UNICEF 2010). If one chooses such a policy, it should be managed very carefully and with respect for privacy and other rights. One could also probe for moral judgement capacities in the job interview. For example, this could involve asking whether or not the candidate has been confronted with an ethical dilemma and how he/she has dealt with it.

Second, we would like to stress the important role integrity should play in the evaluation and the promotion of staff. A club or federation would give a very important signal if it would not only promote on the basis of sport successes or financial performance, but also take 'integrity' into consideration as a criterion. Third, clubs should explicitly formulate standards for sports training, stimulating staff to follow continuing training in this area to improve their skills in identifying and dealing with ethical dilemmas (EUPEA 2002; Boocock 2004).

Function 2: Guiding and coaching towards integrity

Determining and defining integrity is just a first step for building a sound integrity management framework. Both experience and literature are full of warnings that the mere formulation of values and rules, and the mere creation of structures and procedures are insufficient to ensure behaviour of integrity among organizational members. All of this has to become part of daily practice in the organization, requiring three additional functions, the first among these being the object of this section: guiding towards integrity. How can the organizational members be guided and coached so that they know what is expected from them in terms of integrity and they feel stimulated to act accordingly?

Exemplary behaviour by national and international sport bodies, club management, officials and referees

Managers in clubs, national and international federations are of course crucial for the integrity management framework as a whole. That is why they are listed as the first (before 'integrity actors') in the list of actors of integrity management (see p. 21). Here we limit ourselves to emphasizing the importance of exemplary behaviour. Through their own behaviour, managers give an important message about what is acceptable and what is not acceptable that is at least as important as their official communication.

Integrity training

Integrity training is probably one of the most often advertised instruments of integrity management. It is also a very broad concept that includes a wide variety of types of training that can be situated along the continuum of the rules-based and values-based approaches to integrity management. We will briefly discuss three such types, situating them along the continuum.

At one side of the continuum is the purely 'rules-based' type of integrity training. A typical format for this would be a classroom setting where the expert/consultant would be talking most of the time, explaining what is expected from the organizational members according to the laws, rules and codes, and what the consequences are if one does not follow these directions. On the other, values-based, side of the continuum are purely inductive training sessions that are better described as discussion sessions. The trainees will do most of the thinking and talking with the expert/consultant only being there as a facilitator who stimulates discussion, provokes thinking and plays the devil's advocate. In between these two types are many others that combine rules-based and values-based elements. One example of this would be dilemma training sessions. The aim of dilemma training is to recognize that difficult dilemma-type situations are inevitable in organizations, to send the message that organizational members are not alone when they face these dilemmas and to provide them with techniques and advice on how to deal with these situations (see, for example, Cooper 1982; van Luijk 1996).

As with all integrity management instruments, the choice of a particular training type will depend on local circumstances and on the overall balance of rules-based and values-based instruments. In any case, it is important to bear in mind that training should not be limited to new recruits and that the effectiveness of a training session will drastically increase if there is some kind of follow-up. This could consist of a regular update training, where the new elements of the normative framework are presented and where the techniques are practised again.

Integrating integrity in the regular discourse of the organization

One of the key success factors for an integrity management framework is the impact it has on the ground, the extent to which it stimulates the members of the organization to act with integrity in their day-to-day activities. This sub-section focuses on a number of instruments that are particularly effective in achieving this goal.

One could announce the integrity policy and the contents of the code through channels of external communication. Examples of this include the organization's magazine, website, newsletter and targeted mailing. This is, of course, a useful tool for ensuring trust among the organization's stakeholders but it could also have an important yet indirect effect upon the integrity of the organizational members themselves. The fact that the external stakeholders are now better informed could help to prevent certain types of integrity violations or problems. Stakeholders, such as sponsors who directly contact trainers, putting inappropriate pressure on them, might now be less likely to put managers and trainers in difficult situations or be more critical of organizational members' behaviour, because they know what is expected from them.

As mentioned, one could organize regular discussions of ethical dilemmas or other ethical questions and issues in the official internal communication channels of the organization. Examples of this include the organization's internal magazine, intranet and newsletters. One could also institutionalize regular discussions of ethical issues in staff meetings, as well as in individual meetings between the manager and his or her staff. The latter could be done through instruments of personnel management (particularly in the evaluation cycle). Forcing manager and supporting staff to discuss the topic of integrity in these formally required conversations would serve as an excellent vehicle for institutionalizing the integrity discourse.

Coaching and counselling for integrity

This instrument implies the appointment of an actor or a number of actors within or outside the organization whose task it is to provide content-based support to staff members with ethical concerns. In the context of youth sport, these counsellors could also specialize in, for example, identifying signs of abuse and harm in young athletes and in providing necessary support. This could take several degrees of institutionalization, ranging from the informal appointment of certain organizational members such as sport scientists, sport medicine staff and paediatricians and sport psychologists to establishing a formal body, with some independence from the organizational hierarchy, that provides written advice to organizational members facing integrity issues.

Function 3: Monitoring integrity

It is not sufficient to merely define integrity and then guide organizational members and other stakeholders towards applying those norms and values in their daily actions. The organization should also monitor to what extent this actually occurs. This refers to the third function of the integrity management framework. There are many instruments to monitor integrity, including whistle-blowing arrangements and complaint systems but also more active monitoring instruments such as early warning systems or, simply, daily supervision by supervisors. Given the space constraints, we limit ourselves here to the monitoring instrument that probably receives most attention: whistle-blowing.

'"Whistle-blowing" can be defined as organization members' disclosure of illegal, immoral, or illegitimate practices under the control of their employers, to parties who may be able to effect action' (Miceli and Near 1985: 525). It is a complex affair. On the one hand it is obvious that managers, trainers, parents, supporting staff or other actors in the sports field who take this kind of risk, with the public interest or the prevention of harm (particularly physical or mental abuse of children in sports clubs) as their goal, deserve respect. On the other hand, it is clear that the act of whistle-blowing usually damages the image of the organization concerned, which might in turn lead to decreasing trust among the public in the organization itself, but often also in sports as a whole. Whistle-blowing policies therefore have the aim of maintaining the desirable effects of whistle-blowing (the fact that the wrongdoing is reported to actors who can stop it) while trying to reduce the undesirable effects upon the image of the organization. Such a whistle-blowing policy therefore essentially consists of two components: (1) a system for reporting wrongdoing; and (2) a system for the protection of those who make use, in good faith, of these channels.

The very idea of a whistle-blowing policy often provokes resistance because it is often associated with big scandals (that were indeed often made public by whistle-blowers) or with 'witch-hunts' and paranoia. These concerns are unnecessary, at least on the condition that the whistle-blowing policy is well developed. Whistle-blowing policies are actually intended to prevent public scandals. By providing additional reporting channels, they offer employees a way to report the wrongdoing without having to turn to the press or other public reporting channels.

Function 4: Enforcing integrity

However important prevention and guidance are, every integrity management framework will need a significant component of enforcement. If the rules are clear for the organizational members and one observes significant transgressions of those rules, then sanctions will be necessary if the integrity management framework is to maintain its overall legitimacy. The specific investigating and sanctioning mechanisms will differ largely from organization to organization and it is not useful to elaborate them in this context.

We limit ourselves to one important recommendation: ensure that both the procedures and the sanctions are perceived as fair (see, for example, De Schrijver *et al.* 2010). Clear guidelines for responding to disclosure, suspicions and allegations, for example, should be elaborated as well as reporting procedures and other principles for dealing with allegations, confidentiality, and anonymous complaints and rumours. The sanction should be consistent with the seriousness of the violation and with the sanctions for other colleagues who committed similar violations.

Processes

Instruments might perhaps be the most visible and best-known component of an integrity management framework, but they are by no means sufficient on their own. They also need to be brought to life and subsequently be kept in good health through development processes. To successfully proceed through a process, one should move through a cycle of plan, do, 'check' and adapt.

At the level of the integrity management framework as a whole it is important to design a development process that ensures that plans are not only implemented (do), but also evaluated (check) and, if necessary, adapted through a recurring process that should be institutionalized. One could, for example, think of an 'integrity plan' (or integrity section in the strategic plan of the organization) that is approved by senior management and the implementation of which is regularly evaluated, if necessary leading to adaptations of the plan. Some kind of institutionalization that ensures that integrity and its management is regularly thought about is really essential, even in the smallest sport organization.

In the sport sector it would be particularly useful not only to institutionalize processes at the organizational level but also at the inter-organizational level where organizations cooperate (be it at regional, national or international level). A sector as complex as sport has many different actors on very different levels, with very different perspectives, interests and responsibilities, including regional, national and international sport federations covering both recreational and competitive sports; Olympic Committees; international, European, national and local sport governing bodies; sport scientific associations; media; sponsors; sport educational organizations; and specialist sport schools. If all the relevant actors in this broad and diverse sport landscape could meet to work on a common integrity plan and could all be involved in the implementation and regular evaluation of it, then this would stimulate them to cooperate. This would then drastically increase the chance that the different instruments would fit with each other and within an overall strategy. This would also contribute to raising awareness in wider society about the commitment of the sport sector to address integrity issues.

Structures

By 'structures' we refer to the institutional aspect of integrity management. Who is responsible for what in integrity management and how are the different tasks coordinated? Of course, integrity is ultimately the responsibility of all organizational members, yet some actors have more important roles than others.

The most important actors are the line managers. By being a moral person (exhibiting exemplary behaviour) and a moral manager (stimulating staff to behave ethically), managers can play a crucial role in shaping the organizational members' integrity (Brown and Treviño 2006). Second in importance are the 'integrity actors', such as compliance officers, ethics officers or integrity administrators. As important as the role of managers in stimulating integrity might be, it is not sufficient on its own. It is essential that the integrity management framework also acquires a clear place within the organizational structure and that it is visible in the organizational chart in the form of the appointment of an 'integrity actor'. Stimulating integrity is the main task of the 'integrity actors' and they are typically responsible for core integrity instruments like the ethics code, integrity training and communication about integrity. Which form this structural anchoring will take will depend on all kinds of organizational characteristics, including, of course, size. Third in importance from the perspective of integrity management are actors in support functions such as personnel management, financial management and information management. These usually do not have integrity as their primary responsibility, but the instruments that are under their responsibility can play an important part in integrity management (see above). They should therefore be involved in integrity management.

Just as important as the individual commitment and expertise of these individual actors will be the coordination among all these efforts. This is important at the organizational level such as in a sports club or sports federation, where line managers and staff in supporting functions need to cooperate, often under the coordination of an integrity actor, to ensure synergies. Yet, as mentioned above, this will also be important at the higher level of inter-organizational cooperation, for example, at regional or national level. A case in point is the Child Protection in Sport Unit (CPSU) in the UK. This unit works with the active support of sport bodies, statutory agencies and government departments to promote, facilitate and support the safeguarding of children in partnership (Boocock 2004). It can thus play a stimulating and coordinating role.

The discussion on the organization of integrity management is very technical and quickly becomes very complex because the appropriate structure will strongly depend on local/sector circumstances, so we limit ourselves to two general remarks. First, while supra-organizational bodies at national or international level can play a very important coordinating and stimulating role, it should be emphasized that they can never entirely replace an integrity framework at local, organizational level. A basic structure at organizational level remains necessary. The organization needs somebody who has it in his or her job description to think about integrity and integrity management when all other organizational members, including managers, are focusing their attention on something else, such as a crisis or a big sport competition. Second, however useful an 'integrity actor' might be, there is one important risk. Because they know 'somebody is taking care of integrity', the organizational members might feel less responsible for integrity. This would of course be highly problematic, because integrity management will only be effective when all organizational members share some kind of co-ownership of the integrity management framework. Both managers and the integrity actor will have to be very careful to avoid something like a ritualized 'devil's advocate' scenario. This is where the integrity actor is allowed to come on stage now and then and do his/her little performance (for example, launching particular instruments, pointing at particular integrity problems, etc.), after which it's all back to work and nothing really changed. This is not a reason not to appoint an integrity actor, but it is a risk one should be aware of. Thus, one could conceive of the organization of the integrity management framework as a balancing act between two undesirable extremes. One is where, if somebody is responsible for something, then the other organizational members will think it is not their responsibility, and the other is where, if everybody is responsible for something, then nobody will be responsible in practice.

Conclusion

Reports of serious integrity violations are often met with defensive reactions or denial by youth sport managers and this chapter proposes some elements of an alternative response. Youth sport managers could also respond by recognizing that, as in any other area of society, youth sport will always face the risk of integrity violations. Rather than something that should remain hidden or be denied, this is something that could be managed, if done appropriately. Specifically, we argue that declarations, charters and/or standards are a good starting point, but that they require implementation if they are to have a real impact and provide an appropriate and positive response to the integrity challenges facing youth sport. Such implementation is made possible by developing an integrity management framework consisting not only of instruments but also of processes and structures. Importantly, such a framework will not only prevent serious integrity violations, but will also support those in the youth sports domain who have to deal with complicated ethical dilemmas. Integrity management can help youth sport to reduce the inherent risks of causing serious physical, social and psychological harm, and thus help it in realizing its impressive potential for making a positive contribution towards social, political and moral development.

Discussion Questions

1. Integrity management is not only about preventing serious misbehaviour but also about supporting staff in dealing with complicated ethical dilemmas. Can you give some examples of such dilemmas in the area of youth sport, perhaps inspired by the examples in the text?

2. Imagine a sport manager who argues that he does not need to develop an integrity management framework because he has not heard about any serious integrity violations in his organizations. How would you respond to that manager? What arguments can you draw from the text (or from elsewhere) to convince this manager that not only his organization and its stakeholders, but also he himself would benefit from a well-developed integrity management framework?

3. Think of a specific sport organization (or network of organizations) that you are familiar with. Go through the different instruments, processes and structures that were presented in the text and assess the feasibility and desirability of applying them in that organization.

Note

1 This chapter draws significantly from Maesschalck and Bertok (2008).

References

Boocock, S. (2004) 'Child abuse in sport: Developing a strategic response in the UK', in Y. Vanden Auweele (ed.) *Ethics in Youth Sport*. Leuven: LannooCampus, pp. 159–68.

Brackenridge, C. (2006) 'Women and children first? Child abuse and child protection in sport', in R. Giulianotti and D. McArdle (eds) *Sport, Civil Liberties and Human Rights*. London: Routledge, pp. 30–45.

Brown, M. E. and Treviño, L. K. (2006) 'Ethical leadership: A review and future directions', *Leadership Quarterly*, 17: 595–616.

Cooper, T. L. (1982) *The Responsible Administrator: An Approach to Ethics for the Administrative Role* (1st edn). Port Washington, NY: Kennikat.

Council of Europe, Sports Department of the Directorate IV-Education, Culture and Heritage, Youth and Sport (2001) *European Sport Charter: Recommendation nr. R(92) 13 Adopted by the Committee of Ministers of Member States on 16 May 2001*. Strasbourg: Council of Europe.

David, P. (2004) *Human Rights in Youth Sports*. London: Routledge.

De Schrijver, A., Delbeke, K., Maesschalck, J. and Pleysier, S. (2010) 'Fairness perceptions and organisational misbehaviour: An empirical study', *American Review of Public Administration*, 40(6): 691–703.

DeSensi, J. T. and Rosenberg, D. (2003) *Ethics and Morality in Sport Management*. Morgentown: Fitness Information Technology.

Donnelly, P. and Petherick, L. (2006) 'Worker's playtime? Child labour at the extremes of the sporting spectrum', in R. Giulianotti and D. McArdle (eds) *Sport, Civil Liberties and Human Rights*. London: Routledge, pp. 9–29.

EUPEA (2002) EUPEA Code of Ethics and Good Practice Guide for Physical Education. Available at: http://www.eupea.com/public/uploads/files/documents/Eupea%20Code20% 20%of20%%20Ethics.pdf (accessed 12 January 2012).

Karssing, E. (2001) *Morele competentie in organisaties* [Moral competence in organizations]. Assen: Koninklijke Van Gorcum.

Lewis, C. (1991) *The Ethics Challenge in Public Service.* San Francisco, CA: Jossey Bass.

Maesschalck, J. (2004–5) 'Approaches to ethics in the public sector: A proposed extension of the compliance-integrity continuum', *Public Integrity*, 7(1): 21–41.

Maesschalck, J. and Bertok, J. (2008) *Towards a Sound Integrity Framework: Instruments, Processes, Structures and Conditions for Implementation.* Report to the Organisation for Economic Co-operation and Development. Paris: Organisation for Economic Co-operation and Development.

Maesschalck, J. and Vanden Auweele, Y. (2008) 'Integrity management in youth sport: How to ensure that the Panathlon declaration makes a real difference?', paper presented at the World Conference on the Panathlon Declaration, 'Implementation of Ethics in Youth Sport', Ghent, November.

Miceli, M. P. and Near, J. P. (1985) 'Characteristics of organisational climate and perceived wrongdoing associated with whistle-blowing decisions', *Personnel Psychology*, 38: 525–44.

Morgan, W. J. (2006) *Why Sports Morally Matter.* London: Routledge.

Paine, L. S. (1994) 'Managing for organisational integrity', *Harvard Business Review*, March–April: 106–17.

Panathlon Flanders (2004) 'Children harmed by sport: On the threat to positive values in children's and youth sport', in Y. Vanden Auweele (ed.) *Ethics in Youth Sport.* Leuven: Lannoo Campus, pp. 19–29.

Panathlon International (2004) *Declaration on Ethics in Youth Sport.* Ghent: Panathlon International.

UNICEF (2010) *Protecting Children from Violence in Sport: A Review with a Focus on Industrialized Countries.* Florence, Italy: UNICEF, Innocenti Research Centre.

Vanden Auweele, Y. (ed.) (2004) *Ethics in Youth Sport.* Leuven: Lannoo Campus.

Vanden Auweele, Y., Opdenacker, J., Vertommen, T., Boen, F., Van Niekerk, L., De Martelaer, K. *et al.* (2008) 'Unwanted sexual experiences in sport: Perceptions and reported prevalence among Flemish female student-athletes', *International Journal of Sport and Exercise Psychology*, 6(4): 354–65.

van Luijk, H. (1996) 'Stapvoets door een dilemma: Opzet en achtergronden van een bewerkingsmodel' [Stepwise through a dilemma: Purpose and background of a process model], *Filosofie in Bedrijf (Philosophy in Business)*, 22: 33–40.

Walsh, A. J. and Giulianotti, R. (2001) 'This sporting mammon: A normative critique of the commodification of sport', *Journal of the Philosophy of Sport*, 28(1): 53–77.

2 Putting the child back in children's sport

Nurturing young talent in a developmentally appropriate manner

Gretchen Kerr and Ashley Stirling

Introduction

Children in today's western societies hold special status as a function of their rights and unique developmental needs. Although it has not always been the case throughout history, childhood is now viewed as a distinct stage of life in which early life experiences form the foundation, affecting later developmental outcomes. As such, significant attention and resources have been devoted to enhancing the quality of childhood experiences through policies and laws governing such things as health care, mandatory education and parental leave. With millions of children participating in organized sport annually, it forms a potentially important influence on child development and therefore should also be a focus of inquiry and scrutiny.

In this chapter, we will begin by reviewing the historical changes in society's views of children and child development. We will then turn our attention to a critique of children's organized sport programmes. Finally, using theories of child development, considerations will be proposed for the design and delivery of developmentally appropriate sport models for children.

An historical view of child development

An historical review of society's views of children illustrates the ways in which philosophies about children and child development have changed over time. These philosophies are important as they have implications for the ways in which adults interact with children as well as for structural and programmatic outcomes such as education and legal status. Across time, there have been three predominant views of children, each of which will be addressed in turn.

In the middle ages, the philosophy of original sin prevailed in which children were viewed as essentially evil beings. The goal of child rearing therefore was salvation and removal of sin. Also, at this time children were viewed as miniature adults, without distinction from adults in terms of legal status, class of citizen or developmental needs (Verhellen 1989). This historical period saw the extensive use of corporal punishment and use of children to work long days in deplorable conditions with no rights to education.

This early philosophy was replaced with the tabula rasa view. As children were assumed to be born as 'blank slates', adults therefore had an important role to play in contributing to the developmental outcomes, both positive and negative, of young people. At this point, children began to be viewed as persons rather than property (Hart 1991). During the first half of the twentieth century, a 'child-saving era' (Hart 1991) prevailed, in which attention was devoted to ensuring the health and welfare of children. While this progression led to significant reforms to child labour, compulsory education and the legal system, it still viewed children as objects of protection. It was only in the latter half of the twentieth century that children began to have status as persons with rights to protection and self-determination (Hart 1991).

The more contemporary philosophy of children is one of innate goodness. With this perspective, children are viewed as inherently good, therefore the goal of parenting and development is to foster a child's potential. Further, the developmental stages of childhood and adolescence are viewed as very distinct times of life that are separate from adulthood and in which young people are to be nurtured in developmentally appropriate ways. Child development is now viewed as resulting from the interaction between the child and external influences, with young people seen as being active agents in their own development (Santrock *et al.* 2005).

The United Nations (UN) Convention on the Rights of the Child, which was ratified in 1989, is a strong indicator of the special status ascribed to children. As a legally binding international human rights treaty, it aims to ensure that children are to enjoy fundamental human rights. It recognizes nurturance and protection rights as well as participatory rights which children can exercise in a developmentally appropriate manner. The Convention covers four basic principles: (1) the right to non-discrimination, (2) the obligation to have the best interests of the child as the primary consideration, (3) the right to life, survival and development, and (4) the right of the child to have input into decisions that affect him or her. This Convention clearly recognizes the unique needs and rights of children and the responsibility of adults to promote these (United Nations 1989).

The contemporary view of child development also maintains that early life experiences, both positive and negative, have implications for developmental outcomes later in life. Early life experiences can affect one's health, ability to learn, one's sense of self and abilities to have healthy relationships as some of many examples (Rutter 1989; Cassidy and Shaver 1999; Clarke and Clarke 2000). The attachment relationship an infant forms with a primary caregiver, for example, is known to affect one's later susceptibility to stress and the quality of subsequent relationships (Bowlby 1989). The importance we attribute to childhood experiences is evidenced in part by the current laws and policies that govern mandatory accessible education, health care and parental leave, as well as restrictions on young people's involvement in employment.

Furthermore, as a society, we have adopted a shared responsibility to ensuring child protection and healthy child development. As an example, we have structures and mechanisms in place to protect children when the family unit fails to do so. Although laws differ geographically, most western societies attribute some level of duty and responsibility to adults to intervene when there is suspicion or knowledge of child maltreatment. The UN Convention on the Rights of the Child also recognizes the responsibilities of adults to protect children from all forms of physical or mental violence, injury or abuse, neglect or negligent treatment, maltreatment or exploitation.

We will now turn our attention to competitive sport, a practice in society in which millions of children participate annually, and in which we posit a more attuned focus on the developmental needs of children is needed.

The case of children's sport

An extensive body of evidence exists that illustrates the potential short- and long-term indicators of positive development associated with sport participation for young people. When delivered in a developmentally appropriate manner, sport participation for children is associated with enhanced physical development (Bar-Or 1983), educational outcomes, school engagement, academic performance, pro-social behaviours and psychological adjustment, lower drop-out rates from school and lower delinquency rates, as some of many examples (Larson 2000; Mahoney 2000; Marsh and Kleitman 2002; Eccles *et al.* 2003; Fredricks and Eccles 2006). The National Research Council and Institute of Medicine (NRCIM 2002) identified the main areas of youth development as physical, intellectual, psychological and social; evidence exists to support the potential positive contributions that sport participation can make to each of these (for a review, see Fraser-Thomas *et al.* 2005).

When not delivered in a developmentally appropriate manner however, sport participation also has the potential to be associated with negative outcomes for children's health and well-being. There are numerous examples of potential violations of children's developmental needs in sport, including, among others: overly intensive training, early specialization, overuse injuries, eating disorders, trafficking of athletes, sexual abuse and exploitation, emotional abuse, and doping, which have been addressed in detail by others (Donnelly 1993; Brackenridge 1997, 2001; David 1999; Kidd and Donnelly 2000; Coakley 2001; Bringer *et al.* 2006; Stirling and Kerr 2007, 2008; Stirling 2009).

At the core of these examples of negative developmental experiences is often the misuse of power by the coach (Kidd and Donnelly 2000; Brackenridge 2001; Burke 2001; David 2005; Stirling and Kerr 2009). Further, given that many of these violations occur in public speaks to the normalization of these harmful experiences in sport. For example, when a coach engages in emotionally abusive practices in training, other athletes, coaches and often parents are present and observing. Previous research indicates that many athletes and parents, while having some discomfort about these observations, also learn to accept them as part of the game and simply 'what it takes' to be a successful athlete (Stirling 2011; Kerr and Stirling 2012). The 'bystander' phenomenon, which has become popularized through the study of bullying (Smith *et al.* 1999), also applies to the use of negative coaching practices of some coaches.

As evidence of the normalization of emotional abuse in sport, one need only to consider potential parental reactions should their child be treated in emotionally abusive ways in other realms of society. How would parents respond if their child's teacher told the child he or she was useless or stupid? What would happen to the teacher if he or she threw a book across the room out of frustration? It is quite likely that such examples would elicit very different responses from parents and that there would be repercussions for the teacher in question. And yet such behaviours tend to be accepted as part of the sport culture (Stirling and Kerr 2007).

The research indicating that adults observe harmful treatment of children and yet fail to intervene suggests that the view of shared responsibility does not always prevail in sport. The focus of the UN Convention on the Rights of the Child on adults' responsibility to protect children from harm is reinforced by the Medical Commission of the International Olympic Committee through the following statement: 'everyone in sport shares the responsibility to identify and prevent instances of abuse to assure the health and safety of each participant in the sport environment'. Furthermore, specific to the context of sport, in 2004, the Panathlon Declaration on Ethics in Youth Sport was issued. This declaration represents a commitment of members of the sports community to 'establish clear rules and conduct in the pursuit of positive values in sport'. The Panathlon Declaration declares a commitment to five specific principles: (i) to promote the positive values in youth sport more actively with sustained effort and good planning, (ii) to continue efforts to eliminate all forms of discrimination in youth sport, (iii) to recognize and adopt the fact that sports can also produce negative effects and that preventive and curative measures are needed to protect children, (iv) to welcome the support of sponsors and media but believe that this support should be in accordance with the major objectives of youth sport, and (v) to formally endorse the rights of the child in sport. The following section focuses on ways in which adults, specifically coaches and parents, can promote sport as an avenue for healthy child development.

Nurturing young athletes' talents and interests in a developmentally appropriate manner

Previous research in the general child development literature highlights the important role adults need to play to ensure positive developmental experiences for children (Bronfenbrenner 1999; Larson 2000). Within sport, the adults in positions of power, particularly the coaches and parents, have responsibility to ensure children reap the potential benefits that sport has to offer and to intervene should young people's developmental needs not be met. In determining ways in which adults can facilitate positive youth experiences in sport it is useful to consider the research on children's motives for participating in sport and what children have to say about why they participate in sport and what they enjoy about sport experiences.

Children's motives for participation in sport

An extensive body of research exists on this subject and the evidence that children participate in sport to have fun, to develop their skills and fitness, and to be with friends is compelling (Brustad 1993; Weinberg and Gould 2003; Light and Curry 2009; Light and Lemonie 2010). Interestingly, when children are asked why they participate in sport, the notion of winning is conspicuously absent from their accounts. Although adults typically frame competitive sport for children around the concept of winning, a desire or need to win was the lowest ranked reason given by young competitors for playing sports in a study conducted by the English Sports Council (1998). This and other research with similar findings (see, for example, Barber *et al.* 1999) suggests that, in competitive sport, children are often treated as 'miniature adults' and a means of meeting the aspirations and needs of the adults involved rather than those of the children themselves.

Over-emphasis on winning

Much has been written about the over-emphasis on winning, sometimes at all costs in children's sport (Crone 1999; Cook and Cole 2001). As the emphasis on winning increases, so does the likelihood that children will be viewed as property or a means to an end. As Donnelly (1993: 14) writes:

> the body has become an instrument, an object to be worked on, trained, tuned, and otherwise manipulated in order to achieve performance. Those close to the athlete (coaches, trainers, commentators) and even athletes themselves refer to the athlete's body as if it or the performance it produces exists distinct from the person (in some cases even substituting for the person). Detachment of the body and its performance from the person legitimizes the use of drugs and other techniques, even violation and abuse, in the name of improved performance.

Similarly, Tofler and DiGeronimo (2000) explained that potentially abusive situations can result when adults lose their ability to differentiate their own needs and goals for success from that of the child. In many cases, a coach maintains his or her place on the roster if winning performances are produced; as such, coaches need athletes to perform well if they wish to continue to coach, even as volunteers. Similarly, parents often place their children in organized sport because of the belief that sport enhances the child's overall health and well-being, but once immersed in a sport culture that emphasizes winning, the likelihood that these aspirations of health promotion are replaced by winning increases. Bringer *et al.* (2001: 229) also refer to the 'win-at-all-costs' culture increasing athletes' being at risk for abuse as, once athletes are willing to do anything to achieve their goals, they justify any means to reach the goal. These examples highlight the potential for developmentally harmful practices to exist in children's sport.

Child-centred coaching approaches

Within the literature on the nature of children's participation in sport, calls for child-centred, developmentally appropriate approaches to sport programmes have been common (Ogilvie 1979; Valoriote 1986; David 2005; Kidman 2005; Kerr and Stirling 2008). In 1976, the American Alliance for Health, Physical Education and Recreation developed a visionary Bill of Rights for Young Athletes that outlined basic principles for the design and delivery of child-centred sport, including, for example: the right to play as a child and not as an adult; the right to have qualified adult leadership and the right to participate at a level commensurate with each child's developmental level (Martens 1978: 360). The need for a more child-centred approach to sport has since been regularly voiced:

> The sport experience should be designed in a form that would permit every child to develop strong positive feelings about their bodies ... contribute positively to the child's ability to identify more sensitively with others through shared experiences both physical and emotional ... [and] should condition attitudes that health maintenance through some form of physical expression does increase one's joy of living.
>
> (Ogilvie 1979: 58)

Pooley (1986) criticized the highly competitive model for athlete development and proposed an alternative, more inclusive model focusing on maximizing opportunities for participation, skill development and leadership at different stages of a child's growth and development. This strategy was first designed to reduce competitiveness in Canadian organized youth soccer (Pooley 1986), and has resulted in the development of mini-soccer, which is characterized by a reduced length of game, size of playing area and other modifications. Similarly, Valoriote (1986: 202) suggested that the delivery of sport programmes should be centred around a 'holistic approach which addresses the physical, mental, emotional, and social needs of participants'.

More recently, researchers have suggested specific characteristics and trajectories for the positive development of children in sport. Côté *et al.* (2008) suggested that there should be a progression from play to practice in youth sport; children should have the opportunity to sample several sporting activities; the delivery of youth sport programmes should focus on the developmental assets of the child; issues of physical and psychological safety, appropriate structure, supportive relationships, opportunities to belong, positive social norms, support of efficacy and mattering, opportunities for skill building, and integration of family, school and community efforts should be addressed; and attention should be paid to how playing and training activities of the child change over time.

From a human rights perspective, David (2005) proposed the following principles as fundamental to a child-centred sport system: (1) equity, non-discrimination, fairness; (2) best interests of the child: children first; (3) evolving capacities of the child; (4) subject of rights: exercise of rights; (5) consultation, the child's opinion, informed participation; (6) appropriate direction and guidance; (7) mutual respect, support and responsibility; (8) highest attainable standard of health; (9) transparency, accountability, monitoring; and (10) excellence.

Furthermore, in describing an athlete-centred coaching approach, Kidman (2005: 16) asserts that: 'The key to the athlete-centred approach is a leadership style that caters to athletes' needs and understandings where athletes are enabled to learn and have control of their participation in sport.' Similar to the recommendations of advocates for the child-centred coaching approaches described above are the key components of the athlete-centred approach outlined by Kidman (2005), including developing thinking and decision-making in athletes through questioning, pursuing a sport culture in which athletes gain responsibility for establishing and maintaining goals for themselves or a team, and the use of role rotation on teams to enhance empathy, understanding, trust and decision-making skills. Within the framework of an athlete-centred approach to coaching, 'empowered athletes have the authority and are enabled to engage actively and fully in shaping and defining their own direction' (Kidman 2005: 16).

Although there are similarities in the recommendations made for the respective child- and athlete-centred approaches, there is a paucity of literature that integrates child development theories with the design and delivery of sport programmes for children. This is perplexing as there is an extensive body of evidence in the developmental psychology literature that addresses ways to ensure healthy child development. If we turn our attention to sport, a domain which is highly child-populated, it seems reasonable to suggest that for sport programmes to contribute to healthy child development, they need to be designed and delivered based upon this evidence. It is with this context in mind that we now turn our attention to potential contributions sport can make to the development of young people if we align the design and delivery of sport programmes with developmental theory.

Application of child development theory to sport

Numerous theories of child development have been proposed, ranging from psychodynamic theory to learning theory, cognitive theory, ecological approaches and others (Santrock *et al.* 2005) with each approach offering specific contributions to our understanding of their development. The psycho-social perspective to life-span development proposed by Erikson (1963) has been widely used in developmental psychology and considers human development to be the result of the dynamic interplay between individual needs and abilities and societal expectations and demands. We assert that this psychosocial perspective may be a valid theory to apply to children in sport as it complements previous research-based recommendations for child-centred coaching approaches. Notably, the psychosocial developmental perspective maintains that the developmental needs of the child must be considered in order to promote holistic growth and well-being, and that the child should have agency over her or his own development (Newman and Newman 1995). Furthermore, Erikson's psychosocial developmental theory was selected as the developmental theory for application to sport because of its focus on the interaction of the person and the environment. Similarly, the literature on healthy and unhealthy athlete development also considers this interaction (Fraser-Thomas *et al.* 2005; Stirling 2011).

According to Erikson (1963), at each stage of life, one is presented with unique problems or challenges that require the integration of one's needs and skills with the social demands of one's culture. More specifically, he proposes that at each stage of life one is presented with a psychosocial crisis in which one must make psychological efforts to adjust to the demands of one's social environment. For Erikson, the word 'crisis' refers to a normal set of strains rather than an extraordinary event. The ways in which these crises are resolved affect one's orientation to subsequent stages of life. Erikson presents each crisis as a polarity or contrasting conditions. For example, forming an identity with a group is an important developmental task for those in the early phases of adolescence and Erikson represents this psychosocial crisis as group identity versus alienation. As young people navigate adolescence, the theory posits that tension is created as youth fluctuate between both ends of the pole but that most resolve the crisis in the positive direction with a sense of group identity. A positive resolution of each stage provides greater resources to help meet the demands of the subsequent stage. If someone has difficulty forming associations with peers however, he or she may resolve this crisis towards the negative pole of feeling a sense of isolation and alienation.

In the following section, Erikson's theory of psychosocial stages will be applied to the design and delivery of sport programmes. In Table 2.1, the psychosocial crises or developmental challenges associated with various stages of life are described, along with suggestions for appropriate sport delivery. More specifically, recommendations are made for ways to design and deliver youth sport in such a way as to encourage movement towards the positive pole of each developmental challenge. Given that the focus of this chapter is the participation of young people in sport, the stages of life addressed range from early childhood to late adolescence or the ages from 4 to 22.

Table 2.1 Recommendations for children's sport programmes based upon developmental needs

Developmental stage	Psychosocial challenges (Erikson 1963)	Recommendations for sport programme design and/or delivery
Early childhood (4–6 years)	*Initiative versus Guilt* *Initiative* = the active investigation of the world, an expression of agency and the self *Guilt* = a sense that one has been responsible for an unacceptable thought or action	– encouragement of exploration and stretching of one's own capabilities – establishment of environments that allow for and encourage risk-taking (within limits), creativity and questioning of accepted practices
Middle childhood (6–12 years)	*Industry versus Inferiority* *Industry* = acquisition of skills and knowledge valued by the culture, development of concentration, perseverance, work habits and goal-directedness, curiosity, pride in one's efforts *Inferiority* = feelings of inadequacy and worthlessness, enhanced through shaming, criticisms of a child's motivation or effort ('if only you had tried harder'), or abilities	– provision of positive external sources of feedback and reward – presentation of challenges of manageable and increasing difficulty – provision of opportunities to practise new skills without penalties – recognition and reward of effort in addition to performance outcomes
Early adolescence (12–18 years)	*Group Identity versus Alienation* *Group Identity* = sense of being connected to others, desire to be connected to others, extension of connectedness beyond the family, need for social approval, affiliation, leadership, status and power *Alienation* = social estrangement, absence of social support and meaningful connectedness	– encouragement of group affiliations outside of sport – bringing marginalized children into the group – teaching and reinforcement of skills of inclusion among young people – encouragement of group decision-making
Late adolescence (18–22 years)	*Individual Identity Formation versus Identity Confusion* *Identity Formation* = determination of one's own uniqueness, values, beliefs, roles, qualities, significance placed upon various roles *Identity Confusion* = lack of commitment to values, beliefs, roles, etc.	– acknowledgement and encouragement of the developmental need to explore various roles, beliefs and values – provide room to develop identities beyond that of an athlete

Looking ahead: recommendations for sport organizations in promoting a child-centred sport model

To advance the type of developmentally appropriate sport model that is recommended in Table 2.1, sport organizations will need to assume leadership roles. The following section suggests some recommendations for sport organizations in efforts to advance developmentally appropriate sport models for young people. Recommendations are posed in accordance with the UN Convention on the Rights of the Child and the Panathlon Declaration on Ethics in Youth Sport.

Prioritization of the best interests of the child

Sport organizations could promote a child-centred model of sport by advocating a sport culture for children that prioritizes the best interests of the child. The ways in which this priority may be actualized would then be clearly communicated to coaches and parents. In a child-centred model, the programming or curriculum of specific activities would be designed on the basis of children's developmental needs and challenges at each particular stage of life. Everything from the frequency and intensity of training demands, adaptations of equipment, facilities and rules, and athlete involvement would be based upon the particular stage of child development. Furthermore, the expressed purpose of children's sport programmes would be the development of life skills; this would not preclude the attainment of athletic performance outcomes, but these would be a by-product of life skill development rather than the explicit goal. Contrary to the common misconception that tailoring a sport programme to children's needs is inconsistent with performance excellence, a child-centred approach to sport advocates for the development of the child's fullest potential (David 2005). 'Winning' may be a by-product of focusing on the process of fully developing one's skills and abilities, physically, psychologically and socially. Sport organizations and researchers need to address the common assumption, particularly among coaches and parents, that developmentally appropriate sport is incompatible with medal-earning athletic performances.

Appropriate guidance and direction

A developmentally appropriate children's sport model would also see coaches receiving education and training for the important roles we expect them to play. In many countries, coaches at the grassroots level are provided with little or no training in areas of child development. Even in countries such as Canada, which has an extensive coach education programme, challenges exist in enlisting sport organizations and individual coaches to participate in such programmes. Questions also remain about the balance of technical versus child development content presented in coach education programmes. Just as teachers of young children are trained in both their subject area and child development, so should coaches. More specifically, if sport is geared to helping prepare children for life, then coaches should be assisted in finding ways to teach and model life skills.

Imagine, as well, a system in which coaching is recognized as a profession, along with a regulatory body. In North America for example, there is no overseeing governing body for coaching that determines the scope of practice, outlines professional qualification requirements and codes of conduct, or ensures accountability when such codes are breached. It is odd that in other professions that involve working with children, such as teaching and medicine, there are such regulatory bodies that ensure consistent educational requirements and accountability.

Extended responsibility

If one supports the view that sport helps to prepare young people for various life challenges, then the development of life skills through sport becomes a priority. As conveyed in the writings about athlete-centred coaching (Kidman 2005), adults in sport have a moral responsibility to consider how the decisions they make for the child will affect the child in the short term as well as in the long term, long after their sport career is over. Sport organizations would do well to communicate this mandate clearly to coaches and parents as a framework within which decisions are made.

Attending to the athletes' voices

Recommendations are made for sport organizations to develop ways in which young athletes have opportunities to contribute in a developmentally appropriate manner to making decisions that affect them. This does not mean that children may decide, for example, whether or not to participate in conditioning exercises. It means that children are first adequately informed about the need and purpose of conditioning. Then, in a developmentally appropriate manner, they may be offered the opportunity to contribute to the decision about which exercises are used for conditioning. As David (2005: 239) writes: 'Consulting children so as to integrate their opinion in any decision that affects them is not an option, it is an obligation.' Adults need to find creative ways to convey information and involve children in developmentally appropriate ways in decisions that affect them.

In children's sport today, it is almost unheard of that children are provided with the opportunity to evaluate their own experiences in sport. A future direction for both sport organizations and researchers is to examine ways in which children's voices can be heard in evaluating their own experiences.

Conclusion

Following on from the literature that advocates for a more child-centred approach to sport, this chapter highlights the importance of designing and delivering developmentally appropriate sport programmes for children. A substantial body of research exists within the general child development literature with respect to the developmental needs and challenges of children at each stage of life and there would be greater likelihood of realizing the potential benefits that sport has to offer for children if sport programmes were aligned with these developmental needs. Adults, in their roles as parents, coaches and sport administrators, play important roles in ensuring that sport is delivered in accordance with these developmental needs and the best interests of children.

Discussion Questions

1.   Discuss the ways in which competitive children's sport is consistent or inconsistent with the contemporary view of children.
2.   Describe the philosophy that underlies a child-centred model of sport.
3.   With specific reference to a particular stage of child development, recommend methods for designing or delivering sport in a manner that is consistent with the developmental needs and challenges of that stage.

References

Barber, H., Sukhi, H. and White, S. A. (1999) 'Parental influence on children's cognitive and affective responses to competitive soccer participation', *Pediatric Exercise Science*, 11: 44–62.

Bar-Or, O. (1983) *Pediatric Sports Medicine for the Practitioner: From Physiologic Principles to Clinical Application*. New York: Springer Verlag.

Bowlby, J. (1989) *Secure and Insecure Attachment*. New York: Basic Books.

Brackenridge, C. H. (1997) '"He owned me basically … "': Women's experience of sexual abuse in sport', *International Review for the Sociology of Sport*, 32: 115–30.

Brackenridge, C. H. (2001) *Spoilsports: Understanding and Preventing Sexual Exploitation in Sport*. London: Routledge.

Bringer, J. D., Brackenridge, C. H. and Johnston, L. H. (2001) 'The name of the game: A review of sexual exploitation of females in sport', *Current Women's Health Reports*, 1: 225–31.

Bringer, J. D., Brackenridge, C. H. and Johnston, L. H. (2006) 'Swimming coaches' perceptions of sexual exploitation in sport: A preliminary model of role conflict and role ambiguity', *Sport Psychologist*, 20: 465–79.

Bronfenbrenner, U. (1999) 'Environments in developmental perspective: Theoretical and operational models', in S. L. Friedman and T. D. Wachs (eds) *Measuring Environment across the Lifespan*. Washington, DC: American Psychological Association, pp. 3–28.

Brustad, R. (1993) 'Who will go out and play? Parental and psychological influences on children's attraction to physical activity', *Pediatric Exercise Science*, 5: 210–23.

Burke, M. (2001) 'Obeying until it hurts: Coach–athlete relationships', *Journal of the Philosophy of Sport*, 28: 227–40.

Cassidy, J. and Shaver, P. (1999) *Handbook of Attachment: Theory, Research and Clinical Applications*. New York: Guilford.

Clarke, A. and Clarke, A. (2000) *Early Experience and the Life Path*. London: Jessica Kingsley.

Coakley, J. (2001) 'Sports and children: Are organized programs worth the effort?', in J. Coakley (ed.) *Sport in Society: Issues and Controversies* (7th edn). Toronto: McGraw-Hill, pp. 109–37.

Cook, D. T. and Cole, C. L. (2001) 'Kids and sport', *Journal of Sport and Social Issues*, 25: 227–8.

Côté, J., Strachan, L. and Fraser-Thomas, J. (2008) 'Participation, personal development and performance through youth sport', in N. L. Holt (ed.) *Positive Youth Development Through Sport*. New York: Routledge, pp. 34–47.

Crone, J. A. (1999) 'Toward a theory of sport', *Journal of Sport Behavior*, 22: 321–2.

David, P. (1999) 'Children's rights and sports', *International Journal of Children's Rights*, 7: 53–81.

David, P. (2005). *Human Rights in Youth Sport: A Critical Review of Children's Rights in Competitive Sports*. New York: Routledge.

Donnelly, P. (1993) 'Problems associated with youth involvement in high performance sport', in B. R. Cahill and A. J. Pearl (eds) *Intensive Participation in Children's Sports: American Orthopaedic Society for Sports Medicine*. Windsor: Human Kinetics, pp. 95–127.

Eccles, J., Barber, B., Stone, M. and Hunt, J. (2003) 'Extracurricular activities and adolescent development', *Journal of Social Issues*, 59(4): 865–89.

English Sports Council (1998) *Young People, Sports and Ethics: An Examination of Values and Attitudes towards Fair Play among Youth Sport Competitors*. London: English Sports Council.

Erikson, E. (1963) *Childhood and Society*. New York: Norton.

Fraser-Thomas, J., Côté, J. and Deakin, J. (2005) 'Youth sport programs: An avenue to foster positive youth development', *Physical Education and Sport Pedagogy*, 10(1): 19–40.

Fredricks, J. and Eccles, J. (2006) 'Is extracurricular participation associated with beneficial outcomes? Concurrent and longitudinal relations', *Developmental Psychology*, 42(4): 698–713.

Hart, S. (1991) 'From property to person status: Historical perspectives in children's rights', *American Psychologist*, 46(1): 53–9.

Kerr, G. and Stirling, A. (2008) 'Child protection in sport: Implications of an athlete-centred philosophy', *Quest*, 60: 307–23.

Kerr, G. and Stirling, A. (2012) 'Parents' reflections on their child's experiences of emotionally abusive coaching practices', *Journal of Applied Sport Psychology*, 24: 191–206.

Kidd, B. and Donnelly, P. (2000) 'Human rights in sport', *International Review for the Sociology of Sport*, 35: 131–48.

Kidman, L. (2005) *Athlete-centred Coaching: Developing Inspired and Inspiring People*. Riccarton, New Zealand: Innovative Print Communications.

Larson, R. (2000) 'Toward a psychology of positive youth development', *American Psychologist*, 55: 170–83.

Light, R. and Curry, C. (2009) 'Children's reasons for joining sport clubs and staying in them: A case study of a Sydney soccer club', *ACHPER Healthy Lifestyles Journal*, 56: 23–7.

Light, R. and Lemonie, Y. (2010) 'A case study on children's reasons for joining and staying in a French swimming club', *Asian Journal of Exercise and Sport Science*, 7: 1–7.

Mahoney, J. (2000) 'School extracurricular activity participation as a moderator in the development of antisocial patterns', *Child Development*, 71: 502–16.

Marsh, H. and Kleitman, S. (2002). 'Extracurricular school activities: The good, the bad, and the non-linear', *Harvard Educational Review*, 72: 464–514.

Martens, R. (1978) *Joy and Sadness in Children's Sports*. Champaign, IL: Human Kinetics.

NRCIM (National Research Council and Institute of Medicine) (2002) *Community Programs to Promote Youth Development*. Washington, DC: National Academies Press.

Newman, B. and Newman, P. (1995) *Development through Life: A Psychosocial Approach*. New York: Brooks/Cole Publishing Co.

Ogilvie, B. (1979) 'The child athlete: Psychological implications of participation in sport', *Annals of the American Academy of Political and Social Science*, 445: 47–58.

Panathlon International (2004) *Declaration on Ethics in Youth Sport*. Ghent: Panathlon International.

Pooley, J. (1986) 'A level above competition: An inclusive model for youth sport', in M. Weiss and D. Gould (eds) *The 1984 Olympic Scientific Congress Proceedings*, vol. 10: *Sport for Children and Youth*. Champaign, IL: Human Kinetics, pp. 187–95.

Rutter, M. (1989) 'Pathways from childhood to adult life', *Journal of Child Psychology and Psychiatry*, 31: 23–51.

Santrock, J., MacKenzie-Rivers, A., Leung, K. and Malcolmson, T. (2005) *Life-span Development*. Toronto: McGraw-Hill Ryerson.

Smith, P., Morita, Y., Junger-Tas, J., Olweus, D., Catalano, R. and Slee, P. (1999) *The Nature of School Bullying: A Cross-national Perspective*. London: Routledge.

Stirling, A. (2009) 'Definition and constituents of maltreatment in sport: Establishing a conceptual framework for research practitioners', *British Journal of Sports Medicine*, 43: 1091–9.

Stirling, A. (2011) 'Initiating and sustaining emotional abuse in the coach–athlete relationship: Athletes', parents' and coaches' reflections', unpublished dissertation, Toronto, Ontario: University of Toronto.

Stirling, A. and Kerr, G. (2007) 'Elite female swimmers' experiences of emotional abuse across time', *Journal of Emotional Abuse*, 7(4): 89–113.

Stirling, A. E. and Kerr, G. A. (2008) 'Defining and categorizing emotional abuse in sport', *European Journal of Sport Science*, 8: 173–81.

Stirling, A. and Kerr, G. (2009) 'Abused athletes' perceptions of the coach–athlete relationship', *Sport in Society*, 12: 227–39.

Tofler, I. and DiGeronimo, T. F. (2000) *Keeping Your Kids Out Front without Kicking them from Behind: How to Nurture High-achieving Athletes, Scholars, and Performing Artists*. San Francisco, CA: Jossey Bass.

United Nations (1989) Convention on the Rights of the Child. UN General Assembly resolution 44/25. New York: UN. Available at: http://www.unhchr.ch/html/menu2/6/crc/treaties/crc/htm (accessed March 2012).

Valoriote, T. (1986) 'The development model in Canadian sport', in M. Weiss and D. Gould (eds) *The 1984 Olympic Scientific Congress Proceedings*, vol. 10: *Sport for Children and Youth*. Champaign, IL: Human Kinetics, pp. 201–5.

Verhellen, E. (1989) 'A strategy for a fully fledged position of children in our society', in E. Verhellen and F. Spieeshchaert (eds) *Ombudswork for Children*. Leuven: ACCO, pp. 9–33.

Weinberg, R. S. and Gould, D. (2003) *Foundations of Sport and Exercise Psychology* (3rd edn). Windsor, ON: Human Kinetics.

3 The first Youth Olympic Games

Innovations, challenges and ethical issues

Jim Parry and Steffie Lucidarme

Introduction

In 1991, the President of the European Association of National Olympic Committees, Jacques Rogge, opened the inaugural European Youth Olympic Festival (EYOF) in Brussels, where athletes aged 15 to 18 years from 33 different countries competed in ten summer sports. Two years later the first EYOF for winter sports was held in Aosta (Italy) and, since then, the event has taken place both in summer and winter every two years. After the success of the Sydney 2000 Olympic Games the Australian Olympic Committee decided to follow suit by organizing the Australian Youth Olympic Festival (AYOF), first held in January 2001 and every two years thereafter. From a modest beginning in 2001 with participants competing in ten summer sports, the festival has grown significantly into 22 sports, with 2,500 athletes between 13 and 19 years of age from over 20 countries competing in 2009. In the wake of the success of these events, during the 119th Session of the International Olympic Committee (IOC) in Guatemala City in July 2007, the IOC decided to introduce a new sporting event for young athletes – the Youth Olympic Games (YOG; IOC 2009).

The inaugural YOG was held in Singapore, 14–26 August 2010, with 3,500 athletes aged 14 to 18 years (birth years 1992–5) from all 205 National Olympic Committees competing. The sports programme encompassed all 26 sports on the programme of the London 2012 Summer Games, albeit with a limited number of disciplines. Altogether there were 201 events, some introducing new game forms to the Olympics, and some introducing mixed-gender and mixed-nationality team competitions (IOC 2009, 2010). Innsbruck is the venue for the first Winter YOG in 2012, and future editions of the YOG will follow the traditional four-year cycle with the Summer YOG being held in the year of the senior Winter Olympic Games and the Winter YOG in the year of the senior Summer Olympic Games.

The aims of the YOG are to educate, engage and inspire young people around the world to participate in sport and adopt the Olympic values. Obviously, the aims will include bringing together the most talented athletes from around the world to participate in high-level competitions as a possible stepping-stone to the Olympic Games. But the idea is also that the sporting competitions should be held in an educational and cultural environment where athletes are provided with experiences to support learning (IOC 2007, 2010) while staying alongside each other within a Youth Olympic Village.

Rogge reinforces the aims of the YOG as being educational, saying that:

> The vision of the Youth Olympic Games is to inspire young people around the world to participate in sport, and to teach the traditional values of the Olympic Games, which are the pursuit of excellence, friendship and respect for each other, respect for social values like the environment. We also want them to learn about important issues such as the benefits of a healthy lifestyle, the dangers of doping or their role as sports ambassadors in their communities.
>
> (Rogge, quoted in Shokoohi 2010)

Notwithstanding the good intentions the IOC has in creating the YOG, it would be surprising if there were no problems to iron out, or no unintended and undesirable consequences of this innovation. Below we consider some of the issues and challenges that have to be met in organizing the YOG in order to preserve the fairness and integrity of the Games and make it a learning experience for the young athletes competing.

The sports programme

Some of the YOG events differ from the Games in that they have been modified (see also Chapter 7 by Harvey, Kirk and O'Donovan) to be more suitable for young athletes and appealing for spectators, and these events have been very well received. Of significance for this chapter, many encourage a more ethical competition, in line with the Panathlon Declaration on Ethics in Youth Sport (2004; see also the Introduction to this book). The highly popular basketball competition in Singapore was played in a half-court using a three-on-three format, which helped to differentiate the YOG from the Olympic Games. This also presented an exciting spectacle and was very popular with the audience. However, the most important particularity of the 2010 YOG was the number of mixed-gender team events in archery, athletics, cycling, equestrian competitions, fencing, judo, modern pentathlon, swimming, table tennis, tennis and triathlon as an innovation aimed at being more inclusive and addressing gender inequality issues.

The qualification system for each YOG sport and discipline strives to guarantee the participation of the best athletes in their age category. For all disciplines, athletes are able to qualify for the YOG through competitions such as Junior World Championships or official junior rankings. In the four team sports (handball, hockey, volleyball and football) only one national team from each continent is allowed to participate in the six-team tournaments. Therefore, continental qualification events are organized to select the teams. The sixth place is reserved for the host country or can be proposed by the relevant international federation. In each individual sport, a specific number of 'Universality Places' will be reserved to ensure that at least four athletes of each NOC (National Olympic Committee) have the possibility to partake in the YOG. This means that some athletes will get a 'wild card' to enter the competitions. With the participation of all the NOCs, the IOC tries to ensure the universality of the YOG.

Participation and equality of opportunity

One of the main aims of the YOG is to give the world's talented youngsters the opportunity to compete against their peers from around the world and gain international competitive experience. It appears to be very inclusive and open to all youth in the world (theoretically) since the cohort is of four age years (14 to 18), and an Olympiad is held every four years. However, as the regulations stand now, it is not as open and inclusive as it appears for the reasons discussed below.

There are no age groups that include 14-year-olds.

1. The YOG is to be held every four years, and by limiting the age groups for each event to maximum two birth years, there will always be two birth years that are excluded from participation. For example, in 2010 the age group for rowing was limited to the birth years 1992 and 1993. Supposing these age groups were to be kept in 2014, only athletes born in the years 1996 and 1997 would be allowed to participate. Thus, all talented rowers born in 1994 and 1995 would never have a chance to take part in the YOG.
2. For football this restriction is even tighter, since, at the 2010 YOG, only players born in 1995 were allowed in the teams. Almost certainly, the IOC has chosen these restrictions to limit the number of participants but there are other possible ways to achieve this aim. For instance, the IOC could have decided to limit the number of sports instead of having the same number as the Olympics.

Age and fairness

Another possible reason for limiting the age groups to two birth years may be to ensure that age differences will have less effect on the outcomes of the competitions. If all the YOG events were accessible for 14 to 18-year-olds, it is obvious that the older athletes would have an advantage. The narrower the age groups are, the more likely it is that there will be fair competitions. However, we are still left with the problems arising from early-year births and early maturers. It is frequently observed that teenagers born in the first months of the calendar year are over-represented in most youth sport competitions; and early maturers have an advantage in age-limited contests (for example, see Cobley *et al.* 2008 and Chapter 5 of this book by Cobley, Miller, Till and McKenna). Consequently there is a high probability that during the YOG the chronologically older and/or the early maturers will be over-represented and go home with most of the medals.

On the other hand, there are some sports where late maturers are favoured. This is especially the case in gymnastics. In the 1980s and 1990s virtually all female gymnasts competing at an international (adult) level were aged between 14 and 18 years of age. In order to compete at this level, gymnasts had to start serious training of 20 to 35 hours a week by about 6 years of age. As a result, most gymnasts retired by 19 because they had trained for too many hours at too young an age, plagued by injuries and psychologically exhausted. Thanks to the efforts of federations and the IOC, currently gymnasts must be at least 16 years of age to compete in senior-level events. As a result, many international gymnasts are now competing throughout their late twenties with success. By creating the YOG there is a real risk that some nations, national federations, clubs, coaches and even parents could bring gymnastics back to the 1980s by having athletes as young as 14 training and competing as they did before this issue was redressed by the IOC.

Talent identification and early specialization

By maintaining a high-level competition for youth aged 14 to 18, the YOG creates a serious risk of reinforcing the practice of early talent identification and early specialization. Many young athletes show signs of expert sporting potential quite early and most countries worldwide attempt to develop structures to identify exceptionally gifted athletes at an early age in order to focus their resources on these particularly promising individuals. As the efforts and resources invested in these programmes have escalated in recent decades, the pressure on policy makers, trainers and coaches to create more successful athletes has multiplied. All these stakeholders could interpret the new YOG as an endorsement or approval of early talent identification and early specialization. There is a possibility that they could use the YOG to intensify their efforts, despite the fact that early selection and early specialization carry risks for the health and well-being of young athletes. These risks include overuse trauma, growth repercussions, diverse nutritional deficiencies and psychological problems. The age at which there is the highest probability of these problems occurring is estimated to be around puberty, accompanied by intensive training of over 15 hours a week. Many of the athletes participating in the YOG are part of this target group. These are areas of concern but, on the other hand, this may offer an exceptional opportunity for the IOC to raise this matter with the global sporting community and to discourage such early specialization and overtraining, but scepticism on this would be understandable.

Exploitation of young athletes

The responsibility for the young athletes competing at the YOG is largely in the hands of their national delegation, their trainers and their parents. Given the international prestige associated with the YOG it is highly likely that some nations would want to excel in order to advance their own nation's status or the status of a particular sport within that country. Second, parents, coaches and trainers are often so blinded with fanaticism that the desire for their children to achieve becomes more important than respect for their child athletes, or even consideration of their well-being. We see this as 'achievement-by-proxy' syndrome, whereby parents and coaches project their own (often unachieved) ambitions onto their young athletes. So the danger exists that nations, trainers and parents want to achieve excellence at any cost, leading to obsessive overtraining, the obligatory use of drugs and the forging of identification papers. For the young athletes, it is almost impossible to stand up against these forms of dishonesty and abuse, and these are serious ethical issues.

Selection of sports for the programme

On ethical grounds, and considering that the YOG are for young people, there are some YOG sports that could have been omitted because of their unsuitability for youth participants. It may be said that boxing is still a violent sport and therefore not suitable for youth. Likewise, there can be genuine ethical objections to shooting as a sport. Weightlifting and triathlon might also be seen as being unsuitable because they are extremely physically exacting sports. These sports might require training that is too hard and demanding for youth, and potentially be damaging for young bodies, as is the case with the modern pentathlon of excellence in five very different sports, which is too demanding for young athletes. Instead of including the very same sports that have traditionally been included in the Olympics, the YOG could have provided an opportunity to remove certain sports that could be deemed less ethical.

The sports

Sport rules (adaptations)

Adaptations of the senior rules for young athletes are ethically important in several ways. In differentiating court sizes, playing time, equipment and the rules to be applied, events become first of all more suitable to the physical and psychological abilities of these young athletes and therefore fairer (once again, see Chapter 7 by Harvey, Kirk and O'Donovan). Second, by changing the senior rules, the IOC recognizes that youth are not 'mini-adults' and emphasizes to the entire world that it cannot be expected that they perform as adults. Finally, there is also a possible indirect form of protection of the young athletes against excessive and inappropriate training in preparation for the YOG.

Winning and losing

The stress placed upon winning in children's and youth sport has been identified as an ethical issue (Cook and Cole 2001), but as an elite-level competition this is less of a concern for the YOG as it is an event for the best young athletes. The YOG brings together the most talented youngsters from all over the world, but only a few collect a medal. In the classic system of the Olympic Games, most competition schedules include direct elimination. This means that some athletes who have trained for years, who have made a lot of sacrifices, who have believed in and dreamed of their chances and who have travelled thousands of kilometres to achieve them are sent home after only one lost match. Although losing is one of the fundamental outcomes of sport, and learning to cope with loss is an important aspect of growing up and learning, we cannot ignore the possible psychological impact of elimination on young athletes. So we might recommend the development of competition schedules where each athlete can play a number of matches, and where the race for the medals is kept open for a larger number of athletes as a useful change that should be made.

For many countries, winning at the Olympic Games, being an Olympic Champion, even if it is only the YOG, is a real matter of honour. This might generate contradictory interests between the IOC and participating nations, resulting in a serious discrepancy between the IOC's 'official' aims and what actually happens on the pitches, tracks, courts and in the pool. For example, let's say that, seeing the opportunity of the YOG, a new sponsor wants to invest in a certain youth sport. On the one hand the young athletes will have more opportunities to develop their abilities and improve their performances, but on the other hand, the resources invested in the programme increase the expectations on the young athletes and coaches, and this might increase the possibility of abuse (violence, ill treatment, overtraining, eating disorders, a high dependency between athletes and trainers, and a higher risk of injuries). This is of course one major issue with the YOG tensions between an officially articulated and commendable aim of providing education and positive development for young athletes and the hyper-competitive nature of the Olympics that affects the YOG.

Age falsification

In the same month that the first YOG took place, the United States (US) Olympic women's gymnastics team of 2000 finally received their gold medals from the Sydney Games, after a lengthy investigation by the IOC had concluded that a Chinese gymnast, who was supposedly 17 years of age, was in fact 14 at the time (Author unknown 2010a). Despite promises from the Chinese for 2010, the US gave up its women's gymnastics place at the YOG, citing problems with the limitation on coaching accreditations (Normile 2010). This has led some to speculate that the real reason for the US withdrawal was a reluctance to compete at this level with the Chinese. Age falsification prejudices the whole point of the competition, which is to permit a fair and good contest (Fraleigh 1984) under agreed conditions. It damages sport in bringing the integrity of contest into question, and raises issues of trust and tacit contract. An inevitable response to non-compliance is suspicion, mistrust and reluctance to compete again.

This is part of the more general problem of contest-limitation. We see (or have seen in the past) limitations on who is to be regarded as a legitimate opponent, described in terms of weight category, gender, nationality, employment history (professional/amateur), pharmacological status and so on. In Paralympic sport, of course, it is universal because all contests are open only to those within a certain range of disability. Contest-limitation inevitably brings problems of categorization, supervision, detection and policing – and this applies to age as much as doping.

Cultural and religious diversity – football and the hijab

Law four of Association Football permits headgear to be worn only by the goalkeeper, presumably in order to keep dress to a uniform minimum and perhaps also for safety reasons. In March 2007, FIFA passed a ruling on a Canadian case, confirming Law four as above, and forbidding the wearing of the Islamic hijab (Mackay 2010a). In 2010, Iran's women's football team qualified to compete in the YOG competition but were informed by FIFA that they would not be allowed to compete wearing the hijab, a ruling that the IOC supported. After a period of controversy, FIFA and Iran agreed on a kit that includes a cap, below-the-knee pants, long stockings and long-sleeved shirts, and the ban was lifted (Reynolds 2010). This raises some ethical issues related to culture and religion that we look at below.

Those who have seen the film *Chariots of Fire* will recall that Christian observers of the Sabbath are not excepted from programme requirements, and that no special arrangements are made for them. If they are scheduled for a Sunday (or a Jew for a Saturday), the problem is theirs. If they can't or won't compete, it's their loss. No one expects that the rules or the schedules will be changed for them. And we can see why: if the organizers had to take account of ALL religious and cultural preferences, it is hard to see how a global event could ever take place. We don't need to believe in the universality of value to notice that anyone who insists upon his local variant might be seen as imposing it on the rest of us. And there are obvious and good reasons why such insistence should be stoutly resisted.

On the other hand, the rules should not, even unwittingly, unreasonably exclude people from competition. And it would be a sign of intolerance and imposition (even if thoughtless or unconscious) if an existing rule were not reconsidered for its relevance and adequacy in light of some difficulty in local implementation. In this case, we should revisit the reasons for a universal ban on headwear, especially for groups for whom headwear is an issue (e.g.

the yarmulka for Jews, or the turban for Sikhs – the latter has raised legal issues in the UK regarding the compulsory wearing of uniform hats for bus drivers, or crash helmets for motor-cyclists).

There seems to be an issue with consistency and the wearing of the hijab because some other athletes had been allowed to wear the hijab:

> Several athletes competed at the Olympics in Beijing in 2008 wearing a hijab, including Bahrain sprinter Ruqaya Al-Ghasara, the 2006 Asian Games 100 metres champion who carried her country's flag in the Opening Ceremony.
>
> (Mackay 2010b)

If so, it might seem unfair to ban footballers. However, this is not simply a question of the clothing item, but also a question of the legitimate requirements of the sport. To begin with, sprinting is not a contact sport, and this might be a genuine reason for treating it differently from football. On the face of it, this seems like an inconsistency, and we can see why the Iranians would be shocked and perturbed when their expectations were overturned. However, the failure to ban the hijab on a previous occasion might have been simply an oversight, which required amendment for an important occasion such as the YOG.

Allegations made against FIFA include those of religious discrimination (that they mistook the religious hijab for mere national dress), of sexism (wanting to stop the sport developing among Islamic women and putting obstacles in the way of the women's progress) and of racism (Mackay 2010c).

The London Olympics will be conducted during Ramadan – which in 2012 runs from 21 July to 20 August, right in the heart of the Games. Singapore 2010 organizers said they were mindful of a similar clash between the YOG and Ramadan when scheduling the Games, but the overlap with Ramadan was unavoidable because of the tight overseas sports calendar and the fact that the IOC stipulated that the Games had to be held in August, and last not more than 12 days (Reynolds 2010). However, no religious exceptionalism does not mean no religious accommodation. The YOG took many steps to accommodate preferences, such as providing early morning breakfasts and snack bags for those who need to break their fast during the competitions, serving halal food at the village, and setting up prayer rooms for the athletes' use. Still, fasting could pose an additional challenge for the athletes, on top of the physical and mental stress of competition. They will not be able to eat or drink from sunrise till sunset each day, while enduring the rigours of training and competition.

Sport and politics – Iran/Israel

At the 2010 YOG, officials of the Iranian team withdrew their 16-year-old finalist in the under-48 kg weight category of taekwondo, when he was pitted against a competitor from Israel in the gold medal bout. Officials cited an ankle injury, and then announced that the athlete would not attend the presentation ceremony to collect his silver medal as he was *en route* to hospital. Iran has a history of avoiding competition with rivals from Israel, because Iran doesn't recognize Israel politically as a state (Magnay 2010a, 2010b).

There are many issues here in this incident, including dishonesty (fake injury), instrumentality (towards the sport), exploitation (of the young athlete) and contest refusal (can someone *choose* who not to play?). Just taking up the last issue, in our view it is impermissible for a country to enter international competition with such an attitude. If the international community does not exclude someone (as it did with South Africa, for example, over the issue of apartheid), the choice is either for a country to withdraw from competition entirely, or to be disqualified and disciplined. We are of the opinion that what cannot be countenanced is that the venue of the sporting event should be used to make such a political point. Iran is either in or out – it should decide. And the IOC should take firm action against such behaviour (Toney 2010).

Sport forms (disciplines and events)

Many values are expressed through sport forms, and the 2010 YOG organizers strove to come up with some striking innovations for youth sport, some of which are presented here and which have ethical significance.

FIBA33

This is a three-on-three form of basketball played on a half-court with one basket and 5-minute play periods. With non-stop music, fast-paced action and a game lasting less than 15 minutes, Prince Albert of Monaco expressed excitement at this 'intense and dramatic' format (Author unknown 2010b; Hula 2010). The president of the international federation, FIBA, Bob Elphinston, commented on plans to include FIBA33 basketball as part of the YOG and it was reported that Carlos Nuzman, a leading official for the Rio 2016 Olympics, wanted three-on-three at the beach volleyball venue on Copacabana Beach, as well as the fast-tracking of other innovations into the Olympic Games (Author unknown 2010c, 2010d; Mackay 2010d).

First moonlit dive

Night diving was a striking and successful innovation at the 2010 YOG. Jesus Mena, FINA's diving technical committee chairman and the 1988 Olympics 10 m platform bronze medallist, said: 'Before it was a myth that you couldn't dive at night in an outdoor pool. Now we know it's possible. This could change the sport' (Ang 2010). Observers at the 2010 YOG diving commented on the sheer beauty of the event, but there is more to it than that. There were worries that divers would have trouble judging the pool's surface under artificial light, but that problem was solved with the use of sprays to agitate the water. Instead, diving at night has added a technical benefit. A bright day can spell trouble for divers who can mistake the blue of the sky for the colour of the water. But, under the stars, 10 m platform world champion Tom Daley said: 'There was better contrast between the sky and the pool. That helps the divers' (Ang 2010).

Gymnastics

Gymnastics planned certain differences between the YOG and the Olympic Games, citing safety grounds: 'The competition rules and difficulty level of the routines to be performed by the male and female gymnasts at the Youth Olympic Games have been modified in order to safeguard the health and proper development of the athletes' (Author unknown 2010e). In particular, the required difficulty elements were reduced in number, and difficulty value restrictions were imposed. This means that the young athletes are only allowed to perform easier and safer vaults, but it also has the 'child protection' consequence that their trainers will have no gain in forcing enhancement of the difficulty level, although they will still be able to focus on improving performance.

First horse draw

For the first time in Olympic history, riders in equestrian events at the 2010 YOG drew lots to determine which horse each would ride. This is a very significant attempt to make competition fairer. The draw was conducted at the Singapore Turf Club Riding Centre. The assigned horse/rider combinations were to apply throughout the competition for the team and individual events (Author unknown 2010f). Of course, there were objections from some to such a procedure. Adjusting to an unfamiliar horse is a novel challenge for many of the riders, and might raise safety concerns – but at least it is the same challenge for all. Drawing horses by lot might seem to make a lottery of the outcome, if you think that a good horse is what makes a winner – but at least it rules out the possibility that one might be able to buy success, by buying the best horse. The horse draw seems to me to make it more likely that the best *rider* will win, and this is what we should be looking for. It's about both the rider and the horse, of course – but it should be *primarily* about the rider, if it is to be an Olympic sport. This is one case of the more general point: the sport should find ways of testing the athlete, not his equipment. The javelin is a contest to find out who is the best thrower, not who has the best javelin.

Pistol shooting with laser pistols

New laser pistol technology was used for the first time in the sport's history at the YOG, replacing the standard pellet-firing air pistols. The issues here are equity, cost, safety and gender. The cost of shooting will be cut by two-thirds because laser guns are lighter and require no pellets. Therefore, more people (and more countries) will be able to compete and particularly less wealthy countries. Since safety issues will no longer be a major concern, competitions can be held in parks, gardens and even shopping malls, thus increasing the visibility and popularity of the sport. And lighter guns mean that there should be no reason why shooting should not become a mixed-gender sport (Kok 2010). Reports say that this experiment at the YOG was so successful that laser guns will be used in the modern pentathlon competition at the London 2012 Olympics (Kok 2010).

Mixed-gender and mixed-nationality teams

Many argue that the focus of the Olympic Games should be individual competition, and that problems of chauvinism and excessive nationalist influence would be reduced if it weren't for the medals tables and international rivalry. One way of countering the effects of nationalism is by organizing mixed-team events. After the individual events, doubles events or continental team events took place in fencing (where the final was between Bangladesh/Spain and Turkey/Singapore), tennis and table tennis, athletics, triathlon and swimming. Fencing and archery, among others, held mixed-gender events too, thus again raising the general issue of open competitions (Degun 2010; Lim 2010; Xinyi 2010). This encourages a focus on youth rather than on nations.

Education

In light of the intended value outcomes, and of the above issues and difficulties, we suggest that there is a great need for an effective educational initiative, for the athletes and the wider sporting community. In this chapter we are not able to reflect adequately upon probably the most important development of the YOG, its educational and cultural programmes, but we make four positive observations:

1. There *was* an educational programme planned and undertaken focused on education and this is a very significant and positive fact. We wonder whether or not we might look forward to something similar one day in the Olympic Games?
2. Somebody had given much thought and planning to it – in terms of both content and method – and the ample resources that were committed to it.
3. There was a genuine attempt to reach out beyond the athletes, as the fortunate few to be directly involved, to the general public (and to youth in particular). This used many innovative methods that included 'new media'.
4. The educational and cultural programmes were genuinely and explicitly organized according to Olympic values and principles.

Those responsible deserve great credit for this but we have some reservations that we very briefly outline here:

1. There should be some attempt to spell out what concept of 'education' is being employed, and this should be more than simple information-transmission, or ideological indoctrination.
2. Anything that calls itself 'Olympic Education' must draw attention to the educative value of sporting competition itself. It is not enough to see the YOG as merely a convenient *venue* for education – ways should be found of also making explicit and highlighting the *internal* values of sport.
3. It is not clear just how much of the programme is accessible by how many of the athletes, and what its effect on them actually has been, given differences in motivation, educational level, language competence and so on.
4. The education of a child or a youth takes place over a very long period of time. No matter how dramatic or powerful a short YOG educational experience might be, Olympic Education requires the participation of many people around the athlete in his/her formative years such as his/her coach, parent(s), teacher(s), friend(s). Ways must therefore be found of influencing these groups too and taking the education programme beyond the duration of the Games.

Reservations and caveats

Many of our sources are 'official' ones, and so may be rose-tinted, so it's probably wise to approach them with a certain amount of caution. But it's difficult to get better information when the major media showed so little interest in the event. Having said that, there is some evidence that some sports and NOCs didn't take the event seriously enough. For example, many national organizations did not send their best athletes, meaning that some of the events did not have world-class quality. Might the event 'feel' rather different if the overall quality rises to the elite level? If the YOG becomes more 'important' for the NOCs, might the values begin to slide in the direction of the Olympics?

It may be that some of the YOG policies contributed to this lack of elite athletic talent at the event. For example, in the team sports, the rules ensured that some top teams were not even eligible because only one team per country across all four sports could compete. There seems to be a contradiction here between the aspiration of 'universality' (= give everyone a chance) and excellence (= admit only the best) here.

Our (admittedly cursory) inspection of media in six European countries suggests that the overriding emphasis in media reporting was (as usual) on results and medals, with national media reporting heavily on their own national participants. The dominant motif emphasized what a good experience the YOG provided, and a good preparation towards the 'real thing' for those athletes expected to go on to an Olympic Games. There was only rare and limited reference to educational and cultural aims, and so the media seemed to regard the YOG as a kind of mini-Olympics. By contrast, the 'official' publications and comments from the direction of the IOC and the Singapore YOG Organizing Committee lost no opportunity to explain the innovative emphasis on education and culture.

Conclusion

Over the history of the Olympics young athletes (even child athletes) have participated, but the YOG represents a new step towards the systematic distribution of elite sport into the youth population. This brings with it serious ethical risks, while also providing opportunities for making youth sport more ethical, in line with the Panathlon *Declaration on Ethics in Youth Sport* (2004; see also the Introduction). In this chapter we have noted a number of ethical issues with the YOG, identifying both positive and negative aspects and making suggestions as to how these can be addressed. Owing to the fact that the YOG is an event for the elite young athletes, the ethical problems that trouble the Olympic Games could easily trouble the YOG, but with more problematic consequences due to the young age of the competitors. On the other hand, the focus on youth and the articulation of admirable educational aims provides an opportunity to establish a cleaner Games that is more ethical and takes into consideration the role that sport plays in the social and moral development of young people across the world.

This means that YOG outcomes should be carefully monitored and, in particular, the various YOG innovations and initiatives should be evaluated from an ethical perspective and consideration given to their significance for the Olympic Games, and world sport as a whole. It is very good to see serious efforts being made towards an effective education programme, and this might provide a model for future youth events, as well as raising general issues about the relation between sport and education. It might offer motivation for the YOG to go further and be an ethical event for the youth of the world, but it seems to us that, while some positive and novel issues are introduced in a 'Youth' edition of the Olympic Games, many of the issues covered simply highlight already existing challenges for the Olympic Movement in a novel form.

Discussion Questions

1. Identify and critically examine the innovations introduced for the inaugural YOG designed to make the Games more ethical.
2. Outline the education programme introduced for the 2010 YOG, the problems identified by the authors and the solutions they suggest. Comment on how effective they may have been and make your own suggestions for improvements in future YOG.

3. Is the YOG an ethical event for the youth of the world or just a 'youth' edition of the Olympic Games, with its existing ethical challenges and problems for the Olympic Movement merely presented in a novel form?

References

Ang, J. (2010) 'World's first moonlit dive impresses all', 23 August. Available at: http://www.singapore2010.sg/public/sg2010/en/en_news/en_stories/en_20100823_worlds_first_moonlit_dive_impresses_all.html (accessed 12 August 2011).

Author unknown (2010a) 'China FINALLY loses 2000 bronze medal', 11 August. Available at: http://gymnasticscoaching.com/new/category/ethics/ (accessed 12 August 2011).

Author unknown (2010b) 'Monaco's Prince Albert praises 3-on-3 basketball', 19 August. Available at: http://www.singapore2010.sg/public/sg2010/en/en_news/en_stories/en_20100819_monacos_prince_albert_praises_3on3_basketball.html (accessed 12 August 2011).

Author unknown (2010c) 'Rio 2016 president calls for sporting innovations at senior Olympics', *Sportsbeat*, 18 August. Available at: http://www.morethanthegames.co.uk/youth-olympics-2010/1812157-rio-2016-president-calls-sporting-innovations-senior-olympics (accessed 12 August 2011).

Author unknown (2010d) 'Junior women's archery world record shattered in Singapore', 19 August. Available at: http://www.singapore2010.sg/public/sg2010/en/en_news/en_stories/en_20100819_daily_wrap_junior_womens_archery_world_record_shattered_in_singapore.html (accessed 12 August 2011).

Author unknown (2010e) 'Differences between the YOG and the OG', issued by FIG Media Operations, 3 August. Available at: http://www.sportcentric.com/vsite/vfile/page/fileurl/0,11040,5240-202655-219878-166493-0-file,00.pdf (accessed 12 August 2011).

Author unknown (2010f) 'Historic first horse draw in Olympics', 15 August. Available at: http://www.singapore2010.sg/public/sg2010/en/en_news/en_stories/en_20100814_historic_first_horse_draw_in_olympics-.html (accessed 12 August 2011).

Cobley, S., Abraham, C. and Baker, J. (2008) 'Relative age effects on physical education attainment and school sport representation', *Physical Education and Sport Pedagogy*, 13, 267–76.

Cook, D. T. and Cole, C. (2001) 'Kids and sport', *Journal of Sport and Social Issues*, 25(3): 227–8.

Degun, T. (2010) 'Bolarinwa and Tagoe win relay medals at Youth Olympics', 10 August. Available at: http://www.insidethegames.biz/youth-olympics/singapore-2010/10366-bolarinwa-and-tagoe-win-relay-medals-at-youth-olympics (accessed 12 August 2011)

Fraleigh, W. P. (1984) *Right Actions in Sport: Ethics for Contestants*. Champaign, IL: Human Kinetics.

Hula, E. (2010) 'New basketball event for YOG', 8 August. Available at: http://aroundtherings.com/articles/view.aspx?id=35381 (accessed 12 August 2011).

IOC (2007) *Youth Olympic Games*. Lausanne: IOC.

IOC (2009) *Factsheet – Youth Olympic Games Update – Feb. 2009*. Lausanne: IOC.

IOC (2010) *The First Summer Youth Olympic Games in 2010*. Lausanne: IOC.

Kok, L. M. (2010) 'Laser pistols to be used at London 2012', 23 August. Available at: http://www.singapore2010.sg/public/sg2010/en/en_news/en_stories/en_20100823_laser_pistols_to_be_used_at_london_2012.html (accessed 12 August 2011).

Lim, L. (2010) 'China glitter in pool as crowd roars', 16 August. Available at: http://www.singapore2010.sg/public/sg2010/en/en_news/en_stories/en_20100816_china_glitter_in_pool_as_crowd_roars.html (accessed 12 August 2011).

Mackay, D. (2010a) 'Iran replaced by Thailand over Olympic hijab row', 5 April. Available at: http://insidethegames.biz/index.php?option=com_content&view=article&id=9348:exclusive-iran-replaced-by-thailand-over-olympic-hijab-row&catid=97:football-news& Itemid=143 (accessed 12 August 2011).

Mackay, D. (2010b) 'Iran angry after women's football team banned from wearing hijab at Youth Olympics', 3 April. Available at: http://insidethegames.biz/index.php?option=com_content&view=article&id=9337:iran-angry-after-womens-football-team-banned-from-wearing-hijab-at-youth-olympics&catid=1:latest-news&Itemid=73 (accessed 12 August 2011).

Mackay, D. (2010c) 'Iran replaced by Thailand over Olympic hijab row', 5 April. Available at: http://insidethegames.biz/index.php?option=com_content&view=article&id=9348: exclusive-iran-replaced-by-thailand-over-olympic-hijab-row&catid=97:football-news& Itemid=143 (accessed 12 August 2011).

Mackay, D. (2010d) 'Rio 2016 wants to stage 3-on-3 basketball on Copacabana Beach', 23 August. Available at: http://insidethegames.biz/summer-olympics/rio-2016/10361-exclusive-rio-2016-wants-to-stage-3-on-3-basketball-on-copacabana-beach (accessed 12 August 2011).

Magnay, J. (2010a) 'Youth Olympic Games (2010) Iranian fighter pulled out of Israeli clash', 15 August. Available at: http://www.telegraph.co.uk/sport/othersports/taek wondo/7946792/Youth-Olympic-Games-2010-Iranianfighter-pulled-out-of-Israeli-clash. html (accessed 12 August 2011).

Magnay, J. (2010b) 'Political row overshadows Youth Olympic Games in Singapore', 16 August 2010. Available at: http://www.telegraph.co.uk/sport/othersports/olym pics/7947737/Political-row-overshadows-Youth-Olympic-Games-in-Singapore.html (accessed 12 August 2011).

Normile, D. (2010) 'Regarding the Youth Olympics', *International Gymnast Magazine*, 2 July. Available at: http://www.intlgymnast.com/index.php?option=com_content& view=article&id=1691:usa-gymnastics-official-statement&catid=2:news&Itemid=53 (accessed 12 August 2011).

Panathlon International (2004) Declaration on Ethics in Youth Sport. Available at: http://www.panathlon.net (accessed 23 July 2011).

Reynolds, T. (2010) 'London 2012 to learn lessons from Ramadan scheduling'. Available at: http://www.morethanthegames.co.uk/youth-olympics-2010/1212036-yog-2010-london-2012-learn-lessons-ramadan-scheduling (accessed 12 August 2011).

Shokoohi, K. (2010) 'Games they can call their own', *IOC Newsletter*, 6 August. Available at: http://www.olympic.org/en/content/Olympic-Games/?articleNewsGroup=-1&articleId=96176 (accessed 12 August 2011).

Toney, J. (2010) 'Sad Soleimani the only loser and Rogge must act', *Sports Beat*, 16 August. Available at: http://www.morethanthegames.co.uk/youth-olympics-2010/1612125-sad-soleimani-only-loser-and-rogge-must-act (accessed 12 August 2011).

Xinyi, L. (2010) 'Best partnership: Gu Yuting and Adem Hman', 10 August. Available at: http://www.singapore2010.sg/public/sg2010/en/en_news/en_stories/en_20100825_Best_partnership_Gu_Yuting_and_Adem_Hman.html (accessed 12 August 2011).

4 Youth sport ethics

Teaching pro-social behaviour

Kristine De Martelaer, Joke De Bouw and Katrien Struyven

Introduction

Over the past decade national and international organizations have paid increasing attention and commitment to promoting ethically sound sport, focusing on specific problems associated with youth sport, codes of conduct, campaigns on fair play, and the identification and exchanging of good practices in youth sport policy. However, while there is interest in ethics in sport, the area is, in many ways, in its infancy (Livingston 2010). According to Livingston, this is due to limited formal training in ethics and, subsequently, the limited knowledge base for those who are central to fostering ethical practice in youth sport. This includes athletes, coaches, medical and allied staff, and those involved in management and business. While there is a significant amount of philosophical literature on sport ethics there is far less on pedagogical applications or philosophy-in-action, which is the focus of this book.

In our view, this lack of attention to philosophy-in-action in ethics needs to be redressed in teacher and coach education, training programmes in higher education and in volunteer training. Therefore, in this chapter we focus on how to enhance learning pro-social behaviour in youth sport. We outline several approaches to fostering the learning of pro-social behaviour and examine possibilities for enhancing it by looking at the education of physical education teachers, coaches and sports leaders.

Throughout the chapter the terms *youth, children, child athletes* and *pupils* refer to the age category from 3 to 18 years old. The term *coach* includes the job of a physical education teacher, often functioning as a coach, and volunteers providing guidance in organized sport. When using the word *teaching*, as in *teaching strategies*, we refer to coaching in youth sport as well.

Concepts of youth sport ethics

Coaches can often be confronted with a confusing range of concepts when they read, talk and write about ethical issues in sport. To provide some clarity on this we outline and discuss the main ethical concepts in the literature without going into phenomenological or hermeneutical depth. They are: fair play, morality and ethics, and physical literacy.

Fair play

This is perhaps the most common concept in sport ethics (see, for example, Lee 1996; Vallerand *et al.* 1997; Boixados *et al.* 2004). It is traditionally seen as a moral goal for sport (Loland 2002) and identified as one of the core principles in the Olympic Charter (Naul 2003). Fair actions (in competitions) can be considered attractive, unblemished and clean, in that they do not merely serve self-interest but are performed from an impartial sense of serving the common good arising from a sense of obligation (Loland 2002). Loland emphasizes that dictionary definitions on fair play agree with official declarations of international organizations and institutions, but often a distinction is made between formal and informal fair play. Formal fair play refers to conforming with the rules and informal fair play to attitudes towards the game, to other competitors and to the officials (Lenk 1993). This analytic distinction covers most of the interpretations of the ideal and so may serve as a normative starting point (Loland).

Morality and ethics

In common-sense understandings, morality and ethics are used interchangeably. However, morality can be understood as a sub-class of values and social norms of a group of people while ethics is the philosophical study of morality (McNamee *et al.* 2007). Ethical questions typically begin with practical situations where critical and systematic reflection is needed. *Values* and *norms* are terms typically used in relation to issues of morality and ethics. Values can be seen as meanings or interpretations of human existence, as social constructions that are viewed as guidelines for actions, while norms can be considered as the 'concretization' of values (Knoppers *et al.* 2001). According to these authors, values and their accompanying norms are explicitly and implicitly visible in coaching athletes, in the development of policies, the way people express themselves, their interactions and how they give meaning to their sport involvement and in the construction of organizations. They make a distinction between the visibility of values and norms on an individual, structural and cultural/symbolic level.

Most studies examining moral issues in sport have focused on negative aspects of morality, which is important, but to support the use of sport as a vehicle for personality development, the study of positive aspects of morality in sport is as important (Sage *et al.* 2006). Pro-social behaviours in sport are defined as being behaviour intended to benefit another individual or group of individuals (Eisenberg 1986) and, according to Sage *et al.*, have received only minimal attention. Sage and colleagues have identified a number of personal and situational variables having the potential to influence pro-social action.

Among the personal variables, personal goals and self-identity are both identified as components of the self-structure (Shields and Bredemeier 1995).
According to Shields and Bredemeier the self-structure is the psychological
conceptual system through which people apprehend their identity and value,
and which has been proposed to influence moral action through its influence
on moral intention (Sage *et al.* 2006). Eisenberg's (1986) model of pro-social
behaviour includes the global concept of personal goals. In sport research,
goals are often investigated from an achievement goal perspective to illuminate and understand the different reasons individuals have for engaging in it
(Nichols 1989). The achievement goal theory of Nichols is a solid theoretical
framework that can explain the relationship between dispositional orientations and moral issues in youth sport (Duda 2001; Roberts 2001). For coaches
and other significant adults in youth sport achievement, goal orientations
would represent the link between the individuals' attitude and the environment (Gonçalves *et al.* 2010). A task orientation represents a concern for skill
improvement and intrinsic facets of sporting experience, while an ego orientation represents the tendency to perceive competence and success relative to
others.

A variable that has to be investigated in relation to morality is moral
identity (Sage *et al.* 2006), being defined as 'a commitment to one's sense of
self to lines of action that promote or protect the welfare of others' (Hart
et al. 1998: 515). This definition represents the importance of a set of moral
traits to the self and has been described as the mechanism that motivates
moral action (Sage *et al.* 2006). The nine traits of the internalized dimension
of the Self-importance of Moral Identity Scale (Aquino and Reed 2002) are:
caring, compassionate, fair, friendly, generous, helpful, hardworking, honest
and kind.

Physical literacy

As the concept of physical literacy is becoming more widely recognized, we
clarify the link between it and sport ethics. According to Whitehead (2010:
11–12): 'As appropriate to each individual's endowment, physical literacy can
be described as the motivation, confidence, physical competence, knowledge
and understanding to maintain physical activity throughout the life course.'
This concept comprises three mutually reinforcing key attributes: (1) motivation;
(2) confidence and physical competence; and (3) fluent interaction with the
environment. As embodied beings we 'live through' our embodied dimension
and embodied interaction with our surroundings is the ground of our
development. According to Whitehead, physically literate individuals
endowed with versatility, confidence and competence with respect to their
embodiment would seem to be in a better position to experience, express and
appreciate different emotions, and also to monitor and control emotions and
conform to cultural expectations. Accumulated movement experiences establish a bank of movement memories that facilitate effective interpersonal

interaction. The movement repertoire supports the sensitive awareness of the non-verbal communication of others as well as that displayed by individuals themselves. The resulting empathy is a necessary attribute in developing socially appropriate interaction with others.

According to Siedentop (2002) literate sportspersons understand and are committed to the rules, traditions, rituals and values of a sport, and they have learned to distinguish between good and bad actions and procedures within a sport. The problem is, there is no comprehensive assessment instrument to measure the multi-dimensional nature of physical literacy (Lloyd *et al.* 2010). Lloyd *et al.* use the following four interrelated core domains: (1) physical fitness; (2) motor skills; (3) physical activity behaviours; and (4) awareness, knowledge and understanding, trying to make decent and complete measurement of all these aspects. In response to the call for objective data on physical literacy, the Canadian Assessment of Physical Literacy (CAPL) is currently being tested and aims to provide a valid, reliable, feasible and informative tool (Tremblay and Lloyd 2010). At this moment it is not clear how socially appropriate interaction in sport will be translated in a valid and reliable instrument.

Learning pro-social behaviour

Coaching should involve fostering pro-social behaviour, help individuals to develop physical literacy and empathy, and contribute towards developing socially appropriate interaction with others. To achieve this learning the coach has to be trained in relevant content and teaching strategies. Before going into the subject of teaching strategies or 'how' to coach pro-social behaviour, this section focuses on 'what' to teach as fundamental ingredients for promoting the learning of pro-social behaviour.

Because of the importance of interaction between the individual and the organization, we recommend using an ecological approach in order to have a complete picture of the relevant content of pro-social behaviour in youth sport. An ecological model emphasizes the importance of considering multiple levels of influence and the influence of the environment on behaviour (Ward *et al.* 2007). Table 4.1 is inspired by Ward *et al.*, and is used to describe strategies/interventions and for research on pro-social behaviour in youth sport. It is provided as a way of summarizing key issues at different levels in order to illustrate the importance of multi-level approaches.

When reflecting on the ideal content for the education and training of professionals and volunteers in youth sport, it is helpful to screen the daily practice of these different levels in combination with the existing research in coaching. Because of the impact of the coach and the environment, illustrations will be given of the interpersonal and organizational influences and the community level. Sometimes, relevant research in physical education will be quoted because one of the main goals of physical education in most settings is the promotion of personality development and socio-ethical growth

Table 4.1 An ecological approach influencing learning pro-social behaviour in youth sport (based on the ecological model of Ward *et al.* 2007)

Influences on pro-social behaviour (constructs from theories)	Increased pro-social behaviour comes when:
Individual – self-efficacy and competence (actual and perceived) – expectations (including perceived benefits and barriers) – intentions to be physically literate, with empathy and effective interpersonal interaction – behaviour, interpersonal skills and capability	*Individuals*: – have confidence in their ability to be literate sportspersons with empathy and effective interpersonal interaction with peers and adults – expect benefits from being socially engaged – intend to be literate sportspersons – have the behavioural skills needed to become and stay socially engaged
Interpersonal – social environment (including modelling and observational learning) – social support/social network – social influences/approaches	*Significant others*: – friends are active together with empathy and effective interpersonal interaction – family provides support (such as emphasis on ethically sound sport) – adults support, encourage, and model socially engaged physical literacy; youth sport instruction is designed to develop behavioural skills for pro-social behaviour
Organizational – organizational change – policies	*Organizations*: – youth sport programmes are modified to increase individual learning possibilities of pro-social behaviour as (1) participant and (2) practitioner with a guiding role (referee, coach, organizer ...) – have policies that support the active use of codes of conduct for coaches, parents, officials, managers ... – staff are skilled at stimulating pro-social behaviour – information on preventive policy for athlete protection is available for the general public – organizations are responsible for protection of youth athletes (report and follow-up of maltreatment and abuse)
Community/policy – inter-organizational relations – community development – advocacy approaches	*Community/policy* – image of sport competitions and communication in the media – national and international cooperation on expertise in sport ethics – organizational collaboration among all stakeholders protecting children's rights

(education through movement; Polvi and Telama 2000). As suggested by Shields and Bredemeier (1995), physical education is probably the most suitable and important physical activity for promoting moral development among children and young people. Pedagogies or instructional models that have been applied with success in school settings could be equally successful in community-based contexts (Kirk 2002; see also Chapters 6, 7 and 12 by Light; Harvey, Kirk and O'Donovan; and Wright, Burroughs and Tollefsen, respectively).

Many factors and competing demands influence the interpersonal interactions in youth sport and especially in competitive sport. These include the behaviour of (child) athletes and their parents, the focus of staff members (managers or those responsible for policy and coaches) and the reactions of parents and spectators (De Martelaer and Vertommen 2008). Each of these interpersonal and organizational elements can affect the decision-making of those involved and lead to actions that can be labelled as 'unethical' and sometimes even as 'unlawful' (Livingston 2010).

The most encouraging findings of research on effective strategies and activities for the development of pro-social behaviour come from school-based studies (Wandzilak *et al.* 1988; Bailey 2009). Intervention studies have generally resulted in positive effects, including improvement in moral reasoning, fair play, sportspersonship and personal responsibility (Bailey 2009). Polvi and Telama (2000) indicate that interventions in physical education with cooperative activities based on interaction show development in the skills needed in pro-social behaviour, such as helping, caring for others, giving feedback and making friends, in addition to the development of motor skills. In their study with four groups (reciprocal work in pairs versus teacher-led), they conclude that teacher dependence decreased when pupils cooperated with each other, and that caring for others and number of friends increased under the conditions where pairs (of pupils) changed systematically. The results of this study support the social learning theory by suggesting that social helping behaviour can be learned by practising in situations specifically organized for that purpose (Polvi and Telama 2000).

This suggests that an essential condition for learning pro-social behaviour is interaction and work with many individuals. The research stresses that goal-oriented teaching methods play a more important role than the context of the lesson. High task orientation has been shown to have a positive link with moral variables that are concerned with fair play (Duda *et al.* 1991; Lemyre *et al.* 2002; Kavussanu and Ntoumanis 2003). Dunn and Dunn (1999) found that high task orientation combined with a low ego orientation was most beneficial for sportsmanship. These and other findings indicate that examining interaction between tasks and ego orientation in predicting moral variables is important (Sage *et al.* 2006). Perceived mastery climate is a predictor of students' sportsmanship attitudes (Gutiérrez and Ruiz 2009).

The study of Mouratidou *et al.* (2007) was designed to explore the effectiveness of a six-week, specially designed moral development intervention in physical education. The intervention's design was based on the creation of a task-oriented motivation climate and on a reciprocal teaching style (students working in pairs). Before and after the intervention the Moral Judgement Test was applied. Results revealed that the experimental group exhibited statistically greater moral reasoning after the intervention compared to the control group. This study supports the idea that an appropriate design of physical education can support moral development. Also, other physical education studies evaluating the effectiveness of a specific teaching strategy or designed curriculum resulted in stimulating social or cooperative learning (Dyson *et al.* 2009).

The last level in the ecological approach (see Table 4.1) is the community/ policy level, which will be illustrated by a study on perspectives of youth on fair play in the Olympic Games and a study on child protection legislation. Naul (2003) assessed fair play among 2,940 European adolescents aged 12 and 15 from four different perspectives: individual assessment of the desirability and reality of fair play in the Olympic Games activities and violence behaviour patterns in sports activities. While young people strongly support the desirability of fair play in the Olympic Games, many of the participants in the survey had serious doubts as to whether fair play is actually practised. Naul (2003) concludes that the moral picture of fair play seems to have two faces for youngsters: high moral thinking, but real actions on a lower, pragmatic level.

Nichols and Taylor (2010) explored the benefits and burdens experienced by volunteers in sports clubs arising from child protection legislation, providing valuable insight into the impact of central legislations and measures on practitioners (volunteers) in the field, including representatives of key agencies, disengaged and potential volunteers. In Scotland, child protection legislation may have stimulated a broader adoption of child protection policies in clubs, but it has also imposed additional burdens on volunteers and voluntary administrators. However, having to comply with child protection procedures is a minor deterrent to volunteers, compared to pressures from lack of time, time at paid work and time with their families. The mixed methods approach in this study is called 'management action science', because it aimed to contribute both to the client's work and to academic knowledge in management. The telephone interviews with representatives of key agencies were combined with an online questionnaire survey among three different types of volunteers (current, disengaged, potential) and representatives in sport clubs. This broad approach offers the opportunity to interpret and compare the opinion of different stakeholders.

Empowering youth to foster learning pro-social behaviour

The coaching and the pedagogy adopted are fundamental to young people learning pro-social behaviour in sport. The most effective coaching actively engages young people in all stages of the learning process, referred to by some as empowering learners (Wild and Everley 2010). We suggest that the following two conditions are necessary for empowering young people to enhance the learning of pro-social behaviour:

1. That coaching is conducted within youth sport and physical education settings with youth as participants and with the teacher/coach promoting appropriate social interaction.
2. That the coach provides increasing levels of responsibilities, giving youth a guiding role, gradually in their own group and to other groups and ages, and introducing them into sports coaching programmes.

Settings with youth as participants and appropriate social interaction

Sport is often seen to be a 'social workshop', within which young athletes will learn pro-social behaviour spontaneously and where coaches will auto-matically guide them towards ethically correct reflection (Maes 2007). Teachers also have a tendency to believe that moral values are 'caught not taught' (Theodoulides 2003), as is also suggested by Harvey, Kirk and O'Donovan in Chapter 7. Indeed, Siedentop's arguments were built on his view of sport as a moral practice, taking into account the fact that benefits do not flow automatically from sports participation.

Here we want to focus on the two crucial aspects of empowerment in youth coaching: (1) teaching styles that provide increasing autonomy for the learner; and (2) the active use of codes of conduct, taking into account the degree of autonomy for the athlete. The smallest pedagogical unit embracing the entire process is O–T–L–O, which is a flow and an interaction of objectives (subject matter and behaviour), teaching behaviour (T), learning behaviour (L) and outcomes, as subject matter and behaviour (O) (Mosston and Ashworth 2002). Mosston and Ashworth stress the importance of reflecting on the effect(s) the teachers' goals and, therefore, their teaching style, has on the participants' physical, social, emotional, cognitive and moral/ethical development.

When social and moral development is the focus of the programme, the chain of decision-making in the whole teaching process will be more learner initiated than those lessons where physical developmental goals are priority. Mosston and Ashworth (2002) offer a spectrum of teaching styles. By estab-lishing who (teachers versus learners) makes which decisions, about what and when, they identify the structure of 11 landmark teaching–learning approa-ches, as well as alternative approaches lying between them on the spectrum. These are clustered in two categories (reproduction and production styles) according to the input of the learners in the decision-making. The reproduc-tion styles are more teacher-led while production styles are child-centred with a serious amount of input and thus autonomy of the learner (child-centred) under the supervision of the teacher/coach.

Another approach focused on the need for autonomy is Self-Determination Theory (SDT). This is a broad-based social theory considering issues of con-trol and autonomy as being paramount to individuals' well-being and adjustment (Soenens and Vansteenkiste 2010). SDT proposes three basic psychological needs that are considered as 'nutriments or conditions that are essential to an entity's growth' (Ryan 1995: 410). They are:

1. Autonomy, implying that people have a natural desire to experience their behaviour as freely chosen and volitional;
2. Relatedness, implying that people want to care for others and feel cared for by them;
3. Competence, referring to the desire to feel effective and skilful in the activities one undertakes.

Autonomy or self-determination is viewed as a universally significant human capacity to act in a volitional manner. Within SDT, autonomous regulation is hypothesized to foster optimal behavioural development and well-being, whereas controlled regulations would forestall psychosocial adjustment and even create a vulnerability to maladjustment and psychopathology (Deci and Ryan 2000). Autonomy-supportive socializing agents are characterized by the provision of a desired amount of choice, the acknowledgement of children's perspectives (a child-centred attitude), and the provision of a meaningful rationale when choice is constrained. Conversely, controlling socializing agents would undermine individuals' propensity for autonomous regulation and would prompt more controlled ways of regulating behaviour, as they force individuals to think, behave or feel in particular ways (Soenens and Vansteenkiste 2010).

Another important feature of socializing agents' interpersonal style within SDT is providing structure, which means helping in communicating rules and supporting decision-making. In Table 4.1, the active use of codes of conduct was mentioned in the organizational category, while the way codes and rules are communicated (mostly) by the coach is at the interpersonal level. Inspired by Soenens and Vansteenkiste (2010), Figure 4.1 graphically displays two dimensions as orthogonal, illustrated in a context of youth coaching pro-social behaviour. At the x-axis the dimension autonomy-supportive versus controlling motivation is described and at the y-axis low versus high structure of codes of conduct.

Starting with the upper left quadrant rules, these can be the rules of a game or the rules in a group to function in the activities. When a youth coach is teaching the rules of a specific game during different exercises, s/he can explain gradually between the exercises the reasons why these rules are important by evaluating the concrete situations and by asking children questions. Concerning rules for discipline during lessons, a popular system in physical education around responsibility is Hellison's (1985) Personal and Social Responsibility Model, designed to help children understand and practise self-responsibility (this is covered in more depth by Wright, Burroughs and Tollefsen in Chapter 12). The intrinsic motivating factor in this model is the innate desire of children to get along with others and take responsibility

	High structure WHAT in rules or code of conduct	
Autonomy-supportive, non-controlling	Clear rules, communicated in an empathic fashion and with provision of a clear rationale	Communication of rules without taking the child's perspective; using externally or internally controlling strategies to enforce rules
	Absence of rule-setting and monitoring, child is granted absolute freedom to choose and behave as he/she sees fit	Inconsistent rule-setting and monitoring, coupled with unpredictable expression of internally and externally controlling coaching
	Low structure WHAT in rules or code of conduct	**Autonomy-inhibiting, controlling**

Figure 4.1 The relation between coaching structure (regulation) and autonomy-supportive vs. controlling coaching

for their own behaviour, rather than relying on the teacher (Graham 2001). Masser (1990) describes four levels in this model, exemplified at home, the playground, the classroom and physical education lessons: irresponsibility, self-control, involvement and caring. When working with such systems there are three important characteristics that contribute to success or failure: (1) the system (discipline, rules) is explained at the beginning of the season; (2) the coach consistently adheres to the criteria; and (3) other significant adults such as parents, are supportive to encourage children to cooperate with the coach and with other children (Graham 2001).

Looking to the upper right quadrant of Figure 4.1, coaches can also communicate rules for behaviour in an externally controlling fashion, such as by threatening to use physical punishment, or by shouting or yelling if the child does not comply, or in an internally controlling fashion such as by giving the silent treatment. In the bottom right quadrant of Figure 4.1, the coach does not provide clear guidelines for behaviour, or is guiding without the intention of regulating the child's behaviour. In this case children will feel pressure without having a notion of the coach's expectations. Finally, as depicted in the bottom left quadrant, coaches can also provide a high degree of choice and freedom (high autonomy support) without communicating any clear guidelines or expectations for behaviour (low behaviour control). In organized sport, and more particularly in competition, this situation is rare because there has to be a structure of rules in order to be able to practise sport together.

Informal play, or a very open task during warming up or cooling down, can be situated in this fourth quadrant. This offers interesting possibilities when the guide has learned to observe not only motor skills and physical aspects but also psychosocial aspects among children. Free play enhances children's cognitive and socio-emotional growth (Singer *et al.* 2006; Pellegrini *et al.* 2007) because the learners have to create solutions themselves to solve problems and to guarantee participation.

The research of Bortoli *et al.* (2011) indicates that creating a mastery-involving climate enhances performers' adaptive emotional responses. Coaches should feel confident that emphasizing a mastery-involving environment will foster among their athletes a variety of pleasant states, enjoyment during the learning process, greater effort to master skills and persistence in the face of difficulties (Bortoli *et al.* 2011). Stimulating for developing values and social skills are situations that arise naturally through activities, guided by suitable trained coaches asking questions and modelling appropriate responses through their own behaviour (Ewing *et al.* 2002).

Wubbels *et al.* (1997) suggested that effective teachers have strong pupil–teacher relationships and are empathic, but are also in control (Chambers and Armour 2011). The adult's role is to fine-tune empathy both in terms of appropriate techniques and in terms of reinforcing the behaviour so it becomes a habit in children's lives (Jones 2005). According to Jones, moral action in general, and in sport in particular, is informed by other concepts and constructs, such as virtue, motivational orientation, maturity, principles, judgement, reasoning, perception, emotions and numerous situational factors. Therefore acquiring moral knowledge is primarily a process of learning how to recognize a wide variety of complex situations and how to respond to them appropriately.

Learning pro-social behaviour with youth in a guiding role

Also the shift from 'participation' to young people's 'engagement with physical culture' is important (Kirk 1997) in order go give young people the opportunity to learn different responsibilities and roles. Empowered learners can help others because they are familiar with productive teaching with enough autonomy and they are used to adopting a guiding role in peer-assisted learning, being a referee in a (small) group (Wild and Everley 2010). Coaches involve the learner by empowering their internal mental process (Chambers 2011). In the description of models of pedagogy the model 'Empowering Sport' foregrounds fair play while learners engage themselves and others in physical activity exploring the interrelationship of sport skills and social responsibility (Kinchin 2010; see also Chapter 7 by Harvey, Kirk and O'Donovan). In being a volunteer, young people can progressively learn different pro-social skills as well. One of the strategies can be enabling young people to begin and sustain involvement in leadership and volunteering through sport. At local level a framework can be created with several partners so that youngsters can experience sports leadership, help during activities, gain leadership qualifications and take up sports volunteering placements in the community (Phillpots 2010).

Eley and Kirk (2002) demonstrated the advantage of using sport and volunteering as a means for encouraging pro-social behaviour and citizenship among young people, and the positive impact this could have on the volunteer personally. The first phase of their investigation took place before a leadership camp and all participants completed two inventories, one designed to measure volunteering motivations (VFI) and the perceived leadership skill inventory (LSI). In the second phase, nine months after the initial data collection, there was a re-evaluation of the volunteers' perceptions of their leadership skills and voluntary orientations in order to evaluate the impact of the volunteer project. This study has practical significance for people or organizations wishing to recruit and maintain young volunteers. Volunteer satisfaction depends on possibilities for fun, learning, qualifications, empowerment and flexibility. Also, through involvement in coaching, management or adminis-tration, sports provide an avenue to learn social responsibility, leadership skills and confidence for life.

Teacher and sport coaching education programmes

In this section we make suggestions for content that might be included in physical education teacher and coach education programmes to assist coaches (and teachers) in fostering pro-social learning. We draw attention to the important link between theory and practice in order to ensure that the process and outcomes of research, including the evaluation of interventions and practices, are of real benefit and value for adults and children through iden-tifying what works for them. The coach is central in the process of developing pro-social behaviour but what is missing in the literature when focusing on methods and strategies is evaluation of the coach's own moral character. With this in mind, we suggest that the (future) coach should be seen as a reflective practitioner.

Glasgow and Hicks (2003) argue that professional development for tea-chers is often done *for* or *to* them instead of *with* or *by* them and we suggest that this is also the case in youth sport coaches and volunteers. There are two dominant pedagogies. One is more behaviourist and autocratic, focused on the education of *what* to coach; the other is more humanistic and is under-pinned by constructivist perceptions of learning (Light 2008) that lead to thinking more about *how* and *who* to coach. Much of a coach's work is linked to a wide range of significant others in a particular social and cultural context (Potrac *et al.* 2002). Therefore coaching is not only concerned with making myriad connections between subjects and methods, but also with making connections between other persons and life in general (Armour and Fernan-dez-Balboa 2000). Coaches' preference for developing their practice is gen-erally for learning through contextualized experience (Jones *et al.* 2004; Wright *et al.* 2007). Taking into account the coach's primary role as educator, we suggest that further development is needed for coaches to understand how their development of knowledge and understanding can be translated into the development of skill in undertaking specified work (Blair and Capel 2011).

Developing pro-social behaviour takes place through inter-individual inter-action, but an important condition is that interaction involves taking into account the other person's needs (Polvi and Telama 2000). The most effective teaching activities engage young people in all stages of the learning process (Wild and Everley 2010) with O'Sullivan and MacPhail (2010) stressing the need to listen to the voices of young people and for this to be increasingly enshrined in public policy and political debate.

The major question for us is where aspects relevant for sport ethics can be coached and the global picture of relevant topics. In order to include lessons filling in the four levels of the ecological approach (see Table 4.1), lessons on 'Ethics in Sport' have to cover individual, interpersonal, organizational and community/policy aspects. Taking into account the research domain covering relevant topics, lessons can focus on philosophical and historical issues, behavioural codes, verbal and non-verbal communication, respecting rules and techniques, campaigns and good practices, laws and decrees (see Figure 4.2).

In teaching or coaching and, in particular, in coaching pro-social behaviour in and through sport, it is very important to create an active learning environment for students to make learning effective. By learning in an active and interactive way during coach education, (future) youth sport leaders will be able to foster youth sport ethics as part of their coaching in a more practical setting among young people too.

The practical setting is of central importance for learning in sport and movement education, particularly when compared to other subject areas in schools. Rather than delivering information, the ultimate goal is to make a connection between the content (theory) and behaviour in real situations (practice) for youth sport ethics. An integrative instruction model suggests that sport skills are logically taught together with mental skills because learning is more efficient, more effective and more meaningful when physical, technical and tactical components of sport skills are integrated with mental skill instruction (Poczwardowski *et al.* 2004).

Ethics scholars have noted a trend in the teaching and practice of ethics to emphasize ethical dilemmas in which students and practitioners are taught to

	Content	**Scientific subject in movement sciences**	
Individual – interpersonal	Individual, developmental approach	Sport psychology	
	Rules, techniques, teaching methods, interaction, communication	**Sport pedagogy, movement education**	
	Phenomenological, philosophical thinking, historical aspects	Sport philosophy, sport history	
Organization policy	Cultural, situational, contextual	Sport sociology	
	Structures, campaigns, policy, management	Sport policy management	
	Justice, official declarations and regulations	Sport law	

Figure 4.2 Content of learning to teach sport ethics related to the scientific subject in movement sciences

rely on reason and analysis to choose the best solution and discard other options. Using rational, objective, universal and impartial principles, this approach is termed *principle ethics* and seeks to answer the question 'What shall I do?' On the other hand, *virtue ethics* emphasizes the character of the professional rather than situational variables and gives an answer to the question 'Who shall I be?' (Aoyagi and Portenga 2010). According to Aoyagi and Portenga, principle ethics is more reactive while virtue ethics is a more proactive system, with both approaches being complementary.

Conclusion and challenges

Coaching practice

Physically literate individuals not only move efficiently, they also move enthusiastically, creatively, competently, ethically in socially responsible ways (Penney and Chandler 2000; Whitehead 2007). This chapter adds value to learning pro-social behaviour in youth sport by focusing on conceptual, content and methodological points of view, helping practitioners to understand, innovate, design and implement appropriate strategies to coach youth in an ethically sound environment, taking into account individual, interpersonal, organizational and community aspects.

By bringing together policy, coaching practice, research and (higher) education in an area such as sports ethics, the gap in evidence-based research can be gradually closed. Central to this process is the need to raise the capacity to make better judgements about practice, policy and research (Thomas and Pring 2004), and higher education. Promising contexts for developing value and social skills are those mediated by suitably trained teachers and coaches who focus on situations that arise naturally through activities, by asking questions and by modelling appropriate responses through their own behaviour (Ewing *et al.* 2002). Practitioners and researchers should take the opportunity to approach the topic of sport ethics not just theoretically but also practically. Countries where coach education, sport leader schemes and junior sport practices are increasingly informed by child protection legislation (for example, the United Kingdom, Australia, New Zealand) (Kirk 2002) provide direction for the pursuit of ethical sport.

In making sport coaching and physical education teaching practice ethical we would ask sport coaches and physical education teachers the following questions:

- What kinds of teaching strategies for stimulating pro-social behaviour in sport do you use that have an effect on the knowledge, insight, skills and attitude of the young people in your charge?
- How do you communicate with young people, parents, staff members, volunteers, public and sponsors concerning: (1) the introduction/use of a sport code for ethically sound behaviour and situations, and (2) a critical incident happening in their own sport environment or in the media?

For those responsible for teachers' and coaches' (lifelong) education, we pose this question:

- What kinds of didactical approaches are actually used in your training programme and is this sufficient from a quantitative and qualitative point of view?

Research

Several research approaches for studying ethics in youth sport are based on questionnaires. The problem with using questionnaires to measure pro-social and anti-social behaviour is that the results refer to (self-) reported data rather than actual behaviour. Individuals, when responding to items tapping moral variables, may portray themselves in a favourable, socially desirable way (Sage *et al.* 2006). In the literature the importance of investigators contributing to the complex realities in a coaching setting is stressed (Côté *et al.* 1995; Potrac *et al.* 2002). In order to increase the understanding of the complex nature of coaching, the examination of the pedagogical strategies used by practitioners within the practice environment is necessary, preferably by using a mixed-method approach. A good example is the study by Potrac *et al.* (2002), where systematic observation and interpretive interview techniques were used to: (1) identify pedagogical strategies within the practice, and (2) investigating how such behaviours were influenced by social, contextual, experiential and situational factors.

Using observations to collect data on the behaviour of coaches in a practice environment has to be spread over the length of a season in order to provide accurate accounts of the coach's pedagogical strategies (Kahan 1999). Observations taken at a single phase of the season provide only a 'snapshot' of a practitioner's coaching behaviour at a particular time (Potrac *et al.* 2002).

Research studies in teaching contexts have mainly been based on group communication, less on activity and conducted over quite short periods of time of, typically, five to ten weeks (Polvi and Telama 2000). Eley and Kirk's (2002) study on (potential) young volunteers encouraging pro-social behaviour and citizenship was conducted over nine months but still measured a short-term effect.

Discussion Questions

1. What do the authors suggest is limiting the ability of sporting organizations around the world making a positive influence on the ethical conduct of youth sport?
2. Explain and discuss the proposed link between physical literacy and ethical conduct in sport and suggest how attention paid to physical literacy could lead to improving ethical practice and learning in youth sport and physical education.

3. Select a sport you are familiar with as a player and/or coach and suggest how these pedagogical strategies could be used to enhance positive social learning in youth sport or physical education settings.

References

Aoyagi, M. W and Portenga, S. T. (2010) 'The role of positive ethics and virtues in the context of sport and performance psychology service delivery', *Professional Psychology: Research and Practice*, 41 (3): 253–9.

Aquino, K. and Reed, A. (2002) 'The self-importance of moral identity', *Journal of Personality and Social Psychology*, 83: 1423–40.

Armour, K. M. and Fernandez-Balboa, J. M. (2000) 'Connections, pedagogy and professional learning', paper presented at CEDAR 8th International Conference, University of Warwick.

Bailey, R. (2009) 'Physical education and sport in schools: A review of benefits and outcomes', in R. Bailey and D. Kirk (eds) *The Routledge Physical Education Reader*, pp. 29–37. London: Routledge.

Blair, R. and Capel, S. (2011) 'Primary physical education, coaches and continuing professional development', *Sport, Education and Society*, 16(4): 485–505.

Boixados, M., Cruz, J., Torregrosa, M. and Valiente, L. (2004) 'Relationship among motivational climate, satisfaction, perceived ability, and fair play attitudes in young soccer players', *Journal of Applied Sport Psychology*, 16(4): 301–17.

Bortoli, L., Bertollo, M., Comani, S. and Robazza, C. (2011) 'Competence, achievement goals, motivational climate, and pleasant psychobiosocial states in youth sport', *Journal of Sports Sciences*, 29(2): 171–80.

Chambers, F. (2011) 'Learning theory for effective learning in practice', in K. Armour (ed.) *Sport Pedagogy: An Introduction for Teaching and Coaching*. London: Pearson, pp. 39–52.

Chambers, F. C. and Armour, K. M. (2011) 'Do as we do and not as we say: Teacher educators supporting student teachers to learn on teaching practice', *Sport, Education and Society*, 16(4): 527–44.

Côté, J., Salmela, J. H. and Russell, S. (1995) 'The knowledge of high performance gymnastic coaches: Competition and training considerations', *The Sport Psychologist*, 9: 76–95.

Deci, E. L. and Ryan, R. M. (2000) 'The "what" and "why" of goal pursuits: Human needs and the self-determination of behavior', *Psychological Enquiry*, 11: 227–68.

De Martelaer, K. and Vertommen, T. (2008) 'Youth sport children's rights in Flanders, International', in Y. Vanden Auweele, K. De Martelaer, M. Maes and T. Vertommen (eds) *Ethics Management in Youth Sport Implementation of the Panathlon Declaration. Strategies and Good Practices*, cd-rom, 5–7 November. Ghent: PVLO.

Duda, J. (2001) 'Achievement goal research in sport: Pushing the boundaries and clarifying some misunderstandings', in G. Roberts (ed.) *Advances in Motivation in Sport and Exercise*. Champaign, IL: Human Kinetics, pp. 129–82.

Duda, J. L., Olson, L. K. and Templin, T. J. (1991) 'The relationship of task and ego orientation to sportsmanship attitudes and the perceived legitimacy of injurious acts', *Research Quarterly for Exercise and Sport*, 62: 79–87.

Dunn, J. G. and Dunn, J. C. (1999) 'Goal orientations, perceptions of aggression and sportspersonship in elite male youth ice hockey players', *The Sport Psychologist*, 13: 183–200.

Dyson, B., Griffin, L. L. and Hastie, P. (2009) 'Sport education, tactical games and cooperative learning. Theoretical and pedagogical considerations', in R. Bailey and D. Kirk (eds) *The Routledge Physical Education Reader*. London: Routledge, pp. 285–99.

Eisenberg, N. (1986) *Altruistic Emotion, Cognition and Behaviour*. Hillsdale, NJ: Lawrence Erlbaum Associates.

Eley, D. and Kirk, D. (2002) 'Developing citizenship through sport: The impact of a sport-based volunteer programme on young sport leaders', *Sport, Education and Society*, 7(2): 151–66.

Ewing, M., Gano-Overway, L., Branta, C. and Seefeldt, V. (2002) 'The role of sport in youth development', in M. Gatz, M. Messner and S. J. Ball-Rokeach (eds) *Paradoxes of Youth and Sport*. New York: State University of New York, pp. 31–47.

Glasgow, N. A. and Hicks, C. D. (2003) *What Successful Teachers Do: Research-based Classroom Strategies for New and Veteran Teachers*. Newbury Park, CA: Corwin Press.

Gonçalves, C. E., Coelho e Silva, M. J., Cruz, J., Torregrosa, M. and Cumming, S. P. (2010) 'The effect of achievement goals on moral attitudes in young athletes', *Journal of Sports Science and Medicine*, 9: 605–11.

Graham, G. (2001) *Teaching Children Physical Education: Becoming a Master Teacher*. Champaign, IL: Human Kinetics.

Gutiérrez, M. and Ruiz, L. M. (2009) 'Perceived motivational climate, sportsmanship, and students' attitudes toward physical education classes and teachers', *Perceptual and Motor Skills*, 108(1): 308–26.

Hart, D., Atkins, R. and Ford, D. (1998) 'Urban America as a context for the development of moral identity in adolescence', *Journal of Social Issues*, 54: 513–30.

Hellison, D. R. (1985) *Goals and Strategies for Teaching Physical Education*. Champaign, IL: Human Kinetics.

Jones, C. (2005) 'Character, virtue and physical education', *European Physical Education Review*, 11(2): 139–51.

Jones, R. L., Armour, K. and Potrac, P. (2004) *Sports Coaching Cultures: From Practice to Theory*. London: Routledge.

Kahan, D. (1999) 'Coaching behaviour: A review of the systematic observation literature', *Applied Research in Coaching and Athletics Annual*, 14: 17–58.

Kavussanu, M. and Ntoumanis, N. (2003) 'Participation in sport and moral functioning: Does ego orientation mediate their relationship?', *Journal of Sport and Exercise Psychology*, 25: 1–18.

Kinchin, G. D. (2010) 'Models of pedagogy', in R. Bailey (ed.) *Physical Education for Learning: A Guide for Secondary Schools*. London: Continuum, pp. 118–28.

Kirk, D. (1997) 'Time commitments in junior sport: Social consequences for participants and their families', *European Journal of Physical Education*, 2: 51–73.

Kirk, D. (2002) 'Junior sport as a moral practice', *Journal of Teaching in Physical Education*, 21: 402–8.

Knoppers, A., ten Boom, A., Buisman, A., Elling, A. and De Knop, P. (2001) 'Values and norms in sport', in P. Steenbergen, P. De Knop and A. Elling (eds) *Values and Norms in Sport: Critical Reflections on the Position and Meanings of Sport in Society*. Oxford: Meyer and Meyer Sport, pp. 17–32.

Lee, M. J. (1996) *Young People, Sport and Ethics: An Examination of Fairplay in Youth Sport*. Technical report to the Research Unit of the Sports Council, London.

Lemyre, P. N., Roberts, G. C. and Ommundsen, Y. (2002) 'Achievement goal orientations, perceived ability, and sports-personship in youth soccer', *Journal of Applied Sport Psychology*, 14: 120–36.

Lenk, H. (1993) 'Fairness and fair play', in V. Gerhardt and M. Lämmer (eds) *Fairness und Fair Play*. Sankt Augustin: Academia Verlag.

Light, R. (2008) '"Complex" learning theory in physical education: An examination of its epistemology and assumptions about how we learn', *Journal of Teaching in Physical Education*, 27(1): 21–37.

Livingston, E. (2010) 'Sport ethics – An oxymoron?', *Journal of Science and Medicine in Sport*, 13S: e87.

Lloyd, M., Colley, R. C. and Tremblay, M. S. (2010) 'Perhaps we're riding the wrong animal: Advancing the debate on "fitness testing" for children', *Pediatric Exercise Science*, 22: 176–82.

Loland, S. (2002) *Fair Play in Sport: A Moral Norm System*. London: Routledge.

Maes, M. (2007) 'Sport en Ethiek in Europees perspectief' [Sport and ethics in a European perspective], in J. Scheerder, C. Van Tuyckom and A. Vermeersch (eds) *Europa in Beweging. Sport Vanuit Europees Persectief*. Ghent: Academia Press, pp. 307–26.

Masser, L. S. (1990) 'Teaching for affective learning in elementary physical education', *Journal of Physical Education, Recreation and Dance*, 61(7): 18–19.

McNamee, M., Olivier, S. and Wainwright, P. (2007) *Research in Ethics in Exercise, Health and Sport Sciences*. London: Routledge.

Mosston, M. and Ashworth, S. (2002) *Teaching Physical Education*. San Francisco, CA: Benjamin Cummings.

Mouratidou, K., Goutza, S. and Chatzopoulos, D. (2007) 'Physical education and moral development: An intervention programme to promote moral reasoning through physical education in high school students', *European Physical Education Review*, 13(1): 41–56.

Naul, R. (2003) 'Fair play as perceived by youngsters', in *Sport, Ethics, Culture: Fair Play, Sponsors, Doping*. Rapallo: Panathlon International, pp. 249–59.

Nichols, G. and Taylor, P. (2010) 'The balance of benefit and burden? The impact of child protection legislation on volunteers in Scottish sports clubs', *European Sport Management Quarterly*, 10(1): 31–47.

O'Sullivan, M. and MacPhail, A. (eds) (2010) *Young People's Voices in Physical Education and Youth Sport*. London: Routledge.

Pellegrini, A. D., Dupuis, D. and Smith, P. K. (2007) 'Play in emotion and development', *Developmental Review*, 27(2): 271–6.

Penney, D. and Chandler, T. (2000) 'Physical education: What future(s)?', *Sport, Education and Society*, 5(1): 71–87.

Phillpots, L. (2010) 'Working with partners', in R. Bailey (ed.) *Physical Education for Learning: A Guide for Secondary Schools*. London: Continuum, pp. 158–71.

Poczwardowski, A., Sherman, C. P. and Ravizza, K. (2004) 'Professional philosophy in the sport psychology service delivery: Building on theory and practice', *The Sport Psychologist*, 18: 445–63.

Polvi, S. and Telama, R. (2000) 'The use of cooperative learning as a social enhancer in physical education', *Scandinavian Journal of Educational Research*, 44(1): 105–15.

Potrac, P., Jones, R. and Armour, K. (2002) 'It's all about getting respect: The coaching behaviors of an expert English soccer coach', *Sport, Education and Society*, 7(2): 183–202.

Roberts, G. (2001) 'Understanding the dynamics of motivation in physical activity: The influence of achievement goals on motivational process', in G. Roberts (ed.) *Advances in Motivation in Sport and Exercise*. Champaign, IL: Human Kinetics, pp. 1–50.

Ryan, R. M. (1995) 'Psychological needs and the facilitation of integrative processes', *Journal of Personality*, 63: 397–427.

Sage, L., Kavussanu, M. and Duda, J. (2006) 'Goal orientations and moral identity as predictors of and antisocial functioning in male association football players', *Journal of Sport Sciences*, 24(5): 455–66.

Shields, D. L. and Bredemeier, B. J. (1995) *Character Development and Physical Activity*. Champaign, IL: Human Kinetics.

Siedentop, D. (2002) 'Junior sport and the evolution of sport cultures', *Journal of Teaching in Physical Education*, 21: 392–401.

Singer, D. G., Golinkoff, R. M. and Hirsh-Pasek, K. (2006) *Play = Learning: How Play Motivates and Enhances Children's Cognitive and Social-emotional Growth*. Oxford: Oxford University Press.

Soenens, B. and Vansteenkiste, M. (2010) 'A theoretical upgrade of the concept of parental psychological control: Proposing new insights on the basis of Self-Determination Theory', *Developmental Review*, 30: 74–99.

Theodoulides, A. (2003) '"I would never personally tell anyone to break the rules, but you can bend them": Teaching moral values through team games', *European Journal of Physical Education*, 8(2): 141–59.

Thomas, C. and Pring, R. (2004) *Evidence-based Practice in Education*. Maidenhead, Berks: Open University Press.

Tremblay, M. and Lloyd, M. (2010) 'Physical literacy measurement – The missing piece', *Physical and Health Education*, spring: 26–30.

Vallerand, R., Briere, N., Blanchard, C. and Provencher, P. (1997) 'Development and validation of the multidimensional sportspersonship orientation scale', *Journal of Sport and Exercise Psychology*, 16: 126–40.

Wandzilak, T., Caroll, T. and Ansorge, C. (1988) 'Values development through physical activity: Promotion, sportsmanlike behaviors, perceptions, and moral reasoning', *Journal of Teaching in Physical Education*, 8: 13–22.

Ward, D. A., Saunders, R. P. and Pate, R. R. (2007) *Physical Activity Interventions in Children and Adolescents*. Champaign, IL: Human Kinetics.

Whitehead, M. (2007) 'Physical literacy: Philosophical considerations in relation to developing a sense of self, universality and propositional knowledge', *Sport, Ethics and Philosophy*, 1(3): 281–98.

Whitehead, M. (ed.) (2010) *Physical Literacy: Throughout the Life Course*. London: Routledge.

Wild, A. and Everley, S. (2010) 'Teaching approaches', in R. Bailey (ed.) *Physical Education for Learning: A Guide for Secondary Schools*. London: Continuum, pp. 93–103.

Wright, T., Trudel, P. and Culver, D. (2007) 'Learning how to coach: The different learning situations reported by youth ice-hockey coaches', *Physical Education and Sport Pedagogy*, 12(2): 127–44.

Wubbels, T., Levy, J. and Brekermans, M. (1997) 'Paying attention to relationships', *Educational Leadership*, 54(7): 82–6.

5 The good and the bad of youth sport today

What about the unforeseen ethical issues?

Steve Cobley, Paul Miller, Kevin Till and Jim McKenna

Introduction

This chapter focuses on the Relative Age Effect (RAE). It considers evidence of participation inequalities, exclusion and subtle forms of indirect discrimination that dominate popular youth sports to illustrate how a preoccupation with talent identification and development is impacting upon and changing local-level youth sport participation. Such processes and outcomes highlight direct transgressions of the cross-national Panathlon Declaration (2004), and present challenges when set against national legislation such as the UK Equality Act, 2010. With the aim of responding to RAE-based discrimination and talent development inefficiencies, the final section of this chapter provides macro-to-micro recommendations for 'positive action' to posit that the needs of youth must be the central concern and placed ahead of unhelpful adult value systems and outcomes. Considered this way, sport may then be better positioned to play a more facilitative developmental role in the lives of youth.

Overview of talent identification and development systems

Tethered by what is seen as 'right at the time' for different ages, sexes and sport context demands, sport organizations and their development systems have long attempted to identify and differentiate particular youth from the broader population in an effort to further prepare and train future Olympic or professional athletes. We argue that the underpinning ideas and practices associated with youth athlete identification and development have become highly rationalized moral activities. However, the ethical problems that surround the implementation of talent development have become highly contextualized to reflect the prevailing social concerns as well as political, economic and social aspirations.

Perhaps the most infamous historical example is provided by the specialist sport schools and centralized training facilities created under socialist regimes within the former German Democratic Republic and Soviet bloc countries. These systems have become notorious for their synergetic mix of Olympic success and unethical exploitation of youth athletes (see, for example, Ungerleider 2001). More recently, and driven by the combination of increasing political, economic and perceived social value attached to sporting success, responses to poor medal/competition performances and/or securing the hosting of international sporting events, many countries, including Australia, the United States, Germany, China and the United Kingdom, have invested heavily in 'talent development' in an attempt to secure their next Olympic/international champions (see, for example, Green and Houlihan 2005). While such investment in future sporting success does not involve the explicit exploitation of youth it does rekindle familiar, and new, ethical concerns.

Whenever talent identification and development systems are discussed, debates about their advantages, disadvantages, benefits and costs emerge. Typically, successful cases of athletes are called upon to uphold and justify a given system, while a host of ethical concerns can generate counter-challenges that question moral reasoning. These often include claims associated with physical and psychological exploitation or abuse (see David 2005), such as over-training (Winsley and Matos 2011), physical injury (American Academy of Pediatrics 2007) labour exploitation (Donnelly 1997), doping (Laure and Binsinger 2005), violence (Tenenbaum *et al.* 1997), psychological (emotional) and sexual abuse (Brackenridge and Fasting 2002). Others point to athlete discrimination on the grounds of gender, race, sexuality, disability, and pre-existing health conditions such as HIV-positive athletes. Thankfully, most of the listed events are relatively rare, or at least, they are assumed to be so. Yet, individually and collectively they generate significant concerns. They encourage questioning of whether or not, with the exception of early specializing sports such as gymnastics, sport should attempt to systematically identify and develop youth at early stages of sport participation (see, for example, Wiersma 2000).

Instead of reiterating these perhaps already known concerns, we highlight emerging empirical evidence that points to a long-standing form of discrimination based on date of birth that is particularly evident in male youth sport contexts. We offer tentative explanations of how a subtle set of processes associated with talent identification and selection practices affect large proportions of youth on a day-to-day basis. Ultimately, these processes constrain sport participation from an early age and stage of development for many young people. Worse, often this exclusion happens in sport contexts that are often admired and promoted on the basis of their positive influence on child development. We provide evidence of forms of discrimination occurring from 'grassroots' levels upward, due to sport systems being preoccupied with competitive performance in youth and elite athlete development, rather than focusing on participation and holistic human development.

Ethical problems in talent identification

Distinct from 'talent discovery', although the terms are often used interchangeably, early talent identification is associated with differentiation, and is equated with non-uniform treatment of youth. This is justified on the basis of demonstrating exceptional performance relative to comparative peer groups, or being most able to resemble performance at adult levels. Depending upon the historical and cultural norms of a sport context, identification has often relied heavily on several strategies used either alone or in combination with other strategies. These include the use of physiological and anthropometric-based tests such as height, weight, 30thsm sprint and maximal oxygen consumption (VO_2max) tests. These tests attempt to replicate performance requirements in a sport context, performance trials or direct competition against similar age/stage peers, and/or subjective assessment procedures such as scout and coach observations at given single time points in a competitive year such as pre-season cross-sectional observation. These data then typically inform the selection of a pre-set/given number or group of 'talented players/athletes' from among the normative, 'non-talented' population. For the minority who are selected, this can often mean greater opportunities to regularly engage, participate, train and compete, as well as having privileged access to more specific coaching knowledge, experience and instruction. Those not identified are less likely to be entitled to equivalent opportunity or access.

Following identification, talent development is associated with the provision of appropriately facilitative environments, such as at sport clubs or regional and national centres, that aim to accelerate the path to becoming an elite performer (Abbott *et al.* 2002). These steps include progressive and intensive training programmes, such as higher volumes, intensities and durations, along with concentrated coaching and sport science support. In recent years these kinds of programmes have expanded rapidly across sports, and have been deployed independently by a combination of clubs, such as professional football clubs, governing bodies like the UK Rugby Football Union (RFU) and national organizations such as Sporting Giants – UK Sport, which have all attempted to reach down to identify precocious athletes.

Related to the ethical principle of beneficence (ensure benefits to others), existing systems have been justifiably criticized for their inability to accurately identify supposedly genuine talent and ineffectiveness in retaining and developing actual elite adult performers (see Vaeyens *et al.* 2008). In identifying talent, there is a widely untested assumption that 'talent' can be accurately and reliably measured in young people and that it exists independently of potentially other influencing factors (e.g. normal biological growth, socio-economic status). Yet it is now clearly established that common markers of athletic youthful talent – such as speed, power and body size – are substantially confounded by growth and maturation (Pearson *et al.* 2006). Normative growth in youth leads to observable step-by-step changes in body size, height, weight and fat per centage, while maturation in adolescence leads to structural and functional changes in the body. Furthermore, the timing and tempo of maturation can vary significantly at ages 13 to 15 between and within males (see Malina *et al.* 2004). This complexity profoundly compromises most – if not all – of the assumptions that are offered in justifying both talent assessment and talent development throughout youth. The evidence we present related to RAEs suggests that, left unaddressed, maturity and/or advanced biological growth creates systematic selection (dis)advantages in the talent identification and development process.

There are multiple explanations for why development systems have been ineffective in developing elite athletes to date. Criticisms of identification point to the singularity of specific physical and physiological parameters. More broadly, sport science as a discipline has been criticized for failing to acknowledge and capture the multidisciplinary nature of sport contexts (Phillips *et al.* 2010). Existing approaches have also failed to consider that some parameters may be more predictive of talented performance at one stage of development and performance (e.g. youth regional level) than in others (e.g. youth/adult national level; Cobley *et al.* 2011). To grasp the relevance of this distinction, consider the increasing need for advanced perceptual cognitive skills in high-level decision-making team sports across and beyond youth stages of sport.

Others argue that existing approaches have failed to consider the predictive effects of antecedent factors, such as psychological self-regulation (Toering *et al.* 2009), on longer term learning and development. Instead, and misguidedly, attention has fallen upon and narrowed towards sole reliance on present performance assessment. Further, approaches have neither repeatedly tracked existing identified youth, nor attempted to identify new emerging youthful talent over the long term, meaning that systems can be seen as being insensitive to change. This also suggests that identification and development practices reinforce, or implicitly accept, a rigid notion of talent, and that once this is observed it will be predictive – or be the best chance – of adult expertise. Such assumptions fail to consider that human development is individualized, dynamic, non-linear and multi-faceted (Abbott *et al.* 2005). Evidence from an array of youth development studies recurrently justifies adopting a fluid, evolving view of athletic capacity.

Relative Age Effects

Put simply, RAEs are associated with the inequalities in opportunity and experience that appear within a given age group as part of a sport or educational system (Wattie *et al.* 2008). For instance, using the dates designated to create annual age groups in UK sport that might typically be 1 September to 31 August, an individual born on 1 September will be the 'relatively oldest' in a sporting year group, such as in Under 10s football, and 'relatively older' when compared to a child born the following calendar year on 28 August but who will be in the same annual age group. Thus, the potential age difference within any given year group is anything up to 364 days.

Problematically, the interaction between time of birth and the dates used for annual age grouping in sport systems is associated with systematic disadvantages for the relatively younger, while at the same time

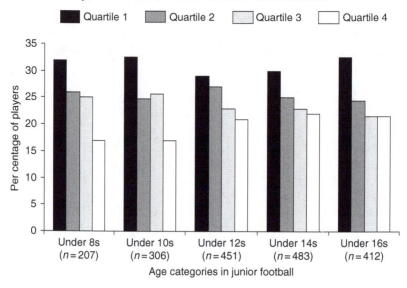

Figure 5.1 Junior football participation trends according to relative age and age-grouping category (Cobley 2009)

disproportionately favouring the relatively older. This simple variation plays out to create immediate inequalities in sport participation, selection and long-term attainment. For instance, relatively younger(est) boys in particular school and sport contexts are consistently identified as being significantly less likely to be selected for school sport teams (Cobley *et al.* 2008), and are less likely to participate in recreational and competitive sports teams at the 'grassroots' junior level (for example, see Grondin *et al.* (1984) on Canadian ice-hockey and volleyball). To provide an illustration, Figure 5.1 shows participation inequalities according to relative age from 'Under 8s to 16s' for a local junior Sunday football league situated within a town in the north of England.

Using the data for Figure 5.1, and after controlling for the number and distribution of live male births in the same town (8,346 during the period of 1985–95 distributed across quartile categories), the relatively youngest (Q4) were, on average, at least 11.5 per cent (i.e. minimum–maximum difference = 8–15.5 per cent) *less likely* to participate in local football across all age categories compared to the relatively older (Q1). This trend increases markedly in representative or developmental sport contexts, especially when those contexts are characterized by a performance emphasis, and contain tiers of selection and identification procedures.

As part of a meta-analytical study of 253 independent samples from studies published between 1984 and 2007, Cobley *et al.* (2009) showed that the overall odds of a relatively older male athlete, compared to a relatively younger athlete (Q1 v Q4) being competitive at the youth representative level (above recreational and local league participation in sports like football and

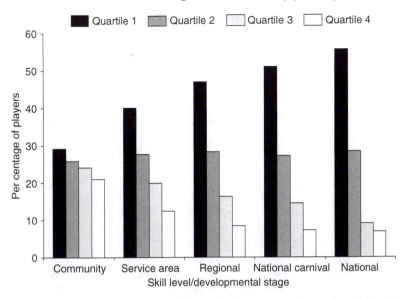

Figure 5.2 Relative age inequalities of junior Rugby League players (i.e. Under 13s to 15s combined) according to skill level/developmental stage (Till *et al.* 2010a, with permission)

ice-hockey) was approximately 2.5 to 1, with this figure varying according to sport context. Figure 5.2 from Till *et al.* (2010a) illustrates the potential change in the likelihood of identification and selection into various stages of a talent development system according to relative age. These data are drawn from junior UK Rugby League, and highlight a substantial participation and selection inequality between the relatively older (Q1) and younger (Q4). Further, these inequalities are initiated at the local community game level, and then intensify progressively across the tiers of the development system at Under 13s to 15s. At the regional, national carnival and national levels of representation, the selection discrepancy between the relatively older and younger becomes more pronounced, being approximately 40, 45 and 50 per cent respectively.

Ethical problems of Relative Age Effects

RAEs emphasize that a high proportion of relatively younger males are missing from participation trends in successive and repeated waves of annual year groups (e.g. Under 8s to 16s) whether in school, local communities or within talent development sport contexts for specific – but highly popular – sporting domains in the UK such as football and rugby. They highlight how a combination of policies, cultural norms and practices create a social reality where participation in 'grassroots' sport is being constrained through a first form of selection (schoolteachers, recreational/club coaches) and, from this point onward, in terms of the stages and levels of sport representation. Furthermore, youth are being (de)selected from various identification and development systems at a relatively early age of sporting involvement. These outcomes are likely related to being delayed in growth and maturation (Sherar *et al.* 2007; Till *et al.* 2010b); subsequent lowered expectations for immediate and/or future performance success relative to others in annual age groups; cultural valuing of immediate competition success in youth sport; and the preoccupation with developing elite athletes. From a motivational point of view, RAEs potentially devastate self-determination in those not selected, which is more likely to be the relatively younger. Their interest and motivation to participate in sport may be dented through externally imposed perceptions of competence, and actively undermined through controlled and regulated access that constrains relatedness and autonomy. On such premises, it is perhaps not difficult to see the human developmental and ethical problems associated with RAEs in youth sport systems.

RAEs and their mechanisms alone are worthy of careful consideration, as they illuminate several unforeseen ethical issues associated with advantage/ disadvantage (Buchmann and DiPrete 2006), inequality (Reay 2006), issues of inclusion and exclusion (Archer *et al.* 2003), meritocracy (Brown and Tannock 2009) and discrimination (Musch and Hay 1999). Sport RAEs clearly constitute a socially created inequality, referring to a situation or state which is not equal, or where there is an unfair distribution of a valued component or quality. They have a long reach in young people, probably because of the centrality of the body in adolescence and early adulthood (see, for example, Light and Kirk 2000). Besides immediate participation and attainment inequalities in youth, sport-based RAEs could also generate substantial social, health and economic dimensions in the long term.

In terms of social inequality, RAEs highlight that relatively younger individuals and groups have denuded social status and, as a result, they are denied equal access to participate within particular activities. In this case, our concern is for access to sporting – and therefore social – networks and facilities, although similar arguments might be made for the provision made for senior citizens, prisoners, ex-offenders and so on. Although yet to be empirically verified, sport-based RAEs could also cause a public health inequality, where the relatively younger may be less likely to engage in physical activity and/or other sports, which also happens in other sub-segments of the population such as low socio-economic groups. Equally, being cut from any system – especially one that is geared around disposing of a majority of its participants despite potentially extensive and invested involvement, as in professional football, is also likely to lead to less preferred outcomes, including compromised psychological health such as emotional disturbance and depression. While existing evidence suggests that the relatively younger are less likely to secure a contract as a professional athlete, in terms of economic inequality they may also be less likely to be employed in the sport-related sector, whether as a coach, officiator or employee of a sport governing body, due to their less favourable experiences in youth.

Whenever inequalities are present, it then becomes appropriate to consider the processes by which they occur, to what degree they challenge contemporary ethical standards and values, and whether they may in fact actually be unfairly discriminatory. In contemporary legislation, the UK Equality Act (2010) attempts to ensure that individuals or a group of people, are treated equally on the basis of a set of '*protected characteristics*'. These characteristics presently include: sex, race, ethnicity, disability, sexual orientation, religion or belief, trans-sexuality, having just had a baby or being pregnant, being married or in a civil partnership, and age. If individuals are treated differently on the basis of a named characteristic, then it is considered unlawful discrimination. To clarify though, relative age is presently not included as a protected characteristic. That said, UK law recognizes two kinds of discrimination: *direct* and *indirect*. Direct discrimination occurs when a protected characteristic is used as an explicit reason for discriminating. In contrast, indirect discrimination occurs when provisions, criteria or practices discriminate by putting groups at a disadvantage compared with others, but which cannot be justified as proportionate. It is not necessary to prove that indirect discrimination is intentional, so long as effects are demonstrable (i.e. via evidence). However, to generally establish whether indirect discrimination is occurring, as in the case of RAEs, four questions – adapted from the perspective of work and employment – should be considered:

Has the selection procedure been applied to all regardless of group?
Does the procedure disproportionately exclude more people from a particular group than people who are not from that group?
Is being excluded a disadvantage to people from a particular group?
Can the employer/sport organization or system prove that the need for the rule which excludes them overrides the disparate effect?

To answer the above questions based on the evidence that we have offered, we contend that RAEs represent a form of indirect discrimination, even though when set against current legislation it is still to be named as a protected characteristic within the Equality Act (2010). We suggest that the selection and/or identification procedures, which are applied extensively across youth, regulate participation trends in the initial stages of sport participation as well as the age stages and tiers of representation beyond it. The effects derive from a combination of static annual age grouping, selection procedures and current sport cultural values/norms, which result in disproportionately excluding the relatively younger in any given age grouping. This is recurrently and consistently indicated by research from particular youth sport contexts (see Figures 5.1 and 5.2). The pathway of disadvantage is clear, beginning by (1) restricting access and participation in local-level provision from an early age, which reduces the likelihood of

(2) access, and subsequently participating and/or being recruited and retained within a sport development system; which reduces even further the chances of (3) participating as an adult, or becoming a professional athlete. Finally, and possibly just as importantly, we contend that no employer or organization, including sport governing bodies, can confirm a coherent, evidence-based theoretical rationale for present practices. Neither can they confirm the requirement for, or effectiveness of early selection and differentiation of youth, especially in open team sport contexts. Those who endorse this practice may conveniently overlook the problems inherent in (1) talent measurement and forecasting; (2) maturational confounding; and (3) may fail to address the multiple factors and developmental needs of the athlete.

Viewed as indirect discrimination, albeit unintentional, institutional macro-level systems can be implicated for being ineffective, inefficient and potentially detrimental to a proportion of youth. At the micro-level, the reality and day-to-day experiences of youth sport highlight an additional ethical problem, known as 'solipsism'. In simplest terms, solipsism exists when an individual or organization holds that their experiences are the only existing objective reality. Within solipsism, there are no other realities including other persons with an independent objective existence. Thus, the effect of solipsism is to deny alternative experiences or existences, even though they may be equally informative and significant. For example, in 'white solipsism' (Rich 1979: 299) an individual will lose their ability to recognize and understand racial discrimination. It is also possible to use this term at an organizational or system level.

We suggest that RAEs may be best understood as a form of solipsism, a 'blind spot' within sport systems. Indeed, it is not unreasonable to assume that some sport organizations may not have recognized their upholding of RAEs' existence or their prevalence. Rather they have been present, but have remained hidden from conscious awareness. This may have occurred due to one or several reasons, including perceived unimportance, concentration on particular values/practices, denial, oversight, or even failure to recognize and value youth experience as well as their needs and perspectives. Historically, society and organizations, for the purposes of logistical and organizational convenience, have tended to group individuals into simplistic groups/categories typified by tangible, observable group differences. This can be easily seen with classic sporting groupings, like Under 13s or Junior–Academy–Senior. Over time these approaches become accepted and reinforced by members as an accurate truthful reality, as opposed to being regarded as a socially created construct. Indeed, even the evolution of discriminatory legislation, culminating in the Equality Act (2010), may also reflect a form of solipsism. Over time it has gradually included additional protected characteristics, based on a shift from between-group to within-group comparisons (see Figure 5.3). For instance, UK law did not formally recognize disability discrimination until 1995. That said, now more complex and intricate within-group characteristics have become protected (see, for example, the Civil Partnership Act 2004).

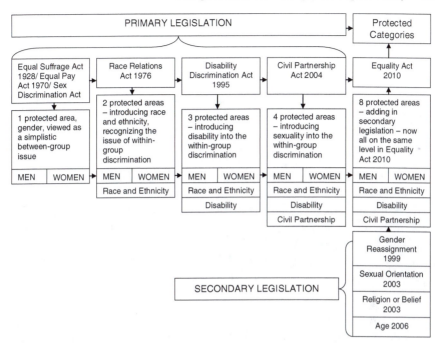

Figure 5.3 Evolution of UK discrimination legislation from 1928 to 2010

In a similar vein, maybe existing practices, such as annual age grouping and standard forms of identification and selection processes, were implemented to help ensure effective organization, fairness and equality for occasions of identifying talent, as well as maximization of youth success. But, at the same time, we also need to identify potential weaknesses and consequences. The two core weaknesses and consequences of present youth sport systems are the minimal consideration of the developmental needs of youth, and potential within-group developmental variation which leads to RAEs. While we are becoming better aware of some of our assumptions within broader organizational systems, we also need to be prepared to change our thinking and actions. For what might be deemed to be acceptable practice right now may not be deemed acceptable, or even legal, in the future, unless – with reference to question 4 in establishing indirect discrimination – it can be proven that early selection and RAEs are necessary to develop adult sporting athletes.

Positive action and implications for youth sport systems

Endorsed by the International Olympic Committee and many other national/ public bodies, the Panathlon Declaration on Ethics in Youth Sport (2004) makes five declarations to establish clear rules of conduct in the pursuit of positive values in youth sport. Declaration 2 asserts the aim of actively removing all forms of discrimination, and explicitly recognizes ethical problems associated with 'late developers' and 'less talented' who should be 'offered similar chances to practice sport and be given the same professional attention available to early developers, able-bodied, and the more talented'. More locally, within the UK Equality Act (2010), '*positive action*' is recommended when someone has a protected characteristic, and may be experiencing – or is about to experience – a disadvantage because of it (Government Equalities Office 2010). Although not currently protected, we can still consider positive action and solutions to reduce and remove socially created RAEs, helping those associated with either local-level youth sport or wider athlete development systems, whether as an athlete, coach or sports administrator.

Remembering that RAEs represent ethical problems of (dis)advantage, inequality, inclusion/exclusion and indirect discrimination, as well as challenges to meritocracy, it can also be stated that they reflect recent changes in modern youth sport. But as RAEs are a socially created manifestation it is reasonable to assume that their impact can be reduced or eliminated by likewise changing social processes. Considering the multiple dimensions of RAEs, it is perhaps not surprising that positive action may also occur at multiple levels and with multiple components. However, thorough forecasting and evaluation will be necessary to assess and determine their respective effectiveness.

Prior research has identified strategies for RAE removal. Generally, these are characterized by their focus on logistical changes in sport systems, although they could be critiqued for lacking comprehensive consideration of (1) present values in youth sport, (2) inherent system processes, and (3) resultant individual behaviours that generate unethical discrimination. Potential solutions have included (i) the rotation and manipulation of age-group bandwidths (Hurley *et al.* 2001), (ii) management of athlete distributions in selection, such as through player quotas, and participation, such as through playing time (Helsen *et al.* 1998, 2000), as well as (iii) the incorporation of height and weight classifications to replace annual age groupings (Musch and Grondin 2001). Raising knowledge and awareness of RAEs among those responsible for the infrastructure and coordination has also been identified as a strategy (Cobley 2009), but until recently there has been little evidence of cultural and practical change other than an increased reporting of RAE trends within sport development systems (Powell 2011). This means that the active ingredients of what produces RAEs remain either unchanged or unaffected, despite knowledge and awareness. The combination of potential solipsism, an institutionalized *modus operandi*, and an inability or unwillingness to adapt sport systems and their inherent practices suggests a need to think more deeply to support the introduction of effective authentic positive change (Verbos *et al.* 2007).

Notwithstanding the problems of applying medicine's core ethical principles (Beauchamp and Childress 1989), these can still provide useful guidance and direction for considering purposeful initial intervention and change. For instance, the principle of autonomy recognizes that individuals should be able to self-determine and make personally informed decisions to provide self-agency, and, as a vulnerable group, youth may share and negotiate autonomy with others such as parents and coaches. While there is not necessarily a 'level playing field' regarding the ability of a young person to self-determine access and participate in local sporting activity such as at a school or club, become a club or society member, or access coaching expertise, and it remains influenced by other factors such as socio-economic status, this should not invalidate necessary action associated with RAEs and autonomy. As UNESCO (1978) states, sport and physical education should be a 'fundamental right to all'.

To achieve autonomy, it is pivotal, from an RAE perspective, for young people to be able to voluntarily access local school or community provision. Therefore, access cannot be constrained, regulated, decided and/or coerced by any form of (de)selection process. Based on informed consent, youth should also determine the nature of their engagement and be able to withdraw without penalty, whatever the level/commitment of sport participation. To aid this outcome, it could be argued that the purpose and emphasis of school and local community sport needs to be distinct from the values and practices of adult elite sport, a point further discussed in Chapter 7 of this volume by Harvey, Kirk and O'Donovan. These values and practices are often associated with the internalization of 'external regulation' (Ryan *et al.* 1994), which runs contrary to the idea of autonomy. It also appears appropriate to consider the perspectives of youth, as well as alternative sport development models such as the Developmental Model of Sport Participation (Côté and Fraser-Thomas 2007) in carefully considering how modifications would impact upon participant autonomy.

Access is also important to the principle of justice, which is concerned with the distribution of resources, and the decision as to who deserves/merits 'treatment'. In modern sport systems, there is an argument to suggest – independent of purchasing access – that access to 'treatment', which typically refers to local coaching expertise and/or sporting facilities, can be difficult (Hillsdon *et al.* 2007). Often, young people are called upon to demonstrate their skills and talent prior to being given access to specialized resources – whether this takes the form of facilities, coaching and/or equipment. No doubt, the resource obstacle will always be difficult to address or overcome, but still, sports systems alongside local public provision need to better consider ways for ensuring that initial exposure, participation and involvement can be stimulated, and that youth autonomy can be supported (Eccles *et al.* 1997) with less constraint or dependence on others. In this case, others may represent people, like parents (and often coaches), whose greater disposable wealth allows children to make the best use of enhanced opportunities for engagement.

Perhaps a more radical but effective option would be to replace competitive structures at the early stages of youth participation, that comprise win/loss point systems and competitive leagues, with a variety of skills-based sport activities that prioritize social inclusion and integration (Rose-Krasnor *et al.* 2006). A less severe modification could involve considering placing a far stronger emphasis on 'small-sided games' in team sports (e.g. 4 vs. 4 in football). Such games may partially reduce RAEs as they appear effective in equalizing activity time, as well as the volume of attempts and time spent rehearsing and developing technical and tactical skills (Owen *et al.* 2004; see also Chapter 7 by Harvey *et al.*). However, these may not be entirely effective in reducing the influence and impact of physical 'maturational' dominance. Further, allowing performance criteria and similar selection processes to remain included in such games will only lead to a continuation of RAE prevalence. The active ingredient in this proposition is greater emphasis on technical skill and tactical competence criteria as part of multi-dimensional assessment (Reilly *et al.* 2000), as opposed to physical and performance criteria. That said, these contentions remain to be empirically verified.

If doubt remains about the power of these strategies to achieve positive action and remove RAE-based discrimination, then the medical principle of non-maleficence might be helpful. This states that our primary concern should be to ensure that no harm comes to others through our actions. For enactment, this may require a policy-level intervention to instigate localized change. Based on the problems of talent identification and RAEs, it may be appropriate to delay selection into tiers of representative and developmental sport until after puberty and maturation, such as 16 years for males. This would be particularly pertinent for 'late-specializing' team sports, where peak performance is usually not attained until the mid-twenties. Likewise, it would be appropriate to only offer local community competitive sport at 16+ years. From an adult system perspective, this may appear a far-reaching step but from a youth perspective it would avoid the potential harm and erroneous effects emerging from early scrutiny, assessment and testing, which leads to both differentiation and exclusion. The case for such substantial change is further strengthened by the lack of robust evidence to suggest that existing practice is either effective or necessary, or that there are no better options for minimizing their potentially harmful effects.

By opening access at a 'grassroots' level, and delaying entry into competitive performance streams, we can then begin to consider how to attain the medical principle of beneficence (i.e. promoting actions towards the well-being of others). Here the aim is to ensure that more young people, of all (relative) ages, can potentially accrue the social, psychological, developmental and health benefits that are linked to involvement in sport (Fraser-Thomas *et al.* 2005), and help youth to make properly informed decisions about engagement into adulthood. To better foster initial youth motivation, a range of further perspectives can be explored and integrated, including social inclusion (e.g. Bailey 2005), positive psychology (e.g. Linley and Joseph 2004), positive youth development (e.g. Holt 2008) and self-determination theory (Deci and Ryan 1985; Vallerand 1997). Each provides valuable insights since they are highly compatible with the aspiration of minimizing RAEs.

So what does this mean from a practitioner standpoint? Well, alongside the steps of positive action highlighted above and in terms of personal interaction, several recommendations can be made from a self-deterministic stance. Considerate of the three key components of self-determination (competence, autonomy and relatedness), practitioners should consider offering activities that promote consistent personalized skill-referenced learning in sport contexts, characterized by comparisons with self as opposed to comparisons against others (Ames 1992). To add, opportunities for self-assessment and external sources of feedback about progress should be frequent to more accurately gauge competence. The participation experience and emotional responses need to be created, especially with other participants, to heighten relatedness. Interactions need to be frequent, positive and supportive to sustain and promote behaviour adaptation which further optimizes social competence. Shared exploration with caring others enhances relatedness, and when this is supplemented by self-choice in exploring and using potential ways of problem-solving, these can all aid in building a sense of autonomy. These actions are best delivered in a low controlling 'growth climate' dominated by positive expectations for improvement and learning, which further develops competence and autonomy. This contrasts with other motivational climates, which may emphasize external control, (de)selection, regulation and minimal relatedness (Potrac and Jones 2010), and which can reinforce the use of fixed judgements about a participant's ability to learn and develop (Dweck and Leggett 1988; Dweck *et al.* 1995).

Conclusion

As a consequence of a performance emphasis within talent identification and development systems, changes in custom and practice are needed to address the unforeseen ethical problems which have emerged to affect 'grassroots' youth sport and beyond. These changes can occur at a variety of levels, from the mind-set of individual coaches and instructors, through to practice and cultural change by sport governing bodies. Whatever the level – and perhaps even the scale – of the required change, it is clear that carrying on with the status quo is no longer acceptable or even justifiable, especially since a number of mediating options have been identified. Yet the recommendations we have offered do not represent utopia. They may not even prove to be especially effective – but they may offer a springboard into more ethically justifiable practices. Importantly, though, each does reflect a principled attempt to modify 'the bad' of contemporary youth sport, which we have presented as having unacknowledged ideological and ethical flaws. Helping organizations to recognize these 'blind spots' by encouraging consideration of their unquestioned practices and norms may help them acknowledge – as the evidence shows – that they themselves may be undermining the very outcomes they seek and even claim to achieve.

Emphasizing such a discrepancy may be the first point in the journey towards fundamental change. Whatever is changed, our concern is that the needs of young people remain at the heart of the sport experience, and that these are always placed ahead of unhelpful adult value systems and outcomes. In that way, sport may be better positioned to positively impact upon youth development as well as performance success in adulthood. On that road, sport has a better chance of delivering on its promise as a powerful social force for changing individual lives.

Discussion Questions

1.   What are the advantages and disadvantages of early talent identification in youth sport systems?
2.   'Relative age effects tell us who we should be identifying early and working with for the future!' (quote from sport a governing body representative about the relatively older) Evaluate the validity of this statement.
3.   How would you change sport systems so that they remove forms of RAE-based indirect discrimination?

References

Abbott, A., Button, C., Pepping, G. J. and Collins, D. (2005) 'Unnatural selection: Talent identification and development in sport', *Nonlinear Dynamics, Psychology and Life Sciences*, 9: 61–88.

Abbott, A., Collins, D., Martindale, R. and Sowerby, K. (2002) *Talent Identification and Development: An Academic Review*. Edinburgh: Sport Scotland.

American Academy of Pediatrics Council on Sports Medicine and Fitness (2007) 'Overuse injuries, overtraining, and burnout in child and adolescent athletes', *Pediatrics*, 119(6): 1242–5.

Ames, C. (1992) 'Classrooms: Goals, structures, and student motivation', *Journal of Educational Psychology*, 84: 261–71.

Archer, L., Hutchings, M. and Ross, A. (2003) *Higher Education and Social Class: Issues of Exclusion and Inclusion*. London: Routledge.

Bailey, R. (2005) 'Evaluating the relationship between physical education, sport and social inclusion', *Educational Review*, 57: 71–90.

Beauchamp, T. L. and Childress, J. F. (1989) *Principles of Biomedical Ethics* (3rd edn). New York: Oxford University Press.

Brackenridge, C. and Fasting, F. (2002) *Sexual Harassment and Abuse in Sport: International Research and Policy Perspectives*. London: Whitting and Birch.

Brown, P. and Tannock, S. (2009) 'Education, meritocracy and the global war for talent', *Journal of Educational Policy*, 24: 377–92.

Buchmann, C. and DiPrete, T. A. (2006) 'The growing female advantage in college completion: The role of family background and academic achievement', *American Sociological Review*, 71: 515–41.

Cobley, S. (2009) *Relative Age Effects in Sport and Education: The Prevalence and Consequences of a Hidden Inequality*. Unpublished thesis, Leeds Metropolitan University, UK.

Cobley, S., Abraham, C. and Baker, J. (2008) 'Relative age effects on physical education attainment and school sport representation', *Physical Education and Sport Pedagogy*, 13: 267–76.

Cobley, S., Schorer, J. and Baker, J. (2011) 'Identification and development of sport talent: A brief introduction to a growing field of research and practice', in J. Baker, S. Cobley and J. Schorer (eds) *Talent Identification and Development in Sport: International Perspectives*. London: Routledge, pp. 1–10.

Cobley, S., Baker, J., Wattie, N. and McKenna, J. (2009) 'Annual age-grouping and athlete development: A meta-analytical review of relative age effects in sport', *Sports Medicine*, 39: 235–56.

Côté, J. and Fraser-Thomas, J. (2007) 'Youth involvement in sport', in P. Crocker (ed.) *Introduction to Sport Psychology: A Canadian Perspective*. Toronto: Pearson, Prentice Hall, pp. 266–94.

David, P. (2005) *Human Rights in Youth Sport: A Critical Review of Children's Rights in Competitive Sports*. London: Routledge, Taylor and Francis.

Deci, E. L. and Ryan, R. M. (1985) *Intrinsic Motivation and Self-determination in Human Behaviour*. New York: Plenum.

Donnelly, P. (1997) 'Child labour, sport labour: Applying child labour laws to sport', *International Review for the Sociology of Sport*, 32: 389–406.

Dweck, C. S. and Leggett, E. L. (1988) 'A social-cognitive approach to motivation and personality', *Psychological Review*, 9: 256–73.

Dweck, C. S., Chiu, C. and Hong, Y. (1995) 'Implicit theories and their role in judgments and reactions: A word from two perspectives', *Psychological Inquiry*, 6(4): 267–85.

Eccles, J., Early, D., Frasier, K., Belansky, E. and McCarthy, K. (1997) 'The relation of connection, regulation, and support for autonomy to adolescents' functioning', *Journal of Adolescent Research*, 12(2): 263–86.

Fraser-Thomas, J. L., Côté, J. and Deakin, J. (2005) 'Youth sport programs: An avenue to foster positive youth development', *Physical Education and Sport Pedagogy*, 10 (1): 19–40.

Government Equalities Office (2010) 'Equality Act 2010: What do I need to know? A quick start guide for private clubs and other associations'. Available at: http://www.equalities.gov.uk/pdf/401727 (accessed 25 June 2011).

Green, M. and Houlihan, B. (2005) *Elite Sport Development: Policy and Political Priorities*. London: Routledge, Taylor and Francis.

Grondin, S., Deschaies, P. and Nault, L. P. (1984) 'Trimestres de naissance et rendement scolaire', *Apprentissage et Socialisation*, 16: 169–74.

Helsen, W. F., Starkes, J. L. and Van Winckel, J. (1998) 'The influence of relative age on success and dropout in male football players', *American Journal of Human Biology*, 10: 791–8.

Helsen, W. F., Starkes, J. L. and Van Winckel, J. (2000) 'Effect of a change in selection year on success in male football players', *American Journal of Human Biology*, 12: 729–35.

Hillsdon, M., Panter, J., Foster, C. and Jones, A. (2007) 'Equitable access to exercise facilities', *American Journal of Preventative Medicine*, 32(6): 506–8.

Hurley, W., Lior, D. and Tracze, S. (2001) 'A proposal to reduce the age discrimination in Canadian minor hockey', *Canadian Public Policy*, 27: 65–75.

Laure, P. and Binsinger, C. (2005) 'Adolescent athletes and the demand and supply of drugs to improve their performance', *Journal of Sports Science and Medicine*, 4: 272–7.

Light, R. and Kirk, D. (2000) 'High school rugby, the body and the reproduction of hegemonic masculinity', *Sport, Education and Society*, 5(2): 163–76.

Linley, A. P. and Joseph, S. (2004) *Positive Psychology in Practice*. Hoboken, NJ: Wiley Press.

Malina, R. M., Bouchard, C. and Bar-Or, O. (2004). *Growth, Maturation, and Physical Activity* (2nd edn). Champaign, IL: Human Kinetics.

Musch, J. and Grondin, S. (2001) 'Unequal competition as an impediment to personal development: A review of the Relative Age Effect in sport', *Developmental Review*, 21: 147–67.

Musch, J. and Hay, R. (1999) 'The Relative Age Effect in football: Cross-cultural evidence for a systematic discrimination against children born late in the competition year', *Sociology of Sport Journal*, 16: 54–64.

Owen, A., Twist, C. and Ford, P. (2004) 'Small-sided games: The physiological and technical effect of altering pitch size and player numbers', *Insight: The F.A. Coaches Association Journal*, 7(2): 50–3.

Panathlon International (2004) Declaration on Ethics in Youth Sport. Available at: http://www.panathlon.net (accessed 23 July 2011).

Pearson, D. T., Naughton, G. A. and Torode, M. (2006) 'Predictability of physiological testing and the role of maturation in talent identification for adolescent team sports', *Journal of Science and Medicine in Sport*, 9: 277–87.

Phillips, E., David, K., Renshaw, I. and Portus, M. (2010) 'Expert performance in sport and the dynamics of talent development', *Sports Medicine*, 40(4): 271–83.

Potrac, P. and Jones, R. (2010) 'Power in coaching', in R. Jones, P. Potrac, C. Cushion and L. T Ronglan (eds) *The Sociology of Sports Coaching*. London: Routledge.

Powell, A. (2011) *Relative Age Distribution in the England Rugby Academy*. Presentation to the Professional Game Board Player Performance Group – Talent Identification and Development Sub-Committee, Northampton (UK), March.

Reay, D. (2006) 'The zombie stalking English schools: Social class and educational inequality', *British Journal of Educational Studies*, 54: 288–307.

Reilly, T., Williams, A. M., Nevill, A. and Franks, A. (2000) 'A multidisciplinary approach to talent detection in football', *Journal of Sports Sciences*, 18: 695–702.

Rich, A. (1979) *On Lies, Secrets, and Silence: Selected Prose, 1966–1978*. New York: W.W. Norton and Co.

Rose-Krasnor, L., Busseri, M. A., Willoughby, T. and Chalmers, H. (2006) 'Breadth and intensity of youth activity involvement as contexts for positive development', *Journal of Youth and Adolescence*, 35(3): 365–79.

Ryan, R. M., Stiller, J. and Lynch, J. H. (1994) 'Representations of relationships to teachers, parents, and friends as predictors of academic motivation and self-esteem', *Journal of Early Adolescence*, 14: 226–49.

Sherar, L. B., Baxter-Jones, A. D. G., Faulkner, R. A. and Russell, K. W. (2007) 'Do physical maturity and birth date predict talent in male youth ice hockey players?', *Journal of Sports Sciences*, 25: 879–86.

Tenenbaum, G., Stewart, E., Singer, R. N. and Duda, J. (1997) 'Aggression and violence in sport: An ISSP position stand', *Journal of Sports Medicine and Physical Fitness*, 37(2): 146–50.

Till, K., Cobley, S., Wattie, N., O'Hara, J., Cooke, C. and Chapman, C. (2010a) 'The prevalence, influential factors and mechanisms of relative age effects in UK Rugby League', *Scandinavian Journal of Science and Medicine in Sport*, 20: 320–9.

Till, K., Cobley, S., O'Hara, J., Chapman, C. and Cooke, C. (2010b) 'Anthropometric, physiological and selection characteristics in high performance UK junior rugby league players', *Talent Development and Excellence*, 2: 193–207.

Toering, T. T., Elferink-Gemser, M. T., Jordet, G. and Visscher, C. (2009) 'Self-regulation and performance level of elite and non-elite youth football players', *Journal of Sports Sciences*, 2: 1509–17.

UK Equality Act (2010). Available at: http://www.legislation.gov.uk/ukpga/2010/15/contents (accessed 20 June 2011).

Ungerleider, S. (2001) *Faust's Gold: Inside the East German Doping Machine*. New York: Thomas Dunne Books, St Martin's Press.

United Nations Educational, Scientific and Cultural Organisation (UNESCO) (1978) International Charter of Physical Education and Sport. Available at: http://www.unesco.org/education/nfsunesco/pdf/SPORT_E.PDF (accessed 20 June 2011).

Vaeyens, R., Lenoir, M., Williams, A. M. and Philippaerts, R. M. (2008) 'Talent identification and development programmes in sport: Current models and future directions', *Sports Medicine*, 38 (9): 703–14.

Vallerand, R. J. (1997) 'Toward a hierarchical model of intrinsic and extrinsic motivation', in M. P. Zanna (ed.) *Advances in Experimental Social Psychology*. Toronto: Academic Press, pp. 271–361.

Verbos, A., Gerard, J., Forshey, P., Harding, C. and Miller, J. (2007) 'The positive ethical organization: Enacting a living code of ethics and ethical organizational identity', *Journal of Business Ethics*, 76: 17–33.

Wattie, N., Cobley, S. and Baker, J. (2008) 'Toward a unified understanding of relative age effects', *Journal of Sports Sciences*, 26: 1403–9.

Wiersma, D. L. (2000) 'Risks and benefits of youth sport specialization: Perspectives and recommendations', *Pediatric Exercise Science*, 12(1): 13–22.

Winsley, R. and Matos, N. (2011) 'Overtraining and elite young athletes', *Medicine and Sport Science*, 56: 97–105.

6 Game Sense pedagogy in youth sport

An applied ethics perspective

Richard L. Light

Introduction

Research and writing in the physical education field over the last decade has seen a rapid growth of interest in pedagogy in games teaching, and particularly in Teaching Games for Understanding (TGfU) and its variants. There is also an emerging and long overdue interest in pedagogy within the sport-coaching field focused on athlete-centred coaching approaches (Kidman 2005; Jones 2006; Kirk 2010; Light and Evans 2010). These approaches have much to offer for improving game-playing ability and making sport more enjoyable and satisfying for children and young people. There is, however, a range of learning arising from the use of these approaches that is often unintended and less tangible, yet likely to be more significant in the educational and life journeys of young people (see, for example, Kretchmar 2005; Light 2008).

Sport can play a very significant part in the overall development of young people as they grow into particular types of people including their social and personal development (see, for example, Fraser-Thomas *et al.* 2005; Danish *et al.* 2006). This includes negative influences, such as those arising from the influence of the discourses of elite-level media sport on moral development, and concerns with the loss of the ludic element of sport through the imposition of adult models of sport upon children (Tomlinson and Fleming 1995; Coakley 2007). Although there has been some attention paid to the affective aspects of learning using a TGfU approach (Holt *et al.* 2002; Light 2002, 2003; Pope 2006) most research on it and other similar approaches focuses on aspects of game performance such as the development of skill, decision-making and tactical knowledge (see, for example, Hopper *et al.* 2009). While developing skills, tactical understanding and decision-making are worthwhile *products* of game-centred approaches, less attention has been paid to the hidden learning arising from the use of TGfU pedagogy.

Implicit learning and youth sport

Kirk's (1992) work on the hidden curriculum in physical education drew attention to the range of unintended and unnoticed learning that can occur in physical education classes, with more recent attention being paid to the idea of implicit (or tacit) learning in the coaching literature (Nash and Collins 2006). Implicit learning refers to that learning which is not immediately evident or quantifiable and which typically occurs at a non-conscious level, where it bypasses conscious scrutiny. It is therefore also very difficult to identify in research but it is important that it figures in research on learning in and through sport, physical education and other physical activity. A recently completed study on coach development as implicit learning over time provides one example of how this might be achieved. In their study on elite-level rugby coaches Light and Evans (2010) identified the *characteristics* of a coaching habitus developed over the participants' lives by operationalizing Bourdieu's (1986) concept of habitus.

A broad conception of learning allows for consideration of the significance of the implicit pedagogy of participation in social practices within particular social and cultural settings that operate at a non-conscious, embodied level (Light 2008). Over time, such embodied learning comes to constitute the habitus that structures the individual's social action, dispositions, inclinations and tastes (Bourdieu 1986). Some constructivist perspectives on learning also highlight the engagement of the body in learning and the implicit learning arising from participation in practice. For example, Lave and Wenger (1991) focus on practice points to a range of cultural learning arising from participation in the practices of a community of practice well beyond the explicit learning of skills and technique. Their analytic concepts of situated learning, communities of practice and legitimate peripheral participation imply the extent of implicit learning arising from participation in practice as well as its durability and significance.

Lave and Wenger's (1991) concepts of situated learning and communities of practice in particular imply an ecological approach to learning suggesting that learning is an inherent aspect of participation in social life involving the whole person and his/her environment. This focus on the centrality of the body in learning through practice makes situated learning a valuable way of looking at learning in and through participation in physical education and sport (see, for example, Kirk and MacPhail 2002: Light 2006). Influenced by the phenomenology of Heidegger (see, for example, 1973) and Merleau-Ponty (see, for example, 1964), Lave and Wenger use the term 'person-in-the-world' to capture the inseparability of the learner and his/her world. Learning is thus more than just knowing *about* the world. It is a way of *being* in the world and adapting to it. As Merleau-Ponty (1964) suggests, the world is not in front of me but is instead 'all round me' (cited in Priest 2003). From this perspective the concept of situated learning implies comprehensive understandings involving the whole person and the world within which they live as they engage in 'Activity with and in the world' (Lave and Wenger 1991: 33). The language used by Lave and Wenger and constructivists in education such as Davis and Sumara (1997, 2003) reflects a view of learning as a holistic process involving the entire person and not just a mind somehow operating independently of the body.

This stream of thinking assumes the importance of context for learning. For Lave and Wenger (1991) the learning arising from participation in practice is specific to the community of practice within which it takes place. They stress the importance of participation in the practices of particular communities, such as a sports club, a school or the workplace, as a means of learning and mastering the understandings and skills required to live in them. For Lave and Wenger this involves learning 'how to do' practices through participating in them and is inseparable from the social, cultural and physical environment. Learning involves co-participation with others and is dependent upon the ability to perform tasks rather than learning in instructional settings removed from actual practice and performance. The philosophic notion of practice used by Lave and Wenger, Bourdieu (see Bourdieu 1977) and others such as Marx emphasizes both the transformative nature of action and the importance of action in relation to thought. As an aspect of practice, learning necessarily involves the whole person and not just the mind. Accepting that learning is a complex, multi-faceted and ongoing lifelong process allows us to see how learning is inseparable from the formation of a person's identity and experiences of day-to-day life. It also highlights the role that participation in youth sport can play in what Dewey (1997 [1916]) refers to as the 'human growth' of young people.

Game Sense pedagogy

One of the factors contributing towards the growth in interest in TGfU over the past decade has been the identification of it being consistent with constructivist perspectives on learning (Gréhaigne and Godbout 1998; Kirk and Macdonald 1998). This offered a valuable means of understanding how learning occurred in games and how it could be shaped and enhanced using game-centred approaches. In particular, socio-cultural constructivism helped explain how important the verbal interaction used in game-centred approaches is for learning. Socio-cultural constructivism emphasizes the nature of all learning as a social and interpretive process and the ways in which the learner's prior knowledge and experience shape his or her interpretation of the learning experience and the knowledge he or she constructs.

Game Sense was developed through collaboration between Rod Thorpe, the Australian Sports Commission and local coaches in Australia during the mid- to late 1990s specifically for sport coaching. It places learning within the context of games that offer opportunities for learning how to play a sport or develop specific aspects of it. In junior programmes that introduce children to the sport this would typically involve starting with a simple game in which skill demands are reduced to allow immediate intellectual engagement in the game and gradually building on this, making the games progressively more complex and demanding as knowledge and skill develop hand in hand. For children and young people who already have a fair understanding of the sport, training would typically focus on a specific aspect of the sport that the coach feels needs attention. To achieve his/her aims the coach would design a game to meet his/her needs as a problem for the players to solve.

For example, in helping players use extra numbers in attack in rugby s/he might have small groups of three attacking players against two defenders in a narrow space where the attackers have to use the space effectively. After allowing the players to play the game and solve the problem the coach would typically bring the players in for some discussion on what tactics could be adopted but could also extend this to discussions on skills such as passing. Rather than tell the players what he/she wants the coach asks questions that generate critical thinking, discussion between the players and the collaborative development of solutions that they then test in the game. This typically involves a process of empowering the players to take command of their own learning and to develop decision-making independent of the coach. This is particularly valuable for athletes playing sports like rugby and football, where the coach has fewer opportunities for direct intervention during the games than in sports like American football, baseball and basketball.

During the modified training games used the coach might make some positive comments on good play and ask a couple of questions 'on the run' moving between the small-sided games being played at the same time (for example, 'where's the space?'). S/he could then build on the knowledge developed to modify the games in ways that are more demanding, or less demanding, by changing the numbers or the space that they have to work in, with the session possibly progressing towards larger games in larger spaces. As with this example, Game Sense follows a pattern of game–reflection and discussion–game, during which players interact with each other, physically and verbally. This is clearly a social process based on critical reflection, dialogue and collaboration requiring and promoting meaningful and purposeful relationships between players and between the coach and players. Light and Fawns (2003) suggest that this process can be seen as an ongoing conversation conducted through action in the game and dialogue and discussion in between games. My own research in this area suggests that such approaches can not only improve playing ability and understanding but can also have a very positive influence on the development of personal identity, self-esteem, a sense of belonging and inclusion, as well as building personal relationships and encouraging consideration of others in and out of school settings (Light 2002, 2003, 2008).

Ethical aspects of Game Sense pedagogy

The following section outlines features of Game Sense pedagogy that address ethical issues in youth sport through:

- the provision of equal opportunity for all players to participate in all aspects of training and to have equal opportunity to develop and improve as a games player through the design of inclusive games that emphasizes really working as a team;

- redressing the unequal power relationships between the coach and the players primarily through the central role of generative dialogue;
- the provision of support for individual and collective endeavour to enhance opportunities for experimentation, expression and creativity.

Provision of equal opportunity

Justification for the playing of team games in schools typically cites notions of teamwork and the ways in which students learn valuable lessons about working productively with others through playing team games. While this is possible and desirable just playing team games does not necessarily develop teamwork or character (see, for example, Weiss and Smith 2002). Indeed, without appropriate coaching team games can promote quite selfish behaviour. For anyone who has watched an under-9s football game at the local school or park there is typically little evidence of teamwork with 20 players crowded like bees around a honey pot hacking at the ball. This is further exacerbated by media treatment of sport that elevates individual achievements over the team as is so evident in the phenomenon of sport celebrities (Jackson and Andrews 2001).

Within physical education settings the modified games used in Game Sense are designed to be inclusive. This involves using rules that limit possibilities for domination by the more capable and confident pupils (therefore excluding the less confident) and designing games that require teamwork for them to be played successfully. This should also be an objective for coaches of young children in sport clubs, where the emphasis of coaching should be on enjoyment and learning about the sport. The modified games are designed to include all players in the team and to foster improvement and the development of all players in the team. For example, in football some players may dominate games due to their superior ability and confidence on the ball, and literally push the less confident to the margins of the pitch. If this is left unchecked the less able are marginalized and deprived of the play they need to improve while the more able players also learn little about playing better and do not improve their play.

There are issues here with fairness, caring and working as a team rather than a collection of individuals, but such modifications to enhance inclusion do not over-compensate to deny the more confident players the chance to learn and improve. To the contrary, preventing them from dominating through superior physical capacities challenges them to engage in the tactical aspects of the game, leading to improvement as players. For example, to address the problem of the better players dominating in football cited above, the teacher could limit dribbling to 3 metres for all players. This has two important effects. The first is that it encourages the 'star players' to look for their team mates and to involve them in the game and to work off the ball.

Players who might have avoided involvement with the ball are thus more likely to call for a reception or position themselves to take a pass by finding space and communicating with the ball carrier. At the same time the 'star players' have to become more intellectually engaged in the game and to think about and be involved with more players in the team. They have to think about to whom they should pass and what type of pass to use, then what they need to do off the ball, such as how they can position themselves to take a reception or act as a decoy runner. This simple modification can both improve the team's play and develop better relationships and communication between players while making the less talented feel more a part of the team. There are certainly good lessons here about a team being more than a collection of individuals and in the different contributions that people of different talents and abilities can make to the collective effort that go well beyond sport.

This emphasis on inclusion and the provision of opportunity for all players to participate, learn and enjoy sport has significant implications for learning to play sport and for what Dewey (1997 [1916]) terms *human growth*. This means that the meaningful engagement all players have in the modified games used in Game Sense leads to improvement for them all. For children and young people who have previously been excluded from meaningful participation in sport this can provide quite strong affective responses and make positive contributions towards the development of identity (Light 2002).

Over the past decade in my teaching of physical education pedagogy to primary school pre-service teachers I have been struck by both the very negative experiences of physical education at school that so many of them recount and their extremely positive responses to Game Sense pedagogy. Indeed, this motivated me to conduct a number of studies that confirm both the extent to which so many of the 'unsporty' are marginalized from physical education as other research has identified (see, for example, Ennis 1999) and deprived of what it can offer while highlighting the potential for Game Sense pedagogy to redress this significant problem (see, for example, Light 2002; Light and Georgakis 2005, 2007). Most of these students were female and had 'dreaded' doing the unit on physical education due to their negative experiences of physical education at school. Invariably they said that they had been excluded from full participation, with some having felt embarrassed and even humiliated (Light 2002; Light and Georgakis 2005). They were all very surprised at how much they enjoyed the Game Sense approach, identifying the ways in which they had been included and had come to feel that they contributed to the team as a major reason for their enjoyment of the experience. Some had quite strong emotional experiences of the unit suggesting that they felt liberated and empowered.

There were similar responses from year six (11 to 12 years of age) primary school children to a Game Sense unit that I conducted over a term with the classroom teacher on cricket (Light 2008). In interviews some of the girls and one boy said that they had been dreading the classes on cricket but, by the end of the term, they were enjoying it very much with many noting how the interaction involved in the Game Sense approach through team talks and debate of ideas had helped them get to know other students in their class and understand them. They felt included and valued, not only in the cricket games, but also in the class as a whole outside physical education lessons (Light 2008).

In his book, *The Pedagogy of the Oppressed*, Freire (1972) focuses on dialogue, social justice and informal adult education, contrasting a 'banking' and 'problem posing' education. He emphasizes the learner's prior experience and knowledge, and argues that the teacher's role should be one of negotiating, mediating between learners' personal meanings and established cultural meanings of the wider community to suggest that pedagogy should have emancipatory potential. Although not originally developed with these ends in mind, Game Sense provides a pedagogy that is capable of realizing Freire's goals of pedagogy. In much of my research on children and young people, some of their responses suggest it can meet his expectation of pedagogy being emancipatory. While children entering a sports club are likely to have had positive previous experience of sport, there is no doubt that there will be differences in confidence and ability and that some will have felt a sense of restraint.

The aims of any youth sport programme and coaching should include making sport enjoyable and accessible for as many as possible and particularly in the younger age groups. This should not only be to 'grow the game' but also to meet the ethical responsibilities of any organized youth-level sport, whether in schools or in community-based clubs that are prominent in countries such as Australia, Great Britain, Germany and Canada. I am not so much referring to opportunity for the development of elite-level sporting pathways but more to opportunities for children and youth to enjoy playing sport as a social practice and to grow as a human through their participation in it.

Dialogue and power relationships

The two most distinctive aspects of Game Sense are the basing of learning in modified games and the use of questioning to stimulate critical dialogue, thinking and reflection. Learning in Game Sense can thus be seen as occurring at both an embodied, non-conscious level through participation in the modified games and at a conscious level through the use of language and conscious reflection to connect abstract thinking with concrete experience (Light and Wallian 2008). This is not to suggest a dualistic division of mind and body because in Game Sense there is an interrelationship between action and speech (Light and Fawns 2003).

As Thorpe and Bunker (2008) suggest in regard to the design of modified games, 'getting the game right' is the most important step for the coach/teacher but the use of language is also central to the Game Sense approach. Learning in games hinges upon the relationship between the body, expressed in action, and the mind, expressed in speech, with the dialogue between players, and between coach and players, forming a central mechanism for learning (Light and Fawns 2003). Indeed, several researchers have recently focused on the role of language in learning through TGfU and its variations when a TGfU approach is used (see, for example, Wallian and Chang 2007; Wright and Forrest 2007). Of course, language is used in all coaching but, more often than not, it is used in a monologue from coach to players to convey information and sometimes from senior players to junior players. Conversely, in Game Sense learning is facilitated through dialogue between players and between the players and the coach. From a socio-cultural constructivist perspective this is where learning occurs and the 'father' of social constructivism, Vygotsky (1978), emphasizes the role of language in learning. Through language in social settings we can learn far more than we can on our own and this extends to learning more than just how to play a particular sport more efficiently.

The dialogue that takes place in Game Sense necessarily requires different relationships between players and between players and the coach. The monologue of directive coaching is based upon a conception of the coach as the expert who passes on knowledge as an object to the players as passive receivers of this knowledge. Inherent in this is an uneven power relationship favouring the coach as the source of knowledge and offering him/her a means of control. A constructivist perspective on learning suggests that learning is more a case of drawing on existing knowledge and sets of inclinations to interpret the learning experience and to construct particular understandings. This significant difference is rooted in the different epistemologies upon which 'traditional' directive coaching and Game Sense coaching sit. This is significant, not only for the coaching approaches adopted, but also for the relationships required and fostered by these two approaches. Game Sense and any other pedagogy informed by social constructivism promotes more equal power relationships between coach and players and between players because they require collaboration and shared learning within a view of the coach/teacher as a co-participant (or co-investigator) in learning (Davis and Sumara 1997; Leach and Moon 2008). Resonating with the ideas of Dewey (1997 [1916]) on teaching and learning, the task of the Game Sense coach is to design an appropriate learning environment and to guide or facilitate learning rather than using direct instruction aimed at internalizing objective knowledge.

Traditional coach-centred coaching tends to disempower players while Game Sense coaching empowers them to make decisions 'on the pitch' and during training. It also empowers them to be independent learners after developing a knowledge base of conceptual understanding (Light and Wallian 2008). Coaches cannot expect players to make informed decisions under pressure in competitive matches unless they have been empowered to make such decisions under similar conditions during training. Game Sense implies that developing as a team over the season is a shared process that is guided by the coach but which also involves providing all players with the power to contribute to the team effort (on and off the pitch) and to take full responsibility, as an individual and as a member of the team. Young players exposed to this sort of coaching over extended periods of time are not only likely to develop as better players but to also learn valuable lessons about some of the core values underpinning democratic societies, including the relationship between freedom and responsibility. While the extreme imbalance in power between coach and players evident in some traditional coaching at the most elite levels might be defensible on some grounds, there is no justification for such relationships in youth sport, and particularly with younger players, regardless of how important winning is. There is an ethical issue here in relation to power and control in which knowledge is used by those seen to hold it as a means of establishing and exerting control over young people.

Foucault's writing on the internalization of social control suggests that the quest for knowledge can be seen as an expression of the desire of individuals to exert power over others (see, for example, Foucault 1977, 1979). According to Foucault, knowledge is always a form of power and is used to establish control. He does not see power as an object that is explicitly wielded but, instead, as something pervasive that is internalized through more subtle strategies such as surveillance. His use of the idea of a *panopticon* in his writing on the history of the prison system shows how such techniques of power work in contemporary societies (Foucault 1977).

While traditional coaches may have a warm relationship with their charges in youth sport and not shout at or intimidate them, the notion of the coach as expert transmitting knowledge to passive players still works at a more implicit level to create 'docile' (Foucault 1977) and passive players and internalize hierarchical relationships. In contrast, when knowledge is seen as being subjective and being constructed through shared effort, along with notions of the coach as a co-participant in learning, it suggests vastly different relationships of power between coach and players. From a constructivist perspective knowledge is not an object but is instead inseparable from the learner. This epistemological contrast has serious implications, not just for learning to play the sport in question but also for the model it presents for young players about how to get things done and about relationships between people of different positions of status and power in society and not just in sport.

Provision of a supportive socio-moral environment

In teaching and coaching informed by a constructivist perspective on learning the teacher provides opportunities for self-directed inquiry, exploration and the, 'freedom of movement and the power to judge, evaluate, select and carry through' (Dewey 1938: 64). Although this may lead to the discovery of a pre-determined, single correct solution in some instances or sports, it also encourages learners to arrive at answers and solutions that are novel and creative and this is particularly so in team sports. In Game Sense this means that, when focusing on tactical aspects of games, the coach may well have some specific tactical solutions in mind but s/he needs to be open to alternative solutions and opportunities for finding solutions that empower learners and allow them to transform the game (Wright and Forrest 2007). This approach implies that learning involves more than knowing the correct answers. Instead, it involves a process of the learners coming up with ideas and solutions that they test. This then requires a supportive social environment within which the learners feel confident to experiment, be creative and take some risks without fear of failing.

In reference to teaching and learning within schools DeVries and Zan (1996) suggest that a cooperative socio-moral environment, in which children feel safe to experiment and make errors from which they can learn, is an essential aspect of a constructivist-informed approach to children who typically learn to play sport beyond the interference of adults (Coakley 2007; Light and Evans 2010). They warn that teachers (and by implication, coaches) should be careful of how their pre-determined ideas about what children should learn can hinder their ability to recognize and appreciate 'the important role of children's constructive errors' (DeVries and Zan 1996: 119) in learning. The same applies to coaching youth sport, and particularly with younger children, where positive feedback from the coach is needed to build confidence, team spirit and to make sport enjoyable. Children not only enjoy the social dimensions of sport but also a sense that they are learning and improving (Light 2008). Rather than telling young players what they are doing is wrong in the quest for mastery of technique, this approach provides for constant positive reinforcements. In Game Sense players should immediately reflect upon experience and learn from their individual and collective 'constructive errors' (DeVries and Zan 1996). This approach is essential for the youngest players but is also important for the long-term development of players in highly competitive leagues. Providing a social environment in which young players feel encouraged to experiment and test out ideas is a good investment due to the ways in which it can develop intelligent, informed players who are empowered to make effective decisions on the pitch or on the court without having the coach constantly scream instructions from the sideline. It is also an approach that can facilitate the development or enhancement of creativity (see, for example, Memmert 2010). Many coaches would likely feel that creativity in team sport is something players are born with or is an innate ability and that it cannot be coached. However, as Leach and Moon (2008: 56) argue, it can be learnt using appropriate pedagogy: 'All people are capable of creative achievements in some areas of activity, provided the conditions are right and they have acquired the relevant knowledge and skills.'

While there will be situations that require direct instruction in coaching, the coach's main focus should be on providing an appropriate learning environment. This refers to both the social and physical environment, and the physical context used to contextualize learning and to facilitate the relevance of tactical knowledge and improvements in performance in training for the competition match on the weekend. This approach can develop better games players, provide more enjoyable experiences for young players and promote long-term player development (see, for example, Mitchell *et al.* 2006). At the same time it can contribute towards the development of young people who have better social skills, can work effectively in groups and who develop skills in negotiation that are necessary in a just society. It can also develop more tolerance for others and a sense of fairness, and make young people a little more inclined to care about and consider others, particularly when all of these learning outcomes are valued and promoted elsewhere in the school, club or community. There are important lessons here for young people in living their lives as they grow up in most contemporary societies that are increasingly complex and experiencing increasingly rapid technological and social change. Learning to make any decisions in life involves reflection upon past errors for anyone, and the experience of feeling secure enough to experiment, be creative and take some risks in learning to play team sports is likely to be invaluable experience for children and young people as they grow up and the consequences of their life decisions become more serious.

Discussion

The three aspects of Game Sense pedagogy that I have discussed in this chapter suggest that it can be seen as ethical pedagogy that can make a contribution towards the socio-moral development of young people participating in youth sport. Providing them with equality of opportunity for involvement and improvement in sport, encouraging more equal relationships of power between coach and players, and establishing a supportive social environment within which children and young people can experiment, explore and create constitutes an ethical approach to teaching and/or coaching that should promote ethical learning. This learning can occur through both conscious cognitive processes and the deeper, embodied learning over time if Game Sense or similar pedagogical approaches are consistently adopted by the teams or clubs of which young people are members.

From sport's development in the schools of the rising middle classes in nineteenth-century England there has been a remarkably enduring belief in it as a vehicle for socio-moral learning (see, for example, Mangan 1981). However, the links between sport and positive social and moral learning are not so straightforward (Sandford *et al.* 2006). Indeed, there is not a great deal of convincing evidence to support the idea that participation in sport *necessarily* 'builds character', and there is a danger in assuming that positive social learning is an automatic outcome from participation in sport (Long and Sanderson 2001; Shields and Bredemeir 1995). The important implication here is that sport has *potential* for fostering positive socio-cultural learning (Sandford *et al.* 2006). This potential can be realized through a number of strategies, including adopting appropriate approaches to coaching/teaching and having such learning as a specific objective of coaching. This is evident in approaches that explicitly use sport specifically to impart particular social learning such as Sport Education (Siedentop 1994), Teaching Personal and Social Responsibility (Hellison 1995) and Sport for Peace (Ennis 1999), some of which are discussed in further detail in this book. Game-centred approaches were not designed with any specific social learning in mind. Bunker and Thorpe (1982) developed TGfU expressly to develop better games players, with Game Sense focused on developing thinking players (den Duyn 1997), but the development of their pedagogy over the past decade has provided practitioners with ways in which they can promote positive social and moral learning through these approaches.

When a player/student-centred, games-based pedagogy like Game Sense is used for youth coaching some of the socio-moral learning that I have discussed should occur, even when the coach doesn't have it in mind as a learning objective. However, if the coach does value these outcomes and is working within an environment where such learning is valued and reinforced, then Game Sense pedagogy can make a more significant contribution towards the human growth of children into ethical adults. As is the case with any influence on the long-term socio-moral development of young people, consistency over time is needed rather than one isolated season unconnected to similar experiences elsewhere. As Mills and Gale (2002) suggest, learning is most effective when the same messages are confirmed in school, at home and in the community.

Discussion Questions

1. The author suggests that traditional, technique-focused, directive acts exclude and marginalize the less skilled and less confident children and young people but that a Game Sense approach is inclusive and can engage young players of all levels. Identify what features of Game Sense are claimed make it inclusive and suggest why this is an ethical issue.

2. Discuss and critically examine the ways in which traditional approaches to sport coaching reproduce unequal power relations and what the consequences are for the players' development and learning.

3. Comment on the author's suggestion that playing team games does not necessarily teach lessons in teamwork and working together, and that appropriate pedagogy and learning objectives are required to ensure this positive social learning occurs. Draw on your own experiences as a participant in youth sport, a coach, teacher, or just interested observer, and the relevant literature to discuss this issue and what you think Game Sense has to offer in helping achieve this positive social learning.

References

Bourdieu, P. (1977) *Outline of a Theory of Practice*. Cambridge, MA: Cambridge University Press.

Bourdieu, P. (1986) *A Social Critique of the Judgment of Taste*. London, Routledge.

Bunker, D. and Thorpe, R. (1982) 'A model for teaching games in secondary school', *Bulletin of Physical Education*, 10: 9–16.

Coakley, J. (2007) *Sports in Society: Issues and Controversies* (9th edn). New York: McGraw Hill.

Danish, S. J., Taylor, T. E. and Fazio, R. J. (2006) 'Enhancing adolescent development through sports and leisure', in G. Adams and M. Berzonsky (eds) *Blackwell Handbook of Development Psychology*. Malden, MA: Blackwell, pp. 92–110.

Davis, A. and Sumara, J. (1997) 'Cognition, complexity and teacher education', *Harvard Educational Review*, 67(1): 105–25.

Davis, B. and Sumara, D. (2003) ' "Why aren't they getting this?" Working through the regressive myths of constructivist pedagogy', *Teaching Education*, 14(2): 123–40.

DeVries, R. and Zan, B. (1996) 'A constructivist perspective on the role of the socio-moral atmosphere in promoting children's development', in C. T. Fosnot (ed.) *Constructivism: Theory, Perspectives and Practice*. New York: Teachers College, Columbia University.

Dewey, J. (1938) *Experience and Education*. New York: Collier Books.

Dewey, J. (1997 [1916]) *Democracy in Education*. New York: Free Press.

Ennis, C. D. (1999) 'Creating a culturally relevant curriculum for disengaged girls', *Sport, Education and Society*, 4(1): 31–49.

Foucault, M. (1977) *Discipline and Punish: The Birth of the Prison*, trans. A. Sheridan. London: Allen Lane.

Foucault, M. (1979) *The History of Sexuality I: An Introduction*, trans. R. Hurley. London: Allen Lane.

Fraser-Thomas, J. L., Côté, J. and Deakin, J. (2005) 'Youth sport programs: An avenue to foster positive youth development', *Physical Education and Sport Pedagogy*, 10(1): 19–40.

Freire, P. (1972) *Pedagogy of the Oppressed*. Harmondsworth: Penguin.

Gréhaigne, J. F. and Godbout, P. (1998) 'Observation, critical thinking and transformation: Three key elements for a constructivist perspective of the learning process in team sports', in R. Feingold, R. Rees, G. Barette, I. Fiorentino, S. Virgilio and E. Kowalski (eds) *Education for Life*. New York: Adelphi University.

Heidegger, M. (1973) *Being and Time*, trans. J. Macquarrie and E. Robinson. Oxford: Blackwell.

Hellison, D. (1995) *Teaching Responsibility Through Physical Activity*. Champaign, IL: Human Kinetics.

Holt, N., Strean, W. and Bengoechea, E. G. (2002) 'Expanding the Teaching Games for Understanding model: New avenues for future research and practice', *Journal of Teaching Physical Education* 21(2): 162–77.

Hopper, T., Butler, J. I. and Storey, B. (eds) (2009) *TGfU … Simply Good Pedagogy: Understanding a Complex Challenge*. HPE Canada.

Jackson, S. and Andrews, D. L. (eds) (2001) *Sports Stars: The Cultural Politics of Sporting Celebrity*. London: Routledge.

Jones, R. L. (2006) 'How can educational concepts inform sports coaching?', in R. L. Jones (ed.) *The Sports Coach as Educator*. London: Routledge.

Kidman, L. (2005) *Athlete-centred Coaching: Developing and Inspiring People.* Christchurch, New Zealand: Innovative Print Communications.

Kirk, D. (1992) 'Physical education discourse and ideology: Bringing the hidden curriculum into view', *Quest*, 44(2): 35–56.

Kirk, D. (2010) 'Towards a socio-pedagogy of sports coaching', in J. Lyle and C. Cushion (eds) *Sport Coaching: Professionalisation and Practice.* Edinburgh: Elsevier.

Kirk, D. and Macdonald, D. (1998) 'Situated learning in physical education', *Journal of Teaching in Physical Education*, 17: 376–87.

Kirk, D. and MacPhail, A. (2002) 'Teaching Games for Understanding and situated learning: Rethinking the Bunker and Thorpe model', *Journal of Teaching in Physical Education*, 21: 177–92.

Kretchmar, R. S. (2005) 'Teaching Games for Understanding and the delights of human activity', in L. L. Griffin and J. I. Butler (eds) *Teaching Games for Understanding: Theory, Research and Practice.* Champaign, IL: Human Kinetics.

Lave, J. and Wenger, E. (1991) *Situated Learning: Legitimate Peripheral Participation.* Cambridge: Cambridge University Press.

Leach, J. and Moon, B. (2008) *The Power of Pedagogy.* Los Angeles, CA: Sage.

Light, R. (2002) 'The social nature of games: Pre-service primary teachers' first experiences of TGfU', *European Physical Education Review*, 8(3): 291–310.

Light, R. (2003) 'The joy of learning: Emotion, cognition and learning in games through TGfU', *New Zealand Journal of Physical Education*, 36(1): 94–108.

Light, R. (2006) 'Situated learning in an Australian surf club', *Sport, Education and Society*, 11(2): 155–72.

Light, R. (2008) *Sport in the Lives of Young Australians.* Sydney: University of Sydney Press.

Light, R. L. and Evans, J. R. (2010) 'The impact of Game Sense pedagogy on Australian rugby coaches' practice: A question of pedagogy', *Physical Education and Sport Pedagogy*, 15(2): 103–16.

Light, R. and Fawns, R. (2003) 'Knowing the game: Integrating speech and action through TGfU', *Quest*, 55(2): 161–76.

Light, R. and Georgakis, S. (2005) 'Integrating theory and practice in teacher education: The impact of a Games Sense Unit on female pre-service primary teachers' attitudes toward teaching physical education', *Journal of Physical Education New Zealand*, 38(1): 67–80.

Light, R. and Georgakis, S. (2007) 'Preparing primary school pre-service teachers to teach physical education through a focus on pedagogy', *ACHPER Healthy Lifestyles Journal*, 54(1): 24–8.

Light, R. and Wallian, N. (2008) 'A constructivist approach to teaching swimming', *Quest*, 60(3): 387–404.

Long, J. and Sanderson, I. (2001) 'The social benefits of sport: Where's the proof?', in C. Graton and I. P. Henry (eds) *Sport in the City: The Role of Sport in Economic and Social Regeneration.* London: Routledge.

Mangan, J. A. (1981) *Athleticism in the Victorian and Edwardian Public School: The Emergence and Consolidation of an Educational Ideology.* Cambridge: University of Cambridge Press.

Merleau-Ponty, M. (1964) *L'Oeil et l'esprit.* Paris: Gallimard.

Memmert, D. (2010) 'Development of creativity in the scope of the TGfU approach', in J. I. Butler and L. L. Griffin (eds) *More Teaching Games for Understanding.* Champaign, IL: Human Kinetics, pp. 231–44.

Mills, C. and Gale, T. (2002) 'Schooling and the production of social inequalities: What can and should we be doing?', *Melbourne Studies in Education*, 43(1): 107–28.

Mitchell, S., Oslin, J. and Griffin, L. L. (2006) *Teaching Sport Concepts and Skills: A Tactical Games Approach*. Champaign, IL: Human Kinetics.

Nash, C. and Collins, D. (2006) 'Tacit knowledge in expert coaching: Science or art?', *Quest*, 58(4): 465–77.

Pope, C. (2006) 'Affect in New Zealand junior sport: The forgotten dynamic', *Change: Transformations in Education*, 9(1): 17–26.

Priest, S. (2003) *Merleau-Ponty*. London: Routledge.

Sandford, R. A., Armour, K. M. and Warmington, P. C. (2006) 'Re-engaging youth through physical activity programmes', *British Educational Research Journal*, 32(2): 251–71.

Shields, D. L. and Bredemeier, B. J. (1995) *Character Development and Physical Activity*. Champaign, IL.: Human Kinetics.

Siedentop, D. (ed.) (1994) *Sport Education: Quality PE Through Positive Sport Experiences*. Champaign, IL: Human Kinetics.

Thorpe, R. and Bunker, D. (2008) 'Teaching Games for Understanding – Do current developments reflect original intentions?' Paper presented at the fourth Teaching Games for Understanding Conference, 14–17 May, Vancouver, BC, Canada.

Tomlinson, A. and Fleming, S. (eds) (1995) *Ethics, Sport and Leisure: Crises and Critique*. Germany: Meyer and Meyer.

Vygotsky, L. S. (1978) *Mind in Society: The Development of Higher Psychological Processes*. Cambridge, MA: Harvard University Press.

Wallian, N. and Chang, C.-W. (2007) 'Language, thinking and action: Towards a socio-constructivist approach in physical education', *Physical Education and Sport Pedagogy*, 12(3): 273–88.

Weiss, M. R. and Smith, A. L. (2002) 'Moral development in sport and physical activity: Theory, research and interventions', in T. S. Horn (ed.) *Advances in Sport Psychology* (2nd edn). Champaign, IL: Human Kinetics.

Wright, J. and Forrest, G. (2007) 'A social semiotic analysis of knowledge construction and games centred approaches to teaching', *Physical Education and Sport Pedagogy*, 12(3): 273–87.

7 Sport Education as a pedagogy for promoting sport as ethical practice

*Stephen Harvey, David Kirk and
Toni M. O'Donovan*

Introduction[1]

It is now relatively easy to discredit the idea, passed down from the elite private schools of England's Victorian and Edwardian eras, that 'sport builds character'. Although cynicism about the moral properties of games was evident even in the heyday of what Mangan (1981) called the 'cult of Athleticism', in England from the 1880s up until around 1920, the fact that 'sport builds character' remains a dominant justification for the time, effort and resources allocated to sport through school-based physical education and organized youth sport in the community.

While the idea that 'sport builds character' has become ubiquitous, we believe that if sport is to provide young people with an education in ethical conduct, it must be designed explicitly and intentionally to do so (Hsu 2004; see also Chapter 8 by Van Veldhoven). Indeed, one of the notions that inspired the development of Siedentop's Sport Education model was 'a response to some of the problems of poor role modelling in professional sports and ... the need to find more educative ways of presenting sport in the school curriculum' (Alexander and Luckman 2001: 246).

We think that in the case of Sport Education there is an opportunity for young people to become 'literate'[2] sportspersons, and to develop ethical conduct by teaching young people about, and where appropriate criticizing, a particular type of ethical conduct that for the most part has been pre-determined by adults. Through engagement in Sport Education, arguably, young people can learn about their conduct on the sporting field in both physical education and youth community sport settings (see Shehu 1998; Penney *et al.* 2002). We believe that this isn't the automatic process our predecessors apparently believed it was.

This chapter reviews the empirical findings of research on Sport Education in order to inform our judgement about the model's capacity to promote the ethical dimensions of young people's sporting experiences (for example, fair play, inclusion, etc.). Following this, we will consider four pedagogical applications designed intentionally to enhance these dimensions of young people's sport experiences: ethical contracts; sports panels; modified games/sports;

awards and rewards. And while the four pedagogical applications are the primary aim of this chapter, we feel that we first need to say a little more about why we believe sport, properly implemented, may have the power to provide young people with experiences of ethical conduct.

Sport as an ethical practice

Underpinning Siedentop's goal for Sport Education and the facilitation of the development of sport literacy is a particular approach to ethics developed by philosopher Alasdair MacIntyre (1985). MacIntyre argues that there exist social practices, including games and sports, that are defined by three characteristics: standards of excellence, 'goods' that are derived from the pursuit of excellence, and virtues such as honesty, justice and courage that are necessary to achieve these goods. In sport, as in other social practices, 'goods' can be internal and external to a practice. Internal goods are unique to the practice itself and cannot be gained in any other way than through wholehearted participation. For example, it is not possible to acquire the goods of being a basketball player, the repertoire of skills and tactics, understanding of etiquette, respect for the rules and traditions of basketball, and respect for opponents, without immersing oneself in the practice of basketball. On the other hand, someone who is an excellent basketballer can gain extrinsic goods such as money and prestige. But these goods are not unique to basketball in the way that the skills, strategies and knowledge of traditions of the sport are.

While the pursuit of external goods is inevitable at most levels of sport and most clearly obvious in professional sport, this only becomes a problem when the desire for external goods outweighs the pursuit of internal goods. In these circumstances, sport as a practice is then in danger of corruption, as cheating, use of illegal drugs and other forms of performance enhancement and athlete abuse can become part of the quest for external goods.

In order to become a more literate sportsperson, Morgan (2006) suggests there is mutuality at two levels. First, he contends we need to appreciate that games and sports are rule-bound activities (Suits 1978; Fraleigh 1984; Kretchmar 2005). Second, Morgan (2006) suggests it is the opponents in any sport contest that provide each other with the test or challenge against these standards of excellence. Without opponents, there is no game. In the context of mutual respect for the game and respect for opponents, Morgan claims that cheating – the breaking of rules with the intention of gaining a competitive advantage *and* getting away with it – is a 'moral offence' in two senses; 'first, they [cheats] fail to show moral respect for my competitors as persons in their own right, and second, they fail to show moral respect for the perfectionist demands of the game itself' (2006: 104).

However, this notion of intent has been challenged by a number of philosophers including Lehman (1981). Lehman argues that 'games are played within a framework of social practices and priorities, and violators of rules must be assessed within this framework to determine whether competition or victory, in the normal sense of the word, has occurred' (1981: 43). Lehman outlines a continuum of ethical practice. At one end of the continuum there are sports purists who would play/spectate and want to see a game where players followed every rule, even though observing every rule would mean the game would be continuously subject to stoppages due to constant infringements of the rules. At the other end of the continuum would be a situation where the game would be played but no longer resemble the original game due to excessive rule violations. Thus, Lehman suggested a middle ground where players may agree to an implicit contract to keep within the spirit of the rules of the game. We elaborate on this notion of playing within the spirit of the game later in the chapter in the formulation of the 'ethical contract' in the pedagogical applications section.

Drawing on the work of Searle (1995), Drewe (2000) suggests a distinction between 'constitutive' and 'regulative' rules which are akin to Fraleigh's (1984) primary and supererogatory guides and ends of right action. Siedentop *et al.* (2004) and Launder (2001) have also made such distinctions between these rules, calling them primary and secondary rules. While constitutive or primary rules must be observed to play the actual game (i.e. in soccer one could not walk onto a pitch and begin wielding a hockey stick or baseball bat), in contrast, regulative or secondary rules are there to simply regulate play and pertain to how you treat your opponents or the way the game is set up in order to give equal chances of winning to both teams (i.e. both teams play with the same number of players – 6 vs. 6). In this way, physical education teachers and youth sport practitioners can manipulate these 'regulative' (superogatory or secondary rules) in order that young people learn how to conduct themselves on the field of play. The manipulation of these secondary rules has been strongly influential in our formulation of propositions set out in the pedagogical applications section later in the chapter.

However, although this literature proposes that sport is at root an ethical activity we suggest that ethical practice is not automatically achieved by mere engagement in games and sport (see also Chapter 8 by Van Veldhoven). Ethical lessons must be taught, since they are not necessarily caught in the sense that they are born out of experience (Twietmeyer 2007). As stated in the Panathlon Declaration that prompted the development of this book, we hope to show through a review of the Sport Education literature how this model can 'promote the positive values in youth sport more actively with sustained effort and good planning' (Panathlon International 2004).

Sport Education as a medium for ethical practice

In this section we provide a brief overview of the research literature on Sport Education examining to what extent Sport Education has been shown to be a medium for the development of ethical practice. In other words, and in

Siedentop's terms, does Sport Education help children to become *literate* sportspeople?

In total 29 studies were reviewed, with most of the research undertaken in school physical education contexts with limited application in community youth sport contexts (see also Wallhead and O'Sullivan 2005). The Sport Education studies we cite have been implemented in the United States (13), Australia (6), New Zealand (3), the United Kingdom (4) and more recently in Russia (2). We explore this literature under the five themes of inclusion, responsibility and ownership, personal and social development, social justice, and fair play that emerged from our analysis.

Inclusion

Inclusion has been the focus of 16 papers, the majority of which have been produced by researchers in the United States (e.g. Hastie 1998a), Australia (e.g. Pill 2008) and the UK (e.g. Kinchin *et al.* 2004). Equality between male and female students has been investigated (e.g. Alexander *et al.* 1993; Alexander and Luckman 2001), opportunities to respond in game play (Carlson 1995; Curnow and Macdonald 1995; Hastie 1998b; Hastie and Sinelnikov 2006), as well as involvement in social interaction and hierarchies of power (e.g. Ennis 1999; Brunton 2003). Some studies have also reported more appropriate competition (Grant *et al.* 1992), involvement of less able students (for example, Hastie 1998a; Clarke and Quill 2003) and a high-skilled student's perception of Sport Education (Kinchin 2001). While the majority of studies reflect positively on inclusion (12 out of 16), three studies have reported mixed findings and one study negative findings. For example, Hastie and Trost (2002) showed that both high- and low-skilled students increased performance in discrete skills. But there were mixed and negative findings pertaining to gender with Alexander *et al.* (1996) reporting concerns that potential for gender marginalization in Sport Education remains. Hastie (1998b) also noted that a gender stereotype socialization existed, with boys dominating power roles and having more opportunities to respond in the competition phase of the season, and boys' domination of roles and opportunities to respond in game play also occurred in the study by Curnow and Macdonald (1995). In addition, girls in Brunton's 2003 study had erratic commitment to role responsibility.

Responsibility and ownership

Six studies reported that students have a preference for the responsibility and ownership offered by Sport Education, again with the majority being from the United States (e.g. Hastie 1996; Bennet and Hastie 1997), one from the UK (MacPhail et al. 2004), one from New Zealand (Grant 1992), and finally one United States and Australia cross-cultural study (Hastie and Carlson 1998). The majority of these six studies revealed positive findings. For example, in Hastie's (2000) study, high levels of student engagement and compliance were borne out of a managerial system, which was supported by content embedded in accountability and the student social system. However, there were some divergent responses to Sport Education from students of both cultures in Hastie and Carlson's (1998) cross-cultural study, albeit that this was due to 'variation in personal history rather than country of origin' (Wallhead and O'Sullivan 2005: 200).

Personal and social development

Seven studies reported developments in personal and social skills such as leadership, trust and cooperation, with three of these being from Australia, two from the United States, one from the UK (Kinchin *et al.* 2004) and one from New Zealand (Pope and Grant 1996). All seven studies demonstrated positive findings. For example, Ennis (1999) targeted disengaged girls with her 'Sport for Peace' model, which used peace theory to extend Sport Education to include aspects of self and social responsibility, negotiation and conflict resolution, and care and concern for others. Ennis employed modifications to game rules (i.e. everyone had to touch the ball before a team could score) and equal playing time. This led the higher skilled girls to teach and nurture lower skilled players, and to use patience and support when coaching those students. Furthermore, these pedagogical strategies reduced pressure on the girls to 'be like the boys' and 'always do it perfectly the first time'. Although Ennis's study and others reported here illustrate an inclusive experience and inclusionary behaviours, none reported a change in students' attitudes towards the exclusionary practices of sport.

In another study, Hastie and Buchanan (2000) extended the work of Hastie and Sharpe (1999) by integrating Sport Education with the Teaching Social and Personal Responsibility (TSPR; Hellison 2003) model, which they called 'Empowering Sport'. The 'hybrid' unit applied Sport Education concerns for fairness and competition using modified and explicitly cooperative games in tandem with TSPR's notions of self-control and respect. Through the use of field notes, daily teacher debriefs and interviews with the students the authors concluded that the 'hybrid' model was effective in facilitating personal responsibility, student empowerment and problem-solving, thus improving the quality of the Sport Education season. Alexander and Luckman (2001: 255) concurred with Hastie's (2000) notions that Sport Education could provide 'an emphasis on student empowerment in decisions regarding play and appropriate social behaviour' by stating that the 'meaning, purpose, enjoyment and justice' that students experienced in 'quality teaching' stood in 'stark contrast to the features and outcomes of the "dominant model" of PE'. An earlier national trial of Sport Education in Australia also concurred with these observations. Teachers' perceptions revealed that what is learned shifted markedly towards personal and social skills aided by the social system constructed by the model and its pedagogy. Although Alexander and Luckman's

(2001) study was restricted to teachers' perceptions via a questionnaire, it highlighted many of the potential links to ethical and moral development.

Social justice

Kinchin and O'Sullivan (2003) extended Sport Education with ninth/tenth grade students in 20 lessons of volleyball, which they named a 'cultural studies' unit and is the only paper reviewed which considered the development of social justice through Sport Education. They 'integrated practical and theoretical study of sport and physical activity with just over half the 20 sessions ... devoted to physical activity' (2003: 248). The aim was to encourage students to become critical consumers of sport through discussion of issues such as body image, gender, race, media in sport, etc. Through non-participant observation, student journals and interviews, Kinchin and O'Sullivan reported both positive and negative findings from their study, with students supportive of opportunities to discuss issues of social justice but resistant to the presentation of content in a classroom-based pedagogical format.

Fair play

Four studies have focused on issues of fair play within Sport Education, with three of these being from the United States (e.g. Brock and Hastie 2007) and one taking place in Russia (Sinelnikov and Hastie 2008). Findings from one study in particular were positive. Hastie and Sharpe (1999) developed work from an earlier study by Carlson and Hastie (1997) to investigate the effect of Sport Education on pro-social behaviour with 'at-risk' male sixth and seventh grade students in 20 lessons of kangaroo ball, a modified version of Australian Rules Football. Through video observation of social conflict behaviours and a social behaviour questionnaire, Hastie and Sharpe found that a formalized 'fair play' accountability system during the 'competition phase' of the season increased compliance, reduced negative peer interactions and increased instances of leadership from the students.

The other three studies reported both positive and negative findings. For example, a study by Vidoni and Ward (2009) focused on a 'Fair Play Instruction' intervention during an 18-lesson Sport Education tag rugby season with eighth grade students. The study revealed that the 'Fair Play Instruction' intervention increased students' active participation and decreased waiting time for all participants. There was little difference in 'helpful behaviours' from baseline, but there was a decrease in 'harmful behaviours'. However, this was only with two of the seven students, leading the authors to claim that results in this regard were 'weak' (2009: 303). Nonetheless, the authors did conclude that positive social behaviour in the classroom is not an automatic outcome and must be explicitly taught.

Findings from the studies on fair play in particular exemplify the need to explicitly teach positive social behaviour in physical education (Drewe 2000).

There is also some advocacy from the other sections in this review, demonstrating that this can be achieved through Sport Education if it is one of the researchers' (and teachers') aspirations for their unit (Penney *et al.* 2005a; Wallhead and O'Sullivan 2005).

Building on the support for Sport Education as a means of promoting ethical practice, in the next section we outline four pedagogical applications that can be utilized within the framework of the Sport Education model in order to develop literate sportspeople (Siedentop *et al.* 2004): 'ethical contracts'; sports panels; modified games/sports; awards and rewards.

Four pedagogical applications of Sport Education

The ethical contract

The 'ethical contract' is informed in part by a notion from the Francophone literature of the 'didactic contract' in which an implicit agreement exists between teacher and students about appropriate behaviour in physical education (Amade-Escot 2006). Players' shared understanding of assumptions about a range of acceptable behaviours and conduct while they are on the field/court of play can be thought of as a contract between them, creating what Kretchmar (2005) termed the 'conventional logic for the artificial test'. It is our suggestion that the ethical contract rarely takes an official or written form, as it did, exceptionally, in Hastie and Buchanan's (2000) study. Nevertheless, despite its usually implicit nature, the ethical contract must exist in order to make a competitive game or 'sport' possible.

This implicit contract may be based upon the 'guides and ends of right action' outlined by Fraleigh (1984) so as to increase the probability of a good contest. For example, the ethical contract will comprise both the primary and secondary rules of the game we highlighted earlier in the chapter. The 'primary guide and ends of right action' constructs, establishes and maintains the 'constitutive' rules (i.e. not walking onto the soccer field wielding a hockey stick). The 'supererogatory guides and ends of right action', or the 'regulative' (secondary) rules can then be used to state what is good to do, but are not obligatory to the primary rules of the game (i.e. giving others positive recognition, mutual respect, courtesy, etc.). Indeed, it might be argued that Sport Education has 'hard-wired' features for constructing this ethical contract, in that it offers the students opportunities to gain rewards for things other than winning, such as points for sportspersonship and fair play, punctuality, wearing the appropriate attire, positive spectatorship, and so on.

Sports panels

Sport Education offers a further level of sophistication to deal with 'breaches' of the ethical contract that cannot be solved by the students themselves while in the act of playing their match/game. Disputes that cannot be agreed on the field/court can be discussed by a sports panel that is made up of representatives of each of the teams competing in the league competition. The panel members adjudicate 'breaches' of the ethical contract. Meetings can be held at lunchtimes if lesson time does not permit. Sports panel members can be nominated from each of the teams and a ballot could be made to select the membership. Teams are then notified of decisions via the notice board or sent a letter signed by the panel chair (who may or may not be a teacher). Sports panel discussions offer the student members of the panel opportunities to debate key ethical issues over the season of Sport Education (Vidoni and Ward 2009), and to share their experiences with their team members outside of panel meetings (Kirk *et al.* 2006).

Discussion within a sports panel means that members engage in what Hsu (2004) calls 'critical' rather than 'intuitive' thinking. As they are made up of representatives of each of the teams, the sports panel further encourages sports panel members to help their own team members reflect on their own and others' actions and to arrive at a collective version of an intended end (i.e. what playing fair is; Fraleigh 1984). Fraleigh's primary and supererogatory guides and ends of right action can form a basis for both the panel's discussions and ultimate decisions as well as discussions within each of the individual teams about their ethical conduct.

'Ethical contracts' and sports panels have been somewhat exemplified in the Sport Education literature so far, for example, in the 'Cultural Studies' version of Sport Education offered and discussed by Kinchin and O'Sullivan (2003; see also O'Sullivan and Kinchin 2009), by Ennis (1999) in her 'Sport for Peace' approach and by Hastie and Buchanan (2000) in their 'Empowering Sport' model. However, we note there have been no studies so far that have specifically examined the functioning and operation of a sports panel.

Practice and conditioned/modified games

Using Csikszentmihalyi's notions of 'flow channels', Kretchmar (2005) noted the need to control the artificial challenges of a game to get the game 'just right' so as to provide an optimum level of challenge for the participants. For example, games that are too easy and that fall to the south and east of the optimum 'flow channel' would be deemed too tedious and create boredom. On the other hand, games that are too difficult fall to the north and west of the optimum 'flow channel' and thus would make the game too difficult, creating anxiety among the participants. This concept is similar to the 'Goldilocks principle' reported by Rovegno *et al.* (2001), who further noted that games needed to be modified to the developmental level of the children in order to 'get a good game going' and create a 'good sports contest' (Fraleigh 1984: 30–3).

As was stated earlier, modifications to a game can be made by adapting the secondary (Launder 2001), regulative (Searle 1995) rules. Modifications can be made to games by applying the notions of representation and exaggeration

(Werner *et al.* 1996) to these secondary rules. In terms of representation, typically, invasion-game play is modified (to get it 'just right'; Kretchmar 2005) by using a smaller playing area, smaller goals, fewer players, shorter duration of play and a smaller ball (Penney and Clarke 2005). Teachers may also decide to modify the game by exaggerating certain aspects of the game. For example, in a pre-Sport Education season of 4 vs. 4 soccer games, we may have established that Team A is stronger than Team B since they have beaten Team B 5–0 on two previous occasions, thus giving an 'uneven contest' (Fraleigh 1984: 5). Consequently, the players decide that Team A will play with only three players while allowing Team B to participate with their full complement of four players. Although the teams may not necessarily be equal in terms of numbers of players, this modification ensures the teams are equitably challenged. In addition, if there is such an occurrence where Team B begins to win the contest (i.e. is leading by a three-goal differential), then Team A can bring back their fourth player onto the field of play to once again even up the contest. Indeed, the utility of this idea of modification can be broadened to apply to other game classifications such as net/wall game contexts where students might compete 1 vs. 2 or 1 vs. 1 but with one player playing in a larger court area than their opponent. This notion of modified or conditioned games relates directly to the Panathlon Declaration on Ethics in Youth Sport (Panathlon International 2004), in that children are able to 'match themselves against children of the same level in suitable competition'.

Modified or conditioned games have been employed in various Sport Education studies (Hastie and Sharpe 1999; Hastie and Buchanan 2000; Brock and Hastie 2007; Vidoni and Ward 2009). For instance, in order to make competition fairer, the teacher intervened and discussed possible approaches to increase inclusion, with teacher and students deciding to have everyone touch the ball before their team was allowed to score (Ennis 1999). Rovegno *et al.* (2001) reported using 'levels of defence' (i.e. hot, warm, cold) to determine how close defending players could get to attackers during their aerial basketball tactics unit, a strategy also employed by MacPhail *et al.* (2005). Hastie and Buchanan (2000) allowed for the two opposing teams to negotiate rules before competition began (i.e. who would referee the game, how many points would be earned for a goal, etc. – see previous section). Launder (2001) has previously outlined the practical application of 'differential scoring' in his *Play Practice* text. Finally, not only may the modification of games provide 'teachable moments' (Vidoni and Ward 2009), which can be reinforced via teacher questioning and via the 'debate of ideas' (Gréhaigne *et al.* 2005), students may also be encouraged to design their own games (Hastie 2010).

Awards

The culminating event and awards presentation is one of the six characteristics of Sport Education. Giving awards for achievements in addition to winning is another pedagogical application that can promote and facilitate learning of ethical behaviour. In Sport Education not only is there opportunity to recognize the 'best' and most talented players, there is also room to reward the success of other players, such as the 'most improved', or the 'best sportsperson' (see also Panathlon International 2004). For example, borrowing a practice from Australian Rules Football, awards can be made to the fairest team and individual players. This idea is based on the 'True Spirit of Sportspersonship' or 'de Coubertin' medals that are awarded by the International Olympic Committee (IOC) to those individuals who demonstrate acts of sportspersonship during competition.

Quill and Clarke (2005) noted a 'champagne moment' was awarded each lesson for a special incident that occurred. They outlined that this was not only awarded for exceptional skilled performances but exemplifications of positive sporting behaviour. This award also enabled teams to discuss and evaluate these 'teachable moments' (Vidoni and Ward 2009) and why they were of interest.

Conclusions

Our purpose in this chapter has been to explore the extent to which Sport Education, as a medium for ethical practice, can facilitate young people's learning of ethical behaviour. We conclude that the evidence available in the literature supports the aspiration of Sport Educators to develop literate sportspeople who understand and are knowledgeable about the rules, traditions and values associated with a specific sport, and who can distinguish between good and bad sport practices. We also conclude that mere participation in sport does not necessarily facilitate this learning and that we need to so arrange young people's experiences of sport to make the ethical dimensions of participation explicit. We need, in other words, explicit pedagogical applications that facilitate ethical development in youth sport so that they are taught and not just caught.

Our proposals for developing Sport Education in order to do this are modest indeed; for instance, progressive teachers and coaches use modified games regularly. But, for example, they are not always deployed explicitly to provide young people with experiences of fair play. It is for this reason that we have chosen to highlight the potential of modified and conditioned games and the judicious use of awards as means of pursuing the outcome of sport literacy. Moreover, since sport is underpinned by what we have called here an ethical contract, we believe there is much to be gained by drawing attention to this contract, in order to show that ethics is, as we have proposed, a 'hardwired', necessary feature of all sport (Kretchmar 2005). Indeed, it is the shared respect for rules and for opponents that makes sport possible, and explains why literate and enthusiastic sportspeople are so outraged when others choose to cheat (Morgan 2006).

Our reading of the research literature prompts us to caution that there is much work yet to be done to hone Sport Education to fully realize its potential as a vehicle for ethical development in youth sport. While excellent examples of developments, including hybrids and combinations with other models, exist, it has been argued (e.g. Curtner-Smith and Sofo 2004) that physical education is still dominated by multi-activity teaching and that significant challenges are present for teachers in their attempts to integrate Sport Education into their practice due to, for example, their own personal biographies and the socio-historical aspects of schools and schooling. This over-reliance on the multi-activity model might restrict teachers' ability to promote the development of literate sportspersons by using the various pedagogical applications suggested above.

We also believe there is an urgent need to take the model, with its explicit focus on issues such as fair play, into community youth sport contexts. This is necessary if young people are to experience consistency of values between sport in and 'beyond the gym' (Hellison 2003), to align the experiences of sport that children have with physical education and youth community sport settings, a criticism previously highlighted by Shehu (1998), Penney and Chandler (2000), and reiterated by Penney *et al.* (2005b). It is also necessary if we are to grow new generations of volunteer coaches, administrators and officials in sport, consistent with recent government policy in the UK, for example. We think Sport Education offers young people opportunities to learn responsibility and accountability in sport contexts, and to shift the locus of power in youth sport from adults towards young people themselves. We suggest that the development of Sport Education in youth sport contexts beyond the school, with an explicitly ethical agenda, is a worthy focus for a forward-looking and progressive programme of research and development.

We acknowledge that the administrative and cultural contexts of youth community sport may well act as barriers to some of our suggestions (for further discussion see Shehu 1998; Penney and Chandler 2000; Penney *et al.* 2005b; Sinelnikov and Hastie 2010) with one major concern around Sport Education being its ability to stimulate 'carry-over' effects (Sinelnikov and Hastie 2010) 'beyond the gym' (Hellison 2003). Nonetheless, we further note that our suggestions can, we feel, continue to promote both participation and elite performance goals associated with youth sport.

Discussion Questions

1. Write a short account of one incident in a youth sport and/or physical education context that you have seen or experienced as a player/coach/ teacher/leader which you felt went beyond the bounds of sport as an ethical practice. Share this account with another person or a small group and discuss what might be some of the implications of this incident for physical education and youth sport.
2. To what extent do you as a sports practitioner use some of these pedagogical applications in your classroom? In what ways do you use them to encourage ethical behaviour by the children that you teach/coach/lead?

3. Discuss what potential changes would need to occur in youth sport if Sport Education and the pedagogical applications associated with this model outlined in this chapter were to become prominent features of this domain.

Notes

1 This chapter is based on Harvey, S., Kirk, D. and O'Donovan, T. M. (2011) 'Sport Education as a pedagogical application for ethical development in physical education and youth sport', *Sport, Education and Society, iFirst Article*: 1–22, DOI:10.1080/13573322.2011.624594.

2 We define a literate sportsperson, using the definition provided by Siedentop *et al.* (2004: 8), as someone who 'understands and values the rules, rituals, and traditions of sports and activities and can distinguish between good and bad practices in those activities'.

References

Alexander, K. and Luckman, J. (2001) 'Australian teachers' perceptions and uses of the Sport Education curriculum model', *European Physical Education Review*, 7(3): 243–67.

Alexander, K., Taggart, A. and Medland, A. (1993) 'Sport education in physical education: Try before you buy', *Australian Council for Health, Physical Education, and Recreation National Journal*, 40: 16–23.

Alexander, K., Taggart, A. and Thorpe, S. T. (1996) 'A spring in their steps? Possibilities for professional renewal through Sport Education in Australian schools', *Sport, Education and Society*, 1: 23–46.

Amade-Escot, C. (2006) 'Student learning within the *didactique* tradition', in D. Kirk, D. Macdonald and M. O'Sullivan (eds) *The Handbook of Physical Education*. London: Sage, pp. 347–65.

Bennet, G. and Hastie, P. A. (1997) 'A Sport Education curriculum model for a collegiate physical activity course', *Journal of Physical Education, Recreation and Dance*, 68: 39–44.

Brock, S. J. and Hastie, P. A. (2007) 'Students' conceptions of fair play in Sport Education', *ACHPER Australia Healthy Lifestyles Journal*, 54(1): 11–15.

Brunton, J. (2003) 'Changing hierarchies of power in physical education using Sport Education', *European Physical Education Review*, 9(3): 267–84.

Carlson, T. B. (1995) '"Now I think I can": The reaction of eight low-skilled students to Sport Education', *Australian Council for Health, Physical Education, and Recreation Healthy Lifestyles Journal*, 42: 6–8.

Carlson, T. B. and Hastie, P. A. (1997) 'The student social system within Sport Education', *Journal of Teaching in Physical Education*, 17: 176–95.

Clarke, G. and Quill, M. (2003) 'Researching Sport Education in action: A case study', *European Physical Education Review*, 9(3): 253–66.

Curnow, J. and Macdonald, D. (1995) 'Can Sport Education be gender inclusive? A case study in an upper primary school', *Australian Council for Health, Physical Education, and Recreation Healthy Lifestyles Journal*, 42: 9–11.

Curtner-Smith, M. and Sofo, S. (2004) 'Preservice teachers' conceptions of teaching within Sport Education and multi-activity units', *Sport, Education and Society*, 9(3): 347–77.

Drewe, S. B. (2000) 'The logical connection between moral education and physical education', *Journal of Curriculum Studies*, 32(4): 561–73.

Ennis, C. D. (1999) 'Creating a culturally relevant curriculum for disengaged girls', *Sport, Education and Society*, 49(1): 31–49.

Fraleigh, W. P. (1984) *Right Actions in Sport: Ethics for Contestants*. Champaign, IL: Human Kinetics.

Grant, B. C. (1992) 'Integrating sport into the physical education curriculum in New Zealand secondary schools', *Quest*, 44: 304–16.

Grant, B. C., Treddinick, P. and Hodge, K. (1992) 'Sport education in physical education', *New Zealand Journal of Health, Physical Education and Recreation*, 25: 3–6.

Gréhaigne, J. F., Wallian, N. and Godbout, P. (2005) 'Tactical-decision learning model and students' practices', *Physical Education and Sport Pedagogy*, 10(3): 255–69.

Hastie, P. A. (1996) 'Student role involvement during a unit of Sport Education', *Journal of Teaching in Physical Education*, 16: 88–103.

Hastie, P. A. (1998a) 'Skill and tactical development during a Sport Education season', *Research Quarterly for Exercise and Sport*, 69: 368–79.

Hastie, P. A. (1998b) 'The participation and perceptions of girls within a unit of Sport Education', *Journal of Teaching in Physical Education*, 17: 157–71.

Hastie, P. A. (2000) 'An ecological analysis of a Sport Education season', *Journal of Teaching in Physical Education*, 19: 355–73.

Hastie, P. A. (2010) *Student-designed Games: Strategies for Promoting Creativity, Cooperation, and Skill Development*. Champaign, IL: Human Kinetics.

Hastie, P. A. and Buchanan, A. (2000) 'Teaching responsibility through Sport Education: Prospects of a coalition', *Research Quarterly for Exercise and Sport*, 71 (1): 25–35.

Hastie, P. A. and Carlson, T. B. (1998) 'Sport Education: A cross-cultural comparison', *Comparative Sport and Physical Education Journal*, 8: 22–30.

Hastie, P. A. and Sharpe, T. (1999) 'Effects of a Sport Education curriculum on the positive social behavior of at-risk rural adolescent boys', *Journal of Education for Students Placed at Risk*, 4(4): 417–30.

Hastie, P. A. and Sinelnikov, O. A. (2006) 'Russian students' participation in and perceptions of Sport Education', *European Physical Education Review*, 12(2): 131–50.

Hastie, P. A. and Trost, S. (2002) 'Student physical activity levels during a season of Sport Education', *Pediatric Exercise Science*, 14(1): 64–74.

Hellison, D. (2003) *Teaching Responsibility Through Physical Activity* (2nd edn). Champaign, IL: Human Kinetics.

Hsu, L. (2004) 'Moral thinking, sports rules and education', *Sport, Education and Society*, 14(3): 339–52.

Kinchin, G. D. (2001) 'A high-skilled pupil's experiences of Sport Education', *Australian Council for Health, Physical Education, and Recreation Healthy Lifestyles Journal*, 47: 3–4.

Kinchin, G. D. and O'Sullivan, M. (2003) 'Incidences of student support for and resistance to curricular innovation in high school physical education', *Journal of Teaching in Physical Education*, 22: 245–60.

Kinchin, G. D., Wardle, C., Roderick, S. and Sprosen, A. (2004) 'A survey of year 9 boys perceptions of Sport Education in one English secondary school', *Bulletin of Physical Education*, 40(1): 27–40.

Kirk, D. (with O'Donovan, T., Kirk, S., Jarram, R., MacPhail, A. and Webb, L.) (2006) 'From theory to practice: Exploring the educational benefits of Sport Education in a UK primary school', Jennifer Wall Keynote Lecture, Annual Conference of the Association of Physical Educators, Quebec, McGill University, November.

Kretchmar, R. S. (2005) 'Why do we care so much about games? (And is this ethically defensible?)', *Quest*, 57: 181–91.

Launder, A. G. (2001) *Play Practice: The Games Approach to Teaching and Coaching Sports.* Champaign, IL: Human Kinetics.

Lehman, C. K. (1981) 'Can cheaters play the game?', *Journal of the Philosophy of Sport*, 8: 41–6.

MacIntyre, A. (1985) *After Virtue: A Study in Moral Theory* (2nd edn). London: Duckworth.

MacPhail, A., Kirk, D. and Kinchin, G. D. (2004) 'Sport Education: Promoting team affiliation through physical education', *Journal of Teaching in Physical Education*, 23(2): 106–22.

MacPhail, A., Kirk, D. and Kinchin, G. D. (2005) 'Sport Education in key stage 2 games', in D. Penney, G. Clarke, M. Quill and G. Kinchin (eds) *Sport Education: Research-based Practice.* London: Routledge, pp. 122–39.

Mangan, J. A. (1981) *Athleticism in Victorian and Edwardian Public Schools.* Cambridge: Cambridge University Press.

Morgan, W. J. (2006) 'Philosophy and physical education', in D. Kirk, D. Macdonald and M. O'Sullivan (eds) *The Handbook of Physical Education.* London: Sage, pp. 97–108.

O'Sullivan, M. and Kinchin, G. (2009) 'Cultural studies curriculum in physical activity and sport', in J. Lund and D. Tannehill (eds) *Standards-based Physical Education Curriculum Development.* Sudbury, MA: Jones and Bartlett, pp. 333–66.

Panathlon International (2004) Declaration on Ethics in Youth Sport. Available at: http://www.panathlon.net (accessed 23 January 2012).

Penney, D. and Chandler, T. (2000) 'Physical education: What future(s)?', *Sport, Education and Society*, 5(1): 71–87.

Penney, D. and Clarke, G. (2005) 'Inclusion in Sport Education', in D. Penney, G. Clarke, M. Quill and G. Kinchin (eds) *Sport Education: Research-based Practice.* London: Routledge, pp. 41–54.

Penney, D., Clarke, G. and Kinchin, G. (2002) 'Developing PE as a "connective specialism": Is Sport Education the answer?', *Sport, Education and Society*, 7(1): 55–64.

Penney, D., Clarke, G., Quill, M. and Kinchin, G. (2005a) *Sport Education: Research-based Practice.* London: Routledge.

Penney, D., Kinchin, G., Clarke, G. and Quill, M. (2005b) 'What is Sport Education and why is it timely to explore it?', in D. Penney, G. Clarke, M. Quill and G. Kinchin (eds) *Sport Education: Research-based Practice.* London: Routledge, pp. 3–22.

Pill, S. (2008) 'A teacher's perceptions of the Sport Education model as an alternative for upper primary school physical education', *ACHPER Australia Healthy Lifestyles Journal*, 55(2): 23–9.

Pope, C. and Grant, B. C. (1996) 'Student experiences in Sport Education', *Waikato Journal of Education*, 2: 103–18.

Quill, M. and Clarke, G. (2005) 'Sport Education in Year 8 games', in D. Penney, G. Clarke, M. Quill and G. Kinchin (eds) *Sport Education: Research-based Practice.* London: Routledge, pp. 140–64.

Rovegno, I., Nevett, M., Brock, S. and Babiarz, M. (2001) 'Chapter 7: Teaching and learning basic invasion-game tactics in 4th grade: A descriptive study from situated and constraints theoretical perspectives', *Journal of Teaching in Physical Education*, 20(4): 370–88.

Searle, J. R. (1995) *The Construction of Social Reality*. New York: Free Press.

Shehu, J. (1998) 'Sport Education: Ideology, evidence and implications for PE in Africa', *Sport, Education and Society*, 3(2): 227–35.

Siedentop, D., Hastie, P. A. and van der Mars, H. (2004) *Complete Guide to Sport Education*. Champaign, IL: Human Kinetics.

Sinelnikov, O. A. and Hastie, P. A. (2008) 'Teaching Sport Education to Russian students: An ecological analysis', *European Physical Education Review*, 14(2): 203–22.

Sinelnikov, O. A. and Hastie, P. A. (2010) 'Students' autobiographical memory of participation in multiple Sport Education seasons', *Journal of Teaching in Physical Education*, 29(2): 167–83.

Suits, B. (1978) *The Grasshopper: Games, Life and Utopia*. Ontario: Broadview Press.

Twietmeyer, G. (2007) 'Suffering play: Can the time spent on play and games be justified in a suffering world', *Quest*, 59: 201–11.

Vidoni, C. and Ward, P. (2009) 'Effects of Fair Play Instruction on student social skills during a middle school Sport Education unit', *Physical Education and Sport Pedagogy*, 14(3): 285–310.

Wallhead, T. and O'Sullivan, M. (2005) 'Sport Education: Physical education for the new millennium?', *Physical Education and Sport Pedagogy*, 10(2): 181–210.

Werner, P., Thorpe, R. and Bunker, D. (1996) 'Teaching games for understanding: Evolution of a model', *Journal of Physical Education, Recreation and Dance*, 67(1): 28–33.

8 Sports from a pedagogical perspective

Nicolette Schipper-Van Veldhoven

Many people participate in and love sports. And rightly so, because sports are unique and beautiful. Sports can be a learning environment. But (s)he who does not fight the negative excesses of sport fails to fulfil his/her obligations.

(Wieldraayer *et al.* 2007: 200)

Introduction

One of the responsibilities of the Netherlands Olympic Committee*Netherlands Sports Confederation (NOC*NSF) is to create a responsible youth sport policy within organized youth sport. This means that this policy is in the best interest of the child, and aimed at creating a pedagogical climate when practising sport. A pedagogical climate is a situation in which children and youngsters can develop themselves cognitively, socially, psychologically and/or physically and which holds educational values (pedagogical perspective).

This is important because it has become clear that organized youth sport, next to family and school, is an important socializing context for children and adolescents (Kay 2009; Light 2010). In this way, sports have become known as the third pedagogical environment (Cotterell 1996; Dekovic 1999).

The sports club is one of the most important sites for sports participation of youth (Coakley 1998). From the ages of 6 to 11 and 12 to 17 years, 66 per cent and 65 per cent of all Dutch children are members of a sports club, respectively (Tiessen-Raaphorst *et al.* 2010). There is, therefore, no doubt that children and adolescents are influenced by the social activity they participate in. Participation offers possibilities to learn, both consciously and subconsciously. Sports are no exception and offer children specific new experiences and new ways to act through engagement in practice (Light 2010; Kelly 2011).

While I have outlined that sports are inherently social practices, researchers agree that pure engagement in sports does not automatically lead to positive outcomes and improved social, psychological and/or moral character (Shields *et al.* 1995; Todd and Hodge 2001; Coakley 2004 [1997]). Sports can also lead to the opposite: egotism, arrogance, bullying, discrimination and injuries, but this effect is largely shaped by the context of youth sport participation. The actual effect of participation in sports on the child's development principally depends on the way the sports are played or how the sports project is executed, and the social context in which it takes place (Krouwel *et al.* 2006; Stegeman 2007).

> Organized sports, informal sports and physical education classes differ significantly in the immediate affective experiences they provide and in the relationships between affect components. Within organized sport, socialization outcomes are mediated by the topics, goals and tone of coach–athlete interactions, and by the social parameters within which the interactions are embedded. These findings suggest it would be misleading to search for effects of sport while ignoring variations among and within sport settings.
>
> (Stegeman 2007: 21)

Sports have an intrinsic value and can offer a safe educational environment in which the positive values of sport can occur, such as developing a positive self-image, cooperation skills, consciousness of norms and values (Shields and Bredemeier 2001; Bailey 2006; Findlay and Coplan 2008). So this is not a priori inherent in sports. As we have acknowledged above, this intrinsic value needs to be taught through the child's engagement in an appropriate context for learning these intrinsic values. The questions we therefore need to ask are: How can the NOC*NSF, the sports federations, the sports clubs, trainers, coaches, parents and athletes make sure that 'sports' is an environment which focuses on the positive effects of participating in sports? And how can they diminish the negative effects? Before I move on to answer these questions, it is pertinent to say a little more about the two faces of sports.

The two faces of sports

Sports are for many people a source of pleasure and can contribute to important social developments as mentioned above. However, organizations such as the NOC*NSF cannot, and should not, close their eyes to the other side of sports, where vulnerable people can become victims of deception and abuse. Vulnerability in sports can be seen, for example, in the relationship between the coach and the athlete. This relationship is usually close and intense, but at the same time can be based on an unequal power relationship. Other characteristic vulnerabilities are the structural pushing of boundaries in elite sport, such as asking the most of athletes, the ambitions of athletes, the moral atmosphere, and the physical and psychological development of the 'young' athlete (Wieldraayer *et al.* 2007). According to Rutten *et al.* (2004), 21 per cent of the anti-social behaviour around the playing field, and respectively 8 per cent and 14 per cent of the differences between anti- and pro-social behaviour in the field, can be attributed to differences between teams and trainers, that is, the sports club. These specific vulnerabilities require specific measures for sports, such as a Sports Code for sportspersonship and respect (NOC*NSF 2004).

The positive values of sports can contribute to cooperation, team spirit, fair play, self-confidence and health (van den Heuvel *et al.* 2007; Steenbergen *et al.* 2010). In particular, the Dutch population is convinced that sports can contribute to better health and social cohesion (Eurobarometer 2004). The sports world in the Netherlands is trying to bring the added value of sports into the spotlight. 'This recognised added value is one of the most important reasons why there is such appreciation for sport and why sport is supported both in the political arena as well as by society at large' (NOC*NSF 2009: 82). Scientific research strengthens the realization that the development of positive values depends on the emotional and motivational atmosphere in which the physical activities are offered (Vanden Auweele *et al.* 2001). Bailey (2006) showed that positive experiences, such as having fun and the involvement of all participants, are important conditions without which the positive effects of sports and physical education (e.g. on self-confidence) do not occur. The ways in which these effects occur can rely on the nature of the interaction between students and their teachers, parents and coaches. Contexts that encourage positive experiences are characterized by fun, diversity (variation) and the involvement of all, and are led by appointed (trusted) and well-trained teachers, trainers/coaches, and supportive and well-informed parents (Stegeman 2007).

In my opinion, we do not pay enough attention to the context in which positive values, which can be associated with participation in sports, can occur. There is insufficient research regarding the factors that provide these positive effects in specific contexts that we, 'the sports world', are so eager to claim. The fact that sport is a pedagogically relevant environment where children/adolescents and adults voluntarily interact raises the question as to whether we 'as sports practitioners' pay enough attention to this pedagogical climate. Is it simply enough to assume that the 'genes' of sports create an emotionally and motivationally healthy sports environment? Or do we as sport practitioners and researchers need to do more to showcase how this pedagogically relevant environment needs to be structured to realize this aim?

In the reality of the sports world it is not customary to dwell on the negative side of sport or to incorporate preventive measures in policies. The world of sport often responds to (suspected) abuses and then creates a policy. For example, in 1996, the Netherlands started a project against sexual harassment after several incidents with professional athletes, which was given blanket coverage by the media. After these incidents measures were enacted to prevent these negative effects in the future. The NOC*NSF supports and advises people in sports who are confronted with abuse by way of a hotline and advisers (see Moget and Weber 2008). However, a lot of sports clubs still claim 'it does not happen in our club' and have no policy on abuse or sexual harassment (Serkei 2011). Also, other undesirable behaviour in amateur sport has been investigated by the Ministry of Health, Welfare and Sport. On several occasions in 2006, the media again drew attention to the negative aspects of sports. Having said that, the occurrence of these abuses was not based on figures. But the coverage provided a reason to examine unwanted behaviour in sports.

Research by Tiessen-Raaphorst *et al.* (2008) found that one out of five Dutch children aged 12 years or over has been the victim or witness of unwanted behaviour in sports, such as vandalism, threats, physical and verbal violence, discrimination and nuisance (smoking, alcohol, noise pollution). The seriousness of these forms of undesirable behaviour varies, as does their impact on witnesses and victims. Witnesses and victims most often report verbal violence. Half the directors of sports clubs have received complaints of unwanted behaviour. These complaints were usually concerning verbal violence (27 per cent), vandalism (22 per cent) and theft (18 per cent). The clubs responded in different ways to these complaints. In more than half the cases, those responsible for the behaviour were spoken to, given a warning or the police were notified. For 13 per cent of the victims and witnesses, the experience with unwanted behaviour provided them with a reason to quit as an athlete, volunteer or spectator. This could have important consequences for a sports club.

The image of sports plays an important role for individuals and young children when choosing a sport. Sports are often considered unsuitable because they are seen as too aggressive or violent (51 per cent of the Dutch gave this reason for not choosing a certain sport) or because potential athletes have heard negative stories about the sport (20 per cent; Tiessen-Raaphorst *et al.* 2008).

The same research by Tiessen-Raaphorst *et al.* (2008) examined the familiarity with, and the use of, materials to avoid or decrease unwanted behaviour. Examples of these are campaigns, house rules, codes of conduct, a telephone line for disclosure and confidential advisers. Only a few clubs (11 per cent) use these supportive means. Yet clubs claim they do much to avoid and decrease unwanted behaviour. House rules are used frequently. Less common are attempts to promote the quality of supervision and guidance. This would include careful selection of trainers and support workers. The research did show that a large part of the population was aware of the campaigns that focused on prevention. This could be a starting point for the sports clubs, leading to the further involvement of athletes when dealing with unwanted behaviour, including a broader implementation of the complaint policies of sports clubs.

Creating policies to avoid abuse: the Sports Code

The Netherlands is advanced when it comes to creating policies to avoid abuse. Since 2001 the NOC*NSF and several other national sports bodies in the Netherlands have worked on a Sports Code for sportspersonship and respect. The Sports Code aims to promote sportspersonship and especially fair play (NOC*NSF 2004). This is done by promoting dealing with rules, as well as interaction with others and equal opportunities. To promote sports-personship, it is best if different channels such as campaigns, media, trainers, etc. influence athletes. The Sports Code stimulates and supports organizations that are trying to structurally create responsible policies. Different supportive materials such as behavioural codes for athletes, trainers and coaches, referees and parents have been developed. NOC*NSF also offers policies for arbitration, discrimination, alcohol, doping, injury prevention, etc.

As a sports environment we (NOC*NSF and sports federations) wish to deliver the message that we see the potential negative effects of sports and want to take a proactive role. The issues are real and must be addressed. Even though some negative behaviour occurs everywhere in society, that does not excuse the sports world of its responsibility to create a safe and responsible sports environment. Just like all other facets of society, sports must create an environment where the physical and emotional safety of people is guaranteed. This must include serious efforts towards prevention, before the abuse occurs.

Preventive policies therefore need to be developed in order to safeguard and protect young people involved in sport. Preventive policies need to be linked to the intrinsic possibilities of sports and its ability to contribute to the personal development of athletes and the context in which this can happen. In many cases youth sports can often simply be a reflection of adult sports, without awareness or knowledge of the psychological development of children or of the pedagogical aspects (see also Chapter 7 by Harvey, Kirk and O'Donovan). Buisman (2002, 2004) has argued for many years that more specific attention needs to be paid to youth sports in this regard. 'Youth sports should in the first place be about the interests of the child and the fun he or she has with sports' (Buisman 2004: 322). For those involved in sport, embracing the 'pedagogical perspective', which holds educational value and creates opportunities for children and youngsters to develop themselves cognitively, socially, psychologically and/or physically, is a chance to shape the positive possibilities of sports and invest in the positive areas highlighted above.

The pedagogical perspective of sports

The unique character of sports and physical education offers many pedagogical possibilities, which currently are not often utilized. The rule-based character of sports (see Fraser-Thomas *et al.* 2005; Burnett 2006) offers many educational possibilities. Children and adolescents learn to use and accept rules, to show consideration for others and to deal with their own talents and limits. They also learn to compare their achievements with the achievements of others in a very immediate fashion (Bardel *et al.* 2010). Metaphorically, sports can be seen as an ideal and typically meritocratic system (Hilvoorde 2004). Sports both reflect and prepare for a society that, to a large extent, is structured and organized based on achievements attributed to the efforts of an individual. Sports (as well as physical education) can only offer these virtues in the right context: the right emotional and motivational climate during sports and physical education, and by embedding sports in education. Research by Dirks *et al.* (2003) shows that the quality of the relationship between the practitioner and the athlete is the key influence on the behaviour of adolescent athletes.

> Many coaches just want to win. There are too many coaches in the Netherlands who only want to win. Because of that talent does not have the opportunity to develop optimally. A coach should inspire and not just give instructions. The Dutch sports world needs specialists who can train talents.
>
> *(Nederlands Dagblad*, 12 February 2007: 14)

The pedagogical function of sports is more than good didactics and methods. Transferring values, respect, relationship-building abilities, communication tools, self-esteem reinforcement and solidifying overall personal and environmental awareness (their body, team, opponent), all play a part. It is necessary to act in the child's best interest. This can be especially important for children, adolescents and young adults who are also professional athletes. The downside of sports can sometimes be strongly witnessed in these cases. So it is important to remember that there is a current curve between the goal of sports to excel on the one hand and the positive effects of sports on the personal development of the child/adolescent on the other. From a pedagogical perspective there is a plea for children's rights: all children have the right to practise sports in (socially) safe circumstances and to be trained and guided by competent people. The child should be allowed (eventually) to choose which sport to participate in, and with what ultimate aims (see, for example, Panathlon International 2004).

In order to increase the assertiveness of the maturing individual/athlete and so that they will eventually become sovereign, a resilient environment is needed; that is, an environment that supports the child as a developing individual, increases their resilience and encourages them to achieve independence at the end of the day. The sovereign athlete makes his/her own choices and can stand up for his/her interests without help (Moget and Weber 2007). For the child to become assertive, the sports environment (and the family and school) guides and supports. Visscher (2008) also feels that the child should play an active and responsible role in the process of learning and improving. In the currently accepted model of upbringing, it is especially a process of interaction between the parent and the child within the overall development, with the child playing an active role. Eventually, the child is responsible for his/her choices. Langeveld (1979) called this self-responsibility and self-determination. Parents and practitioners have to have skills which support this process. All adults in the environment of the (young) athlete should adhere to clear directives as to their role, responsibilities and the boundaries of the mutual relationship. It is important that the power relationship between children and coaches offers space for involvement and growth.

Pedagogical training should be a part of the education of sports leaders, sports teachers and sports coaches. There are three pedagogical (sports) pillars that have been highlighted by Bloem and van Toorn (2008) and Moget and Weber (2007). These are:

1. Moral atmosphere: the moral atmosphere is determined by the values that the trainer/coach and the sports club or school propagates. Trainers often subconsciously propagate a message that is common in their sports culture. It is important to become aware of one's values and the transference of these values.
2. Motivational atmosphere: the coach determines for a large part the motivational atmosphere of a club. This can be improved by coaching methods. Some coaches want their pupils to improve themselves. Others think winning is the main goal. It is important that there is a balance between the two.
3. Preventive and repressive policies against physical and mental abuse: it is very important that there is a policy against bullying or intimidation. If these things do occur it has to be clear to everybody that steps will be taken.

Several studies demonstrate the above, which will now be reviewed in turn to show the extent of the evidence that supports each of these features. First, research shows that the moral atmosphere is influenced by the norms of the trainer. From research among football players we know that the norms of the trainer with regard to fair play and aggression are decisive for the moral choices of the players concerned when they are confronted with sport-related moral dilemmas (Guivernau and Duda 2002). Research by Dirks *et al.* (2003) and Shields *et al.* (1995), for example, also refers to the influence of the trainer on relevant moral behaviour of the players in the sporting context.

Second, the motivational atmosphere promoted by the coach is strongly related to the perception children have of their coach's behaviour. The motivational atmosphere and the communication style of the coaches are very influential in the fun that the players have as well as their engagement in sport (Conde *et al.* 2009; Quested and Duda 2009). Perception of a mastery climate created by a coach promotes greater enjoyment, commitment, involvement and personal investment. The children's commitment is negatively related with the perception of a performance climate (Leo *et al.* 2009). Reinboth and Duda (2006) conclude that for sports participation to facilitate athletes' well-being, the sporting environment should be marked by its task-involving features. Such an approach involves prospective 'taking and giving' rationales for requested activities. For example, Olympiou *et al.* (2008) found that the perceived task-involving coach climate (i.e. important role, cooperative learning and effort improvement) was associated with children's perceptions of feeling close, being committed and interacting in a complementary fashion with their coach. Moreover, coaches in a study conducted by Zomermaand (2010) believed that they had an influence on the motivation of their athletes, all mentioning the need for a generally positive coaching approach, which involved praising the little things, focusing on improvement instead of winning and losing, and the importance of developing relationships. All these findings support the role of the coach in supporting a task-involved motivational climate and positive coaching, giving due regard to the well-being of the athletes.

Third, preventive and repressive policies on physical and mental abuse have not been the subject of any current research. Most research has been conducted on perceptions and reported prevalence of abuse (Vertommen 2009) and the production of theoretical models; for example, the grooming process as described by Brackenridge (2001) and the risk factors model (e.g. Finkelhor 1986). Recently, NOC*NSF started research on their telephone line for disclosure. Over ten years, a number of incidents have been reported to NOC*NSF. Cases of sexual harassment and abuse, violence, unwanted intimacies and abuse of power have all been handled by the counsellors and advisers of NOC*NSF, which produces crucial information on the nature and number of complaints concerning harassment and abuse in sport. The registration forms of the counsellors and advisers contain valuable information about the age, sex and position of victim and accused. Types of harassment, point in time and duration of the incident, and sport discipline can also be found in the documents. With this information the NOC*NSF can check and compare these reports to the theories and models mentioned above. Some initial results indicate that there were, in total, 601 phone alerts between 2001 and 2010. More than half of the victims of the abuse were female and younger than 16. Most of the cases were reported by an administrator of the sports club (Vertommen 2011).

The pedagogical relationship

The central condition for a positive learning atmosphere is the development of the pedagogical relationship. The relationship between the coach and the child should be characterized by an appropriate response of the coach to the wishes and needs of the child. The coach and the child communicate and this continued discussion is based on mutual understanding and respect. The rules are clear and incorporate both the ideas of the coach and the child. Breaking the rules is punished consistently. Quensel (1982, quoted in Stegeman and Janssens 2004: 29) makes the following recommendations with regard to the way in which the learning environment should be shaped and supervised in order to create a positive atmosphere to enhance the pedagogical relationship of the child and their coach:

- Encourage a positive self-image by choosing an approach that takes into account what participants already know or can deal with.
- Use a direct and open style of communication.
- Build up a relationship of trust, whereby clarity and a consistent attitude are the chief attributes.
- Focus on all participants.
- Stay motivated and respond to unexpected situations.
- Work in a practical way and avoid long discussions.
- Emphasize an atmosphere of conviviality and relaxation.
- Be yourself.

Sport policy should mention what is needed for the advancement of the rights, well-being, personal development and protection of the (young) athlete and his/her peers, as well as how trainers, coaches and parents can contribute. Signing a declaration of intent can be a sign of dedication to creating a safe environment of mutual respect (Steenbergen *et al.* 2010).

But, most importantly, adults involved in sport need to talk to each other and begin a dialogue and stand up for the interests of young children. Sports clubs need to communicate what they stand for and role models should express this message. A good example in the Netherlands is the sports club Flik Flak, which has a mission statement which focuses on the children and fun in sport. The club has also adopted a protocol to prevent abuse of power and their accommodation has been set up in such a way that there are no hidden areas in all the halls of residence (see Flik Flak 2008).

We need statements which confirm that we will take responsibility. The sports world needs a public debate with a positive basic attitude, not from a defensive position because of negative events. Where possible, children and adolescents should also be involved in the discussion about the pedagogical content of youth sports.

Best pedagogical practices

The sports environment is willing, but is clearly still searching for how to create a pedagogical ciimate. Research such as *The Pedagogical Role of the Sports Club* by Biestra *et al.* (2001, in Dutch) can contribute to the sports reality by making youth sports practitioners more aware of the possibly relevant aspects in their own sports environment, and of their own actions. Such research can also support the discussion between children, practitioners, parents and other interested parties. Other research, for example, into the description and analysis of important aspects of the pedagogic and developmental psychological learning environment in which professional gymnasts train and compete (NOC*NSF 2008), allows for the examination of the power relationship between the gymnast and the management, the athletes' personal development and the use of mental training. The study revealed that realizing a positive pedagogical climate is the joint responsibility of all those who play a part in the (sports) education of the young athlete. Responsible behaviour does not happen automatically but needs to be actively organized and executed, with monitoring for compliance and efficacy. Without a well-organized overall policy that includes implementation, supervision and practical consequences, the balance between sports and well-being can disappear. Then the positive aspects of sports will not have the priority they should have in the life of a maturing athlete to be of importance to personal growth. Vanden Auweele *et al.* (2001) support this view.

A good example of a branch of sports, which has led the way in its pedagogical responsibility in the Netherlands, is the martial arts and strength sports union. Several years ago they began the projects *Opvoeden op de mat* (Educating in the dojo) and *Samen Sterk* (United we stand) (see, for example, Koninklijke Nederlandse Krachtsport en Fitnessfederatie 2004). These projects focus on the educational task of the martial arts teacher and the pedagogical added value of martial arts and strength sports. The project *Tijd voor Vechtsport* (Time for martial arts) in 2008 is supported by a qualitative training programme, which has been followed by over 250 martial arts and strength sports practitioners. The process of 'pedagogification' is given an extra impulse by a manual, an exercise book and a DVD (Bloem and van Toorn 2008). The manual focuses on the importance of a pleasant and positive pedagogic atmosphere, and the psychological and social development of adolescents. A lot of attention is paid to 'pleasant martial arts education', which is subdivided by target group. In a separate exercise book several ways of teaching are described and the DVD shows the dynamics of these ways of teaching.

Recently, the Dutch government has committed itself to improving sports safety, to ensure that sports remain fun for everyone and the power of sports can be embedded in districts and neighbourhoods. The action plan *Naar een prettig en veiliger sportklimaat* (Towards an enjoyable and safer sports climate) defines this determination (Ministry of Health, Welfare and Sport 2011). NOC*NSF, sports federations, local authorities and several ministerial departments cooperate in stimulating preferred behaviour and tackling excesses. Awareness, proper tools for sports (i.e. code of conduct, house rules, confidential advisers, education of sport coaches) and cooperation with various parties are essential for a successful approach.

Conclusion

A pedagogical discussion is a multi-form discussion in which it is accepted that people have different ideas about education and educational targets. This is normative and needs to be made concrete by both the educator and the child. However, one needs to be careful that education is not idealized so that it no longer has anything to do with reality. It also cannot become a naive idea about the manipulability of people in sports, because eventually children and adolescents determine what works in terms of pedagogy. Education in and through sports can only be realized in the sporting practices that possess – from a pedagogical perspective – many qualities. Awareness and responsibility start with each individual. With you and me!

Discussion Questions

1. How do you act in the best interest of the child? How do you/does your sport organization/school create a safe sporting environment?
2. What is your own style of coaching?
3. How do you describe your own behaviour in coaching/teaching (or let somebody else describe/observe your behaviour)?
4. Does your sport organization/school have preventive and awareness policies against physical, emotional and/or sexual abuse?

References

Bailey, R. (2006) 'Physical education and sports in schools: A review of the benefits and outcomes', *Journal of School Health*, 77: 397–401.

Bardel, M., Fontayne, P., Colombel, F. and Schiphof, L. (2010) 'Effects of match result and social comparison on sport state self-esteem fluctuations', *Psychology of Sport and Exercise*, 11: 171–6.

Biestra, G. J. J., Stams, G. J. J. M., Dirks, E., Rutten, E., Schuengel, C., Veuglers, W. et al. (2001) *De Pedagogische taak van de sportvereniging* [The pedagogical role of the sports club]. Arnhem: NOC*NSF.

Bloem, J. and van Toorn, R. (2008) *Positief Vechtsportonderwijs, theoretische en praktische richtlijnen ten bate van een positief leerklimaat in het Nederlandse vechtsportonderwijs* [Positive martial arts education, theoretical and practical guidelines for a positive learning climate in Dutch martial arts education]. Internal report. Arnhem: NOC*NSF.

Brackenridge, C. H. (2001) *Spoilsports: Understanding and Preventing Sexual Exploitation in Sport*. London: Routledge.

Buisman, A. (2002) *Jeugdsport en fair play in het Nederlandse sportbeleid van de jaren negentig* [Youth sports and fair play in the Dutch sports policy in the 1990s]. Amsterdam: SWP.

Buisman, A. (2004) 'Opvoeding in en door sport?' [Upbringing in and through sports?], *Pedagogiek*, 4: 310–23.

Burnett, C. (2006) 'Building social capital through an active community club', *International Review for Sociology of Sport*, 41: 283–94.

Coakley, J. J. (2004 [1997]) *Sport in Society: Issues and Controversies*. Boston, MA: McGraw-Hill.

Conde, C., Almagro, B. J., Sáenz-López, P. and Castillo, E. (2009) 'Intervention and evaluation of the motivational climate transmitted by a basketball coach', *Revista de Psicología del Deporte*, 18-suppl.: 357–61.

Cotterell, J. (1996) *Social Networks and Influences in Adolescence*. London: Routledge.

Dekovic, M. (1999) 'Risk and protective factors in the development of problem behaviour during adolescence', *Journal of Youth and Adolescence*, 28: 667–85.

Dirks, E., Stams, G. J. J. M., Biestra, G. J. J., Schuengel, C. and Hoeksma, J. B. (2003) *Sport en sociale integratie: Een onderzoek naar de betekenis van sportparticipatie voor de sociale integratie van jongens in de samenleving* [Sports and social integration: A study of the meaning of sports participation for social integration of boys into society]. Utrecht: NIZW.

Eurobarometer (2004) 'Special Eurobarometer 213 / wave 62.0 – TNS Opinion & Social'. Available at: http://ec.europa.eu/sport/index_en.htm (accessed 23 November 2011).

Findlay, L. C. and Coplan, R. J. (2008) 'Come out and play: Shyness in childhood and the benefits of organized sport participation', *Canadian Journal of Behavioural Science*, 40: 153–61.

Finkelhor, D. (1986) *A Sourcebook on Child Sexual Abuse*. London: Sage.

Flik Flak (2008) 'Flik Flak gymnastics and dance club'. Available at: www.flik-flak.nl (accessed 23 November 2011).

Fraser-Thomas, J. L., Côté, J. and Deakin, J. (2005) 'Youth sport programs: An avenue to foster positive youth development', *Physical Education & Sport Pedagogy*, 10(1): 19–40.

Guivernau, M. and Duda, J. L. (2002) 'Moral atmosphere and athletic aggressive tendencies in young soccer players', *Journal of Moral Education*, 31: 67–85.

Hilvoorde, I. van (2004) Sports and education: Between realism and idealism. Draft paper written for Education through Sports: Europe's Speaking. 's Hertogenbosch: Mulier Instituut.

Kay, T. (2009) 'Developing through sport: Evidencing sport impacts on young people', *Sport in Society*, 12: 1177–91.

Kelly, L. (2011) 'Social inclusion through sports-base interventions?', *Critical Social Policy*, 31: 126–50.

Koninklijke Nederlandse Krachtsport en Fitnessfederatie (2004) *The Royal Dutch Fitness Federation: Time for Martial Arts*. Available at: http://www.knkf.nl/tijdvoor vechtsport (accessed 23 November 2011).

Krouwel, A., Boonstra, N., Duyvendak, J. and Veldboer, L. (2006) 'A good sport? Research into the capacity of recreational sport to integrate Dutch minorities', *International Review for the Sociology of Sport*, 41(2): 165–80.

Langeveld, M. J. (1979) *Beknopte Theoretische Pedagogiek* [Brief theoretical pedagogics]. Groningen: Wolters-Noordhoff.

Leo, F. M., Sánchez, P. A., Sánchez, D., Amado, D. and Calvo, T. G. (2009) 'Influence of the motivational climate created by coach in the sport commitment in youth basketball players', *Revista de Psicología del Deporte*, 18-suppl.: 375–8.

Light, R. L. (2010) 'Children's social and personal development through sport: A case study of an Australian swimming club', *Journal of Sport and Social Issues*, 34: 379–95.

Ministry of Health, Welfare and Sport (2011) *Actieplan 'Naar een veiliger sportklimaat'* [Towards a safer sports climate]. Den Haag: VWS. Available at: http://www.rijksoverheid.nl/nieuws/2011/04/22/schippers-komt-met-breed-gedragen-actieplan-voor-veiliger-sportklimaat.html (accessed 23 November 2011).

Moget, P. and Weber, M. (2007) 'De twee kanten van sport' [The two sides of sports], in E. Wieldraaijer, C. van den Brink, P. Moget and M. Weber (eds) *De weerbare sporter: Macht, misbruik en kwetsbaarheid* [The defensible sportsperson: Power, abuse and vulnerability]. Deventer: daM Uitgeverij, pp. 190–221.

Moget, P. and Weber, M. (2008) 'Vulnerabilities, pitfalls and chances in sports: A decade of social security policies in Dutch sports', Application to the Panathlon Conference, Ghent.

NOC*NSF (2004) *Sportcode. Laten we sport sportief houden* [Sports code. Let's keep it sportsmanlike]. Den Haag: Deltahage.

NOC*NSF (2008) *Tussenrapportage onderzoek NTO's Dames Turnen, ten behoeve van de KNGU* [Interim report research NTOs Ladies Gymnastics, for the KNGU]. Internal report. Arnhem: NOC*NSF.

NOC*NSF (2009) *Expertrapport Nederlandse sport naar Olympisch niveau* [Expert report: Dutch sport to Olympic level]. Deventer: daM Uitgeverij.

Olympiou, A., Jowett, S. and Duda, J. L. (2008) 'The psychological interface between the coach-created motivational climate and the coach–athlete relationship in team sports', *The Sport Psychologist*, 22: 423–38.

Panathlon International (2004) Declaration on Ethics in Youth Sport. Available at: http://www.panathlon.net (accessed 23 July 2011).

Quested, E. and Duda, J. L. (2009) 'Perceptions of the motivational climate, need satisfaction, and indices of well- and ill-being among hip hop dancers', *Journal of Dance Medicine & Science*, 13: 10–19.

Reinboth, M. and Duda, J. L. (2006) 'Perceived motivational climate, need satisfaction and indices of well- being in team sports: A longitudinal perspective', *Psychology of Sport and Exercise*, 7: 269–86.

Rutten, E.A., Stams, G. J. J. M., Dokovic, M., Schuengel, C., Hoeksma, J. and Biesta, G. (2004) 'Jeugdsport en morele socialisatie' [Youth sports and moral socialization], *Pedagogiek*, 4: 324–41.

Serkei, B. (2011) *Van blind vertrouwen naar verantwoord beleid – Bruikbaarheid en effectiviteit van beleidsinstrumenten seksuele intimidatie NOC*NSF* [From blind faith to responsible policy – usability and effectiveness of the sexual harassment policy of the NOC*NSF]. Utrecht: Movisie.

Shields, D. L. and Bredemeier, B. J. (2001) *Character Development and Physical Activity*. Champaign, IL: Human Kinetics.

Shields, D. L., Bredemeier, B., Gardner, D. and Bomstrom, A. (1995) 'Leadership, cohesion and team norms regarding cheating and aggression', *Sociology of Sport Journal*, 12: 324–36.

Steenbergen, J., Hilhorst, J., Sluis, A. van der and Gijsbers, M. (2010) *Samen voor Sportiviteit en Respect: Anlayse spel-en gedragsregels* [Together for sportsmanship and respect: Analysis of game rules and rules of conduct]. Nijmegen: Kennispraktijk.

Stegeman, H. (2007) *Effecten van Sport en Bewegen op School. Een literatuuronderzoek naar de relatie van fysieke activiteit met de cognitieve, affectieve en sociale ontwikkeling* [Effects of sports and movement in school: A literature study on the relationship between physical activity and cognitive, affective and social development]. 's Hertogenbosch: Mulier Instituut.

Stegeman, H. and Janssens, J. (2004) 'Introduction', in J. Janssens, H. Stegeman, I. van Hilvoorde, N. van Veldhoven *et al.* (eds) *Education Through Sport: An Overview of Good Practices in Europe*. Nieuwegein: Arko Sports Media, pp. 14–29.

Tiessen-Raaphorst, A., Lucassen, J., Dool, R. van den and Kalmthout, J. van (2008) *Weinig over de schreef. Een onderzoek naar onwenselijk gedrag in de breedtesport* [Little crossed the line. A study on unwanted behaviour in sports for all]. Den Haag: Sociaal Cultureel Planbureau.

Tiessen-Raaphorst, A., Verbeek, D., Haan, J. de and Breedveld, K. (2010) *Sport een leven lang. Rapportage sport 2010* [Sport for life. Report on Sport 2010]. 's Hertogenbosch: Sociaal Cultureel Planbureau/Mulier Instituut.

Tijd voor Vechtsport (Time for Martial Arts) (2008) *Tijd voor Vechtsport is een vijfjarig programma (2006 – 2010) van de Koninklijke Nederlandse Krachtsport en Fitnessfederatie (KNKF) in opdracht van het ministerie van Volksgezondheid, Welzijn en Sport* [Time for Martial Arts is a five-year programme (2006–2010) of the Royal Dutch Martial Arts Confederation, commissioned by the Ministry of Health, Welfare and Sport]. Available at: http://www.tijdvoorvechtsport.nl (accessed 23 November 2011).

Todd, D. and Hodge, K. (2001) 'Moral reasoning and achievement motivation in sport: A qualitative inquiry', *Journal of Sport Behaviour*, 24(3): 307–27.

Vanden Auweele, Y. (ed.) (2004) *Ethics in Youth Sport, Analyses and Recommendations*. Leuven: LannooCampus.

Vanden Auweele, Y., Vande Vliet, P. and Delvaux, K. (2001) 'Fysieke activiteit en psychisch welbevinden' [Physical activity and psychological well-being]. 'Special Edition', *Vlaams Tijdschrift voor Sportgeneeskunde & – Wetenschappen*.

van den Heuvel, M., Sterkenburg, J. van and Bottenburg, M. van (2007) *Olympisch Plan 2028. Uitwerking van de bouwsteen sportwaarden* [Olympic Plan 2028. Elaboration of the brick sports values]. 's Hertogenbosch: Mulier Instituut.

Vertommen, T. (2009) *Risicofactoren, vormen en verloop van seksuele intimidatie in de sport* [Risk factors, course and forms of sexual harassment in sport]. Brussels: VUB.

Vertommen, T. (2012) *Analyse van het Meldpunt voor Seksuele Intimidatie in de Sport* [Analysis into the hotline of sexual harassment in sport]. Arnhem: NOC*NSF.

Visscher, C. (2008) *Jeugdsport. Leren en Presteren, over motoriek, cognitie, tijd, kwaliteit en effectiviteit*. Rede uitgesproken tot benoeming tot bijzonder hoogleraar Jeugdsport [Youth Sports. Learning and performing, on motor skill, cognition, time, quality and effectiveness. Speech on appointment as Professor in Youth Sports], Groningen, 2 September.

Wieldraayer, E., Brink, C. van den, Moget, P. and Weber, M. (2007) *De weerbare sporter. Macht, misbruik en kwetsbaarheid* [The defensible sportsperson. Power, abuse and vulnerability]. Deventer: daM Uitgeverij.

Zomermaand, K. L. (2010) 'The views and roles of coaches in the development of youth athlete motivation: A qualitative approach', *Pumukkale Journal of Sport Sciences*, 3: 11–23.

9 Getting naked

Aspirations, delusions, and confusions about gender equity in youth sport

Jeanne Adèle Kentel

> Momentary insanity, nothing more, nothing less. I wasn't thinking about anything. I thought, 'My God, this is the greatest moment of my life on the soccer field.'
>
> (Brandi Chastain, in FIFA 1999)

Those who follow soccer (football), and in particular women's soccer, are quite familiar with the moment when Brandi Chastain scored the winning goal for team USA in the 1999 World Cup shoot-out over China. Her celebration comprised the removal of her jersey, falling to her knees, and running across the playing field while waving her uniform to over 90,000 stadium fans 30 seconds later. Two minutes after the game-winning goal, she re-clothed herself and continued to celebrate with her teammates.

Following the celebrations a media and public perplexity developed in regard to the sexualization of female athletes (Shugart 2003) and the potential effects on young girls of seeing a sports bra. While Chastain's celebratory response was akin to that of many male footballers, the media response towards her was not. For example, at the English Football Association (FA) Cup semi-final held just months earlier, when Ryan Giggs removed his jersey after scoring the game winner, there was no indication of him being sexualized for the act. However, in the Chastain case, media commentary consisted of references to her breasts rather than her athletic prowess. The focus narrowed on her nakedness and not her skill in finding the top corner of the net. Her team had just won the World Cup but was faced with having to downplay a 'booters with hooters' image (Shugart 2003: 13).

The case, and the subsequent public and media response, raise many questions about gender equity in sport. Why was the practice of removing a jersey so noticeable when carried out by a female? Why was the player's skill and successful goal overlooked? Why did Chastain need to explain herself? In some ways the practice of removing jerseys has been prevented since the implementation of Law 12, which was once relaxed, but has been reinforced by the Fédération Internationale de Football Association (FIFA), with referees required to card players who remove jerseys. The law states that, 'while it is permissible for a player to demonstrate his joy when a goal has been scored, the celebration must not be excessive', going on to indicate that 'a player must be cautioned if ... he removes his shirt or covers his head with his shirt' (FIFA 2011: 118). The power relation is evident, whereby decisions are being made by the officials, and not the players and referees involved in the game. It is also noteworthy that while FIFA tournaments for women have existed for over two decades and the laws of the game have undergone consistent revisions, there have been no changes regarding gender-equitable language in the writing of the rules. Players are automatically referred to as male, and the women's game is overshadowed through policy and masculine-oriented language. While there may be a tendency to blame the media for the under-representation, as well as the misrepresentation of women in sport, the difficulty is much more multifarious in nature. It is highly complex and requires a deepened understanding of power structures, media influence and gender theory in order to disrupt the gender order in and for future generations.

In this chapter I argue that if the face of gender equity in sport is going to be reconceptualized, we must engage youth in conversations which critically address the difficulties they are confronted with and invite them to become analytical readers of media and power structures. Through the threading of narrative and historical media accounts, I explore the focus question for this inquiry: 'In what ways might media and power structures influence societal understandings of females in sport?'

The gender equity myth

Plagued with impedimenta, gender equity in sport has been approached from political, educational and cultural perspectives leading to further difficulties and the near impenetrability of the status quo. Not only are women in sport under-represented by the media (Huffman *et al.* 2004), commercially driven agendas often place beauty and sexuality (in particular, heterosexuality) before athletic aptitude. For example, Anna Kournikova was once considered the most photographed woman in the sports domain, even though her sole major tennis title was a doubles Grand Slam triumph with Martina Hingis. Front-page media coverage predominantly sends the message, 'We do not want women who play well; we want women who look great.' Further to the media gender imbalance, there are the objectifications and subjectivities encountered by females in physical education and sport that are not typically endured by their male counterparts (Cockburn and Clarke 2002; Scott and Derry 2005).

While Title IX as implemented in the United States sought to attain gender equity for young female athletes, such legislation has been both problematic and limited. According to certain critics, 'Title IX at midlife has achieved enormous progress, but its promise remains unmet' (Rhode and Walker 2008: 43).

Sport is typically regarded as masculine and therefore the female athlete encounters shifting understandings of her own identity. Observes Koivula (2001: 377):

> Sports have generally been labelled as masculine, although some sports are considered to be feminine. ... Certain tasks and activities have traditionally been assigned to men and others to women, that is, they have been considered to be masculine or feminine activities. These categorizations are to a large extent social constructions based on our expectations regarding gender, and on our beliefs that gender categories are natural, unambiguous, bipolar, static, and individual.

Despite efforts to shift attitudes and perceptions, sport, and in particular professional sport, belongs to men. Men earn the high salaries, men hold the majority of coaching and administrative positions, and men own the teams (Suggs 2000; Frankl 2005; Mullins 2005).

Framing the claims

In this chapter I do not speak of the gender boundaries that males face in sport or what their experiences might be. I am aware that gender boundaries for men do exist, in particular for males who display any hint of effeminacy in what are considered typically masculine sports, or male athletes who are sexualized due to their appearance and physique. This is not an oversight or lack of concern; it is a deliberate decision to focus on stories of females in sport. As a female I recognize that my life stories figure into my perspective despite efforts to remain objective and inclusive. Stories influence our ways of being. We must tell our stories to each other in order to understand. We must tell our stories in order to be transformed. Within this chapter are stories of young women in sport. Within this chapter are their stories related to my own as I experienced them. The stories are told, interpreted and told again with a view to creating a new, albeit utopic, story – of gender equity in sport.

I do recognize that the gender divide in sport is at the same time an economic divide. Indeed from a transnational feminist perspective, race, gender, sexual orientation, nationhood and economics all intersect even though this perspective primarily exists outside 'master narratives' and comprises the acknowledgement of 'scattered hegemonies' and the deconstruction of 'mythic binaries' (Grewal and Kaplan 1994: 28). Constructions of gender are complex and long debated, and as such I am cognizant that this chapter can in no way provide a comprehensive view of such difficulties. Instead, it is an attempt to further discussion about gender issues in sport in relation to the naked (or rather, partially naked) body.

Methods of understanding

Through reflecting upon and revisiting media trends situated in stories of gender and sport, several unexpected parallels emerge. These stories, which are temporal, spatial and personal-social (Clandinin and Connelly 2000), reveal dimensions of inquiry that are inherent in the stories of the persons experiencing them, but also intersect with the responses. As a critical observer of media coverage in sport, I have a particular view of cases whereby women are not only treated differently, but also in ways that suggest subordinacy. Due to my biases borne from my own experiences as a female athlete, teacher, mother and coach, my reading of these three cases is limited. Due to this predisposition there is no attempt to create a grand narrative of gender issues for youth in sport. Rather, this account recognizes that our stories intersect with each other.

Heidegger (1962) suggests that when we look upon a text, the inherent meaning rests with the interpreter. Our experiences shape our view of the world and, when woven with historical and media accounts of conventional popularity, we are given pause to consider the counter-narratives that suggest that the path to gender equity is a long, convoluted journey that requires perpetual provocation and scrutiny. Because of the difficulties, muddiness and uncertainty of gender matters, hermeneutics is an appropriate method for analysis. Hermeneutical inquiry does not merely pursue transformation; it expects it (Ellis 1998). Hermeneutics can encompass the conflicting empirical and interpretive discourses of gender because its primary task is to understand. For every life occurrence, multiple interpretations are possible as 'each individual understands his or her experience uniquely and differently' (Kentel 2010: 24). Hermeneutics calls on the author to interpret and reinterpret the text, and invites readers to do the same.

Getting naked – an overview

In this section I examine three cases about young women in sport. Gleaned from these events are three premises that I pursue in light of notions of gender equity. The topics for these arguments are: (1) getting naked by choice, (2) getting naked through subjection, and (3) getting naked for profit. Indeed there are other relationships between sport and nakedness to be unfolded which are not discussed here, thus this reading is in no way a comprehensive list; rather, it is a beginning to a dialogue concerning these matters and the ways in which they might inform pedagogy in youth sport.

Getting naked by choice

In 2004, the athletic directors of the Canada West Universities Athletic Association came down with a decision to penalize volleyball teams who changed from their warm-up jerseys into their uniforms courtside. The expectation was that teams would go back into the locker rooms to do this prior to game time and then return courtside for play. The University of Alberta women's team launched a protest refusing to comply. They were penalized a point each match until a supportive referee, Arch Beck, joined the protest.

The practice of switching from warm-up shirts to team uniforms was common among secondary and university teams from at least the turn of the new millennium. The comfort level of individual girls and women with this practice has not yet been fully explored. Some might be completely comfortable, some may not be concerned, and some may be embarrassed or insecure in the practice. Dialogue with all players needs to occur before informed decisions can be made. These, however, are social and cultural issues and are not inherent to the game itself. Penalizing teams and awarding points for matters extraneous to game play invites controversy, and penalizing women and not men for the same practice adds fuel to the debate. In these sorts of situations, players are caught up by the ideals of ways of being, by the ways that they are supposed to act, and by ways about which they are confused. It is unknown whether it was a team or coach decision to protest a top-down ruling; nonetheless, inroads are apparent as boundaries are challenged.

Boundaries are interesting devices whereby humans draw a line around ideas, experiences and emotions. The boundary I see here is more than a simple response to an inequitable rule. This boundary represents something more human, more significant. It is as though the women's team is saying, 'This is our space and this is our game; these are our bodies.' I am left wondering if, whether or not only female spectators were allowed, would the decision any be different? Is exclusiveness necessary in order to have opportunity (Murray 2002)?

Women have long endured 'special' treatment in the sporting world. I recall that as a young girl I was not allowed to partake in one of my favourite track and field activities, the triple jump. Apparently it was contra-indicated for the female physiology. When the teachers were not looking, some of us would triple jump anyway and even challenge the boys. We were not allowed to compete at any official level, however, and had to settle for less than the boys. We were bound within a boundary. The *Oxford* and *Webster* dictionaries define bound as:

> *Oxford*   bound[1] limitation, restriction
>   bound[2] spring, leap, advance
> *Webster*   bound[1] tied, in bonds
>   bound[4] going or intending to go

As female athletes we had to bound through the boundary. We did so with intent, purpose and a leap towards freedom. By critically questioning the scientific basis for triple jump being exclusively for boys, a bounding beyond the boundary occurred. The word bound has a 'twofold sense' (Derrida 1973: 4) with bound indicating *freedom* and bound indicating *limitation*. Bound is its own antonym; it is a contradiction in itself. To bound freely, or to advance restrictively is how some girls relate to the 'other'.

As women are making some gains in international sporting events, new ways of marginalization are coming into being. Some women, by choice, may 'remove the duds' (Starkman 1999: 1) as a means to work towards equity. Undoubtedly, nakedness, whether partial or full, attracts media attention. In women's sport, however, baring skin can draw more attention than the game itself, or detract focus from their athletic performances. Thus women taking a stance for their right to choose find themselves in a double bind whereby the intent of their protests, or the move towards equity, is overlooked.

Heidegger (1962) suggests that discourse makes bare (*bloss*) that which is being talked about. *Logos* (the word; discourse; speech) is the means to 'letting something be seen by pointing it out' (Heidegger 1962: 56). Engaging in discourse with youth from Heidegger's perspective would thus be an essential means to uncover the truth. Might women who are uncovering their bodies by choice be acting in a similar fashion? By baring their bodies are they in turn making bare the inequities they encounter as female athletes?

Getting naked through subjection

When the Olympic Games began, it was reserved for men. After an athlete fell down dead after tripping on his scarf, it was determined that they should compete in the nude (Ferguson-Smith 1998). Women were forbidden to compete or even watch, lest they receive the death penalty. Later, exclusive games were held for women only, but when the Olympics were 'revived in 1896 ... only male athletes competed' (Ferguson-Smith 1998: 363). Several years later, women were gradually allowed to compete in the games, primarily in individual sports like swimming. However, in the 1960s, much speculation and controversy surrounded the authenticity of female athletes. Gender verification began whereby women were required to parade nude in front of a team of gynaecologists or undergo a gynaecological exam (Ferguson-Smith 1998). These tests were considered highly degrading; therefore methods such as chromosome testing emerged (Simpson *et al.* 1993) and continued until gender verification was eliminated in the 1990s (Simpson *et al.* 2000). Despite the erosion of gender verification measures, international athletic committees reserve the right to test if suspicions arise, as was the case with Caster Semenya.

The case of Caster Semenya, and how her genetic make-up led to speculation about her gender and subsequent reprehensible treatment (BBC 2011) is both puzzling and distressing. One of the key difficulties with her case is that she was banned from competition while the investigation took place. It was the 'guilty until proven innocent' approach that was both humiliating and unnecessary. Another conundrum surrounding the case was the way she was subjected to the gender testing (BBC 2009a). The purposes of certain tests were concealed from her, and the decision to clear her took nearly a year to transpire.

During the year awaiting the decision Semenya lost her motivation, her confidence, the athletic heights she had achieved (BBC 2011) and perhaps even her self-worth.

the young girl

                                                                        lost

not knowing who she is

                        yearning for a caring heart

                                        desiring unconditional approval
strengthens her body

                    running, jumping, playing

                                    in her body she finds talent

                                    in her body she finds meaning

amidst her strong exterior

others see her power

                                        yet the little girl remains ...

longing to be accepted for who she is

In interviews following the decision to subject Semenya to gender testing, she insisted: 'God made me the way I am and I accept myself' (BBC 2009b). According to the BBC, she also quipped that the ordeal was a joke and underwent a makeover which emphasized her feminine traits. Nonetheless, being unable to compete for nearly a year weighed heavy on Semenya, and the ordeal eventually took its toll both on her state of mind and her athletic performance (BBC 2011). At the writing of this manuscript, she still struggles to meet the personal best time achieved prior to the gender verification testing she was subjected to.

The complicated gender verification process imposed on Semenya prior to her 800-metre victory in Berlin involved an endocrinologist, a gynaecologist, an internal medicine expert, an expert on gender and a psychologist (Slot 2009). The stated purpose of gender testing is to ensure that no one gains an unfair advantage in female competitions. The determination of gender is, however, scientifically indeterminate. Therefore the questions surrounding Semenya might have been explored differently while leaving her dignity intact. With the ability of mass media to access the private lives of individuals, it is doubtful that the inquiry could have been concealed from the public. However, banning the athlete from competition due to a lengthy process was not only an attack on her dignity, but also on the trajectory of her performance.

Educating the young about these sorts of matters may provide an opening to conversations that address the complex nature of gender, gender identity and gender determination. The inherent difficulty in such matters is that even the most seasoned experts do not fully understand what constitutes gender, making comprehensive and critical gender pedagogy difficult to achieve. According to Freire's (1998) liberatory practice of freedom, however, we must engage the young in discourse about matters that concern them and invite them to critically address the complex issues and power structures facing themselves and others.

Getting naked for profit

In 1998, Katarina Witt, the figure-skating Olympian, became the first female athlete to pose nude for *Playboy*. Since that time, other female athletes have followed suit, and in 2004 a special issue featuring 'Women of the Olympics' was published. Other female athletes refuse to pose nude, indicating their desire to be role models for young girls as backing their decision. The reasons for baring all or remaining clothed are diverse and individual. The question that remains is: are female athletes under financial or public pressure to get naked?

Female athletes have made some gains in the past several decades, but remain plagued by a history whereby sport was exclusively for males. Women and girls, then, must find a way to permeate the boundaries surrounding eligibility, opportunity, pay equity and fair treatment. In doing so, they adapt to their environment.

Heidegger (1962) speaks of the 'thrownness' of factical life. For example, a young girl does not choose her life; she is born into it. Because of this, her game is a different game. Is the 'thrownness' of being female an imposition? Is it accepted to a degree, even as it is rejected on another level? A female creates her own path, her own way of becoming. She disallows the 'other' to determine who she will become. Inherently she changes the meaning of what it means to be a female. She throws herself into her own life, a life in which there are possibilities to reinvent the boundaries, a life where there are opportunities to throw *beyond* the boundaries. How does this connect to the boundaries young women face in sport? Even with the barriers permeated, how far have female athletes come really?

> In professional sport …
>
> Top women tennis players earned 59 cents for every dollar earned by their male counterparts.
>
> Women bowlers earned 70 cents for every dollar earned by a male bowler.
>
> Women golfers earned 36 cents for every dollar earned by their male counterparts.
>
> Female alpine skiers earned 81 cents for every dollar earned by their male counterparts.
>
> Women soccer players earned 33 cents for every dollar earned by their male counterparts.

Female basketball players earned 1 cent for every dollar earned by their male counterparts.

We waited until the third millennium for a female health professional to be hired in pro baseball.

(adapted from Mullins 2005; Frankl 2005)

Is there any question of why young women might turn to endorsements and 'remove the duds' (Starkman 1999: 1) in order to earn a living? How might boundaries which restrict female athletes from attaining the attention and salaries of their male counterparts be permeated? Is this 'thrownness' a means to understanding the ways in which a female becomes an athlete or realizes herself to be an athlete? Must one be sexy in order to attract attention? Is this the message given to young athletic girls?

Women in sport today face a whole different set of barriers, namely 'sexploitation' (Hughson *et al.* 2000). Observes Borrie (2000), 'The pressure on sportswomen to increase levels of sponsorship and media coverage has seen many resort to taking their clothes off just to receive some publicity.' Sporting the outfit has become the sport. Removing the outfit has become the means to earn an income or draw attention to women's sport. According to Starkman, 'in the ever-competitive sports marketplace, female athletes are finding there is one sure fire way to get attention and generate some income: remove the duds' (1999: 1). The steady and very significant growth in the number of female athletes and the new heights women have reached as competitors seem to have had little or no effect on the 'male superiority ideology' (Frankl 2005: 1).

The practice of 'removing the duds' has spawned lines of argumentation which substantiate a woman's right to earn a living from her athletic celebrity in whatever way she sees fit. But if there is a justifiable set of reasons for female athletes posing nude, then why aren't the men following suit? Certainly there are the undergarment endorsements of David Beckham and Michael Jordan, but are male displays of libido as widespread as the sexualization of female athletes? Moreover, what female athletes draw salaries akin to those of male athletes?

Permeating boundaries via critical gender pedagogy

What sort of pedagogy might be embraced by educators, coaches and sporting bodies that will empower young women and men to overcome the difficulties inherent in gender equity pursuits? In order for the female athlete to understand the complexities of the female figure in sport, she must look both inwardly and outwardly to the stories that have shaped women's sport, while engaging in a critical analysis of their meanings. Apart from the aforementioned challenges our young girls face in sport, there are yet more barriers that arise when participating in sport. Remarks about body parts, inappropriate gazes (or even touching) and abuses of power by male coaches are all part of the complex nature of youth sport. Even with emerging policies of having one female coach on all young women's teams, there remain stories of discomfort, inappropriateness and abuse. Might we as women rise up and volunteer to coach and speak out? Might we as pedagogues inspirit more men to rise up and speak out when they see such cases? Might we provide places and spaces whereby our young people feel free to speak and are not silenced?

The process of critical discourse uncovers layers of complexity in terms of gender, athleticism and the commodification of the female body; that is, the uncovering of the body in order to attract media coverage or earn a reasonable living in sport. Sometimes when we take a stance we hurt ourselves, we hurt our own careers, we are blacklisted and cannot seem to escape the marginalization encountered. Must we remain silent in order to advance? Must we have permission in order to play the game? Must we be scantily clothed or disrobe in order to express our athletic prowess? Must we live in a historically patriarchal sports world? Or can we define sport on our own terms?

Progress in women's sport continues to trail behind in relation to the financial support, media coverage and opportunities offered to males (Suggs 2000). Through contrasting a range of narratives within media-driven stories of women in sport, several parallels emerge which uncover the prevailing lack of gender equity. Although sport itself is not gendered, individuals who engage in sport can be subjected to a range of stereotypical limitations imposed by the status quo. The veracities unearthed in this inquiry underscore the need to continue to challenge current gender barriers and work towards ensuring that future generations of women have equal opportunities in sport, naked or not. The ensuing call is for women to become powerful role models for girls in existing pedagogical relationships (such as parent, teacher and coach) in order to provide a safe environment for females to be confident in their masculinity and femininity. Examining and giving full consideration to meaningful stories that shape lives permits a permeation of the gender boundaries inherent in sport involvement and physicality.

Sport is not gendered. Society has built the gendered walls around sport. It is up to members of society to bring down these walls and allow girls to be girls, and women to be women. In my decades as a woman, an athlete, an educator, a researcher and a mother, I am not convinced there has been any significant transformation. Albeit, conversations regarding reconceived gender roles celebrate the sieve-like nature of boundaries, as inclusiveness infiltrates the wall of exclusion, and rebounding becomes a 'reboundary-ing'. A new set of socially coded rules is arranged each time the sphere springs, not backward, but forward. Attempts at egalitarianism have fallen short of de-mythicizing gender equity, despite the evidence that some inroads have been made.

It is questionable whether gender equity is achievable. It is hoped that youth do not feel pressured to get naked in order to achieve their goals in sport and also have the freedom to make informed choices in their sporting and personal lives. It remains unknown as to whether a democratic and liberatory practice of freedom and critical gender pedagogy will transpire in youth sport. The certitude is in what we do not do. If we do not engage youth in conversations, tell our stories and initiate action there will certainly not be any transformation. Such action begins with envisaging a different way of being.

Envisage a world where young girls and women can look forward to a career in sport; a vocation where their views are respected, their talent esteemed and their abilities remunerated. Envisage a world where women and men watch females play, not for the pleasure of the scantily clothed body, but for the love of the game. Envisage a world where finesse, imagination and acumen are as valued as efforts to be faster, higher and stronger. Envisage a world where female athletes have no need to fight for recognition, media attention, equitable salaries and a presence in competition. Envisage a world of females honoured for their athleticism.

Whether or not such a utopian world is reachable, our task as educators is to engage in dialogue in our classrooms, locker rooms, playing fields and in the public sporting sector as a means of uncovering or making bare the gender equity challenges. As Title IX enters its fortieth year, it is apposite to reflect on where we have been delusional, ponder what we remain confused about, and aspire to enact a transformable future. This may not be realized as soon as is desirable, but hope offers us a way to envisage gender equity for the youth of years to come.

Discussion Questions

1. In what ways might the development of critical media pedagogy contribute to transforming current gender equity challenges?
2. Consider your own stories related to gender equity. In what ways do your experiences shape your understanding of gender concerns?
3. What changes can you make in your own practice that will assist to create a more equitable environment for those you coach and/or teach?

Acknowledgement

My heartfelt gratitude is given to Meagan Alton for her assistance in the preparation of this manuscript.

References

BBC (2009a) 'Semenya told to take gender test'. Available at: http://news.bbc.co.uk/sport1/hi/athletics/8210471.stm (accessed 25 August 2011).

BBC (2009b) 'Makeover for SA gender-row runner'. Available at: http://news.bbc.co.uk/1/hi/world/africa/8243553.stm (accessed 25 August 2011).

BBC (2011) 'Too fast to be a woman? The story of Caster Semenya'. Available at: http://www.bbc.co.uk/programmes/b00yrv05 (accessed 10 October 2011).

Borrie, J. (2000) 'Shaping up to the image makers', *Canberra Times*, 27 May, Panorama.

Clandinin, D. and Connelly, F. M. (2000) *Narrative Inquiry: Experience and Story in Qualitative Research*. San Francisco, CA: Jossey Bass.

Cockburn, C. and Clarke, G. (2002) '"Everybody's looking at you!": Girls negotiating the "femininity deficit" they incur in physical education', *Women's Studies International Forum*, 25(6): 651–65.

Derrida, J. (1973) *Speech and Phenomena: And Other Essays on Husserl's Theory of Signs*, trans. D. B. Allison. Evanston, IL: Northwestern University Press.

Ellis, J. L. (1998) *Teaching from Understanding: Teacher as Interpretive Inquirer*. New York: Garland.

Ferguson-Smith, M. A. (1998) 'Gender verification and the place of XY females in sport', in W. Harries, C. Williams, W. Stanish and L. Micheli (eds) *Oxford Textbook of Sports Medicine*. Oxford: Oxford University Press, 355–65.

FIFA (1999) 'FIFA Women's World Cup – USA 1999'. Available at: http://www.fifa.com/tournaments/archive/tournament=103/edition=4644/overview.html (accessed 17 November 2011).

FIFA (2011) 'Interpretation of the laws of the game and guidelines for referees'. Available at: http://www.fifa.com/worldfootball/lawsofthegame/index.html (accessed 16 October 2011).

Frankl, D. (2005) 'Gender bias in sports: Separate and not equal'. Available at: http://www.sports-media.org/newpedimension5.htm (accessed 31 January 2005).

Freire, P. (1998) *Pedagogy of Freedom: Ethics, Democracy, and Civic Courage*. Lanham, MD: Rowman and Littlefield.

Grewal, I. and Kaplan, C. (eds) (1994) *Scattered Hegemonies: Postmodernity and Transnational Feminist Practices*. Minneapolis: University of Minnesota Press.

Heidegger, M. (1962) *Being and Time*, trans. J. Macquarie and E. Robinson. New York: Harper and Row.

Huffman, S., Tuggle, C. A. and Rosengard, D. S. (2004) 'How campus media cover sports: The gender-equity issue, one generation later', *Mass Communication and Society*, 7(4): 475–89.

Hughson, S., Kilpatrick, A., Paton, M. A. and Simms, D. (2000) 'Sexploitation'. Available at: http://www.ausport.gov.au/fulltext/2000/ascweb/sexploitation.asp (accessed 5 August 2005).

Kentel, J. A. (2010) 'The dance of conversation: Movement, language and learning', *Asian Journal of Exercise and Sports Science*, 7(1): 19–26.

Koivula, N. (2001) 'Perceived characteristics of sports categorized as gender-neutral, feminine and masculine', *Journal of Sport Behavior*, 24(4): 377–93.

Mullins, A. (2005) 'Are women athletes getting their fair shake?' Available at: http://www.harlemlive.org/shethang/stories/femaleathletics/athletes.html (accessed 5 August 2005).

Murray, S. J. (2002) 'Unveiling myths: Muslim women and sport'. Available at: http://www.womenssportsfoundation.org/cgi-bin/iowa/issues/part/article.html?record=863 (accessed 5 August 2005).

Rhode, D. L. and Walker, C. J. (2008) 'Gender equity in college athletics: Women coaches as a case study', *Stanford Journal of Civil Rights and Civil Liberties*, 4: 1–50.

Scott, B. A. and Derry, J. A. (2005) 'Women in their bodies: Challenging objectification through experiential learning', *Women's Studies Quarterly*, 33 (1–2): 188–209.

Shugart, H. A. (2003) 'She shoots, she scores: Mediated constructions of contemporary female athletes in coverage of the 1999 US women's soccer team', *Western Journal of Communication*, 67: 1–31.

Simpson, J. L., Ljungqvist, A., de la Chapelle, A., Ferguson-Smith, M. A., Genel, M., Carlson, A. S. *et al.* (1993) 'Gender verification in competitive sports', *Sports Medicine*, 16(5): 305–15.

Simpson, J. L., Ljungqvist, A., Ferguson-Smith, M. A., de la Chapelle, A., Elsas, I. I., Ehrhardt, A. A. *et al.* (2000) 'Gender verification in the Olympics', *Journal of the American Medical Association*, 284(12): 1568–69.

Slot, O. (2009) 'Caster Semenya faces gender test after winning 800 m', *The Times*. Available at: http://www.theaustralian.com.au/news/caster-semenya-faces-gender-test after-winning-800m/story-e6frg6n6–1225764235072 (accessed 25 August 2011).

Starkman, R. (1999) 'Top women athletes take clothes off to get more exposure for their sports', *Toronto Star*, 19 December.

Suggs, W. (2000) 'Women's share of coaching jobs shrink', *Chronicle of Higher Education*, 46(37): A68.

10 Exploring ethics

Reflections of a university coach educator

Tania Cassidy

Introduction

Many government-sponsored organizations, such as the Australian Sports Commission (ASC), Coaching Association of Canada (CAC), Sport and Recreation New Zealand (SPARC) and Sports Coach UK, have produced ethical guidelines in the form of codes and policies as the issue of ethics in sport gains more attention. However, despite this attention we are regularly confronted in the media by examples of members of sporting communities such as coaches, administrators, family members and players, at various levels and age groups, acting unethically. For example, in England, medical and coaching staff in a premier league Rugby Union team conspired to induce bleeding in the mouth of a player to have him replaced as a means of gaining advantage in a match in 2009. This was reported as: 'Bloodgate cover up attempt worse than crime' (Author unknown 2009) and in 2011, in New Zealand, the *Otago Times* published a story entitled 'Rugby coach convicted of assaulting son' (Author unknown 2011). Perhaps one of the most sensational incidents of unethical practice in sport was the disqualification of Canadian Ben Johnson after winning the gold medal in the men's 100m sprint at the 1988 Olympic Games for steroid use. In 1996 junior ice hockey coach Graham James was incarcerated for sexually abusing his young players. These are events that Shogan (2007) suggests triggered increased media interest in sport ethics in Canada. The powerful influence of elite sport as represented in the media on young people in sport and the incidence of ethical violations suggests a significant area of concern in youth sport. Sport coaches can clearly play an important role in shaping the ethical learning arising from young people's participation in sport and, in countries where universities offer coaching degrees or units of study focused specifically on coaching, these provide an ideal opportunity for preparing them to meet the challenges involved in dealing with ethical issues in coaching.

It has been suggested that staff in tertiary institutions should engage students in discussions about ethical principles and practice (e.g. Amade-Escot 2006; Morgan 2007; Jones 2008; McNamee 2008; Hardman *et al.* 2010; Telfer 2010; Denison and Avner 2011; Hardman and Jones 2011; Harvey *et al.*

2011). Various resources to support the teaching of sport ethics have also been published, including descriptions of various ethical frameworks (DeSensi and Rosenberg 2003; Malloy *et al.* 2003; Panathlon International 2004; Morgan 2007), ethical decision-making models (Malloy *et al.* 2003) and the use of scenarios to identify ethical dilemmas (McNamee 1998). These resources are valuable but arguably the frameworks, models and scenarios are informed by a modernist view of knowledge as being stable, and of the coaching and coach education process as being linear and unproblematic. These accounts can raise two questions: (1) how do we problematize the idea of coaching knowledge being stable? and (2) how do we teach sports ethics without taking the moral high ground? These questions were at the forefront of my mind as I attempted to negotiate what it meant to teach ethics to students enrolled in a university sports coaching unit.

Markula and Pringle (2006: 178), drawing on the work of Foucault, suggest that academics can act as an 'active social critic' by critically analysing the practices that occur within their own fields, questioning what is considered self-evident or common sense, examining rules and institutions, and considering the reasons why this is the case or how it has come to be. Importantly, this analysis should include a focus of attention on areas that concern 'one's own interests, one's own objectives and one's own methods of knowledge production'. In this chapter I thus attempt to provide insight into how and why I, as a sport coaching educator, designed, amended, and continue to amend, a sports coaching unit that, in part, focuses on sport ethics. An opportunity arises for us in the sports coaching and coach education fields to examine how and why ethics is practised in particular ways in sport. I view the process of undertaking ethical work to be 'a work in progress', as is evidenced by the organization of the chapter. After a brief introduction on the context of the sports coaching unit, the chapter is organized into two sections of 2010 and 2011, which are the two years over which I have taught the unit. These two sections provide examples of my negotiation of the issues involved in teaching about ethical practice and my own critical reflection practices upon it. I conclude the chapter with considerations for the future, which include ideas for teaching sport ethics in 2012.

Teaching sport ethics (PHSE 330: Sports Coaching)

PHSE 330 is the only sports coaching unit located within a multi-disciplinary, physical education[1] degree in the university. Students enrolled in the four-year degree have a common programme of study for the first two years, after which they can major in areas as diverse as dance, exercise physiology, sociology of sport and exercise prescription. Two of the majors are broadly classified as 'socio-cultural', while the other two are described as 'bio-physical'. PHSE 330 is timetabled for two 50-minute lecture sessions per week for a 13-week semester, with no tutorial or practical sessions scheduled. In the past, the content of PHSE 330 has reflected the disciplinary interests of those assigned to teach it and, because the unit is located within the two socio-cultural majors of the degree, sociology and psychology have been the disciplines of choice. In 2010 I was invited to teach PHSE 330 as a consequence of having a disciplinary background in pedagogy and having a research interest in sports coaching and coach education. I accepted the invitation on the proviso that I could disrupt the disciplinary silos often associated with the study of sports coaching and design the content and assessment with the goal of making the unit meaningful to all students, regardless of their major. In an attempt to achieve this goal I organized PHSE 330 into four sections, the second of which was ethics. I consider ethics to be a topic relevant to all students, although I was somewhat anxious as to how I would teach ethics to 140 undergraduate sports coaching students who, along with me, did not have an academic background in ethics or philosophy.

2010

The focus of the first section in PHSE 330 in 2010 was the New Zealand coaching context, to highlight the way the coaching policies produced by SPARC[2] and national sporting organizations were focused on athlete-centred coaching and encouraging coaches to reflect on their practices (Cassidy and Kidman 2010). Yet, within the first few weeks of semester, accounts of unethical behaviour by athletes, administrators and coaches were being reported in the national and international media. For example, 'Eric Devendorf dumped by Waikato Pistons' (Author unknown 2010) and 'Salary cap breach no storm in a teacup' (Stevenson 2010). These reports juxtaposed the policies and principles being espoused by SPARC and the national sporting organizations. The obvious contradictions provided an ideal rationale for the second section of PHSE 330, which explored ethics in a sports coaching context. All the students appeared to have an opinion on the morality of the practices reported in the media, which, arguably, provided insight into how they connected emotionally with the topic of ethics.

Where to begin when 'teaching' ethics?

Canadian academics and professional bodies are widely recognized for the work they undertake in the area of coaching and coach education. For this reason, I initially turned my attention to the Coaching Association of Canada (CAC) and its National Coaching Certification Program (NCCP) to see what they were doing in the area of ethics. The NCCP is available to all Canadian coaches regardless of the sport they coach or the context in which they coach. All coaches participating in the NCCP are required to be 'trained in ethical decision-making and sport safety' (CAC 2011a). To facilitate this training the coaches are required to complete the 'Make Ethical Decisions' (MED) module. When participating in this module coaches are required to draw on the NCCP's Code of Ethics, which defines 'what is considered good and right behaviour' and 'contain standards of behaviour expected of members' (CAC

2011b). Upon successful completion of the MED module the CAC expects coaches to 'be fully equipped to handle virtually any ethical situation with confidence and surety. MED helps coaches identify the legal, ethical, and moral implications of difficult situations that present themselves in the world of team and individual sport' (CAC 2011c). Moreover, it is claimed that because the MED module is a 'cornerstone' of the NCCP it 'leaves coaches with no doubt as to what to do when the going gets tough' (CAC 2011c).

The development of the MED module was informed by the work of Malloy *et al.* (2000). In the first and the second editions of their text, Malloy *et al.* (2003: 105) outline 'five steps for rendering ethical judgement' which they call 'Model I' and provide a seven-stage ethical decision-making process which is the 'core of Model II'. Yet, when proposing these step-by-step models, Malloy *et al.* (2003: 70) also acknowledge that 'throughout history thinkers have explored and proposed a wide range of sources as the base for ethics' and for this reason they encourage those using their models to generate solutions based on the tenets of three ethical perspectives. To support this endeavour they provide an overview of three perspectives of ethics, which they describe as: teleology (consequentialism), deontology (non-consequentialism) and existentialism (authentic). Others writing in the context of sport ethics have also provided overviews of various ethical frameworks. For example, DeSensi and Rosenberg (2003) and Morgan (2007) describe various deontological and teleological theories, while McNamee (1998) describes virtue-based ethical theories.

In 2010 I introduced the students enrolled in PHSE 330 to the notion of sport ethics by providing them with an overview of various ethical frameworks (DeSensi and Rosenberg 2003; Malloy *et al.* 2003; Morgan 2007) before introducing them to the MED module using fictional but realistic and localized scenarios (McNamee 1998).

Reflecting on 'teaching' ethics

Initially, the MED module appeared to be a useful and pragmatic way to introduce ethics to the students. However, confusion arose when the students were asked to 'identify your options and possible consequences'. The confusion arose for two reasons. First, by requiring the students to identify 'possible *consequences*' their options appear to be restricted to those that reflected a teleological or *consequential* perspective of ethics. Second, the students were encouraged to refer to the CAC's Code of Ethics to guide their decision-making process. This also caused some tension because, as explained above, the CAC (2011b) views a code of ethics as defining 'what is considered good and right behaviour'. Yet, according to Malloy *et al.* (2003), ethical approaches that are described as 'consequential' only focus on what is considered 'good' behaviour. It is those ethical approaches that are described as 'non-consequential' that focus on what is the 'right' behaviour. So while the CAC's Code of Ethics encouraged coaches to consider what is good *and* right, the

MED module encouraged the students to only focus on the consequences of their options, thereby reflecting a consequential ethical approach and only focusing on what is considered to be good behaviour.

Despite my reservations and the tensions associated with teaching sport ethics, the anecdotal feedback I received from many students was that they valued being introduced to ethics. The following comment, anonymously written on the end of semester course evaluation, is indicative of this: 'I sit at home watching TV with flatmates and we talk about the ethical dilemmas present!! – creepy! But they're evidently everywhere! – Not just in sport – so it can be applied in other areas.' The student feedback reminded me of the value of recognizing the importance of emotion and 'knowledgeability' in the pedagogical process, particularly practical consciousness (Cassidy 2000, 2010; Cassidy and Tinning 2004; Tinning 2002). Practical consciousness, as a component of knowledgeability, has been described as the knowledge we require to 'go on' in our daily lives that is not consciously accessible to us; rather it is practical in character (Giddens 1991). According to Giddens the explanatory power of practical consciousness is that it highlights how change will not occur on the basis of a rational argument alone, instead there needs to be 'a corresponding level of underlying emotional commitment' (1991: 38). Therefore, if I desire the students in PHSE 330 to leave the unit more attuned to ethical coaching practices then I need to do more than provide a rational code of ethics by which they, as future coaches, have to abide.

Often, when attempts are made to change a social endeavour, such as the behaviours of sports coaches, the driver of the change is a 'desire for certainty and for getting things "right"' (Cassidy and Tinning 2004: 187). This desire for certainty may be one of the reasons why many national sporting organizations have developed codes of ethics or codes of conduct with the aim of guiding, or controlling, the behaviours of coaches, parents and administrators. However, in this period of late modernity aiming for 'certainty' is less of an option, and increasingly it is recognized that we cannot 'control social life completely' (Giddens 1990: 153). This is possibly why codes of ethics and codes of conduct are ineffective as 'how to' guides or the 'perfect solution' for curbing unethical behaviour in the sports coaching context. This observation had implications for the redesigning of PHSE 330 in 2011 and utilized other reading I was doing to develop my understanding of ethics.

During 2010 I also read Shogan (2007), Denison (2007), and Markula and Pringle (2006), and these scholars introduced me to alternative interpretations of ethics and the relationship ethics has with sporting performance. This raised the intriguing question – how should one 'conduct and practice an ethical life without recourse to a universal set of ethical guidelines' (Markula and Pringle 2006: 21)? While the question piqued my interest, I was not sure how to begin to teach about practising an ethical life *without* using a set of ethical guidelines when I was still not sure how to teach about practising an ethical life *using* ethical guidelines. So it was in the spirit of experimentation that I redesigned and taught PHSE 330 in 2011.

2011

Where to begin when 'teaching' ethics without having a universal set of guidelines?

In preparing to teach PHSE 330 in 2011 I continued to explore the question: how should one 'conduct and practice an ethical life without recourse to a universal set of ethical guidelines?' (Markula and Pringle 2006: 21) and more attentively read the work of Denison (2007, 2010a, 2010b), Denison and Avner (2011), Kelly and Hickey (2008), Pringle (2007), Pringle and Hickey (2010), Markula and Pringle (2006) and Shogan (2007). Initially I was drawn to Shogan's (2007) text because of its title – *Sport Ethics in Context*. In this text, the chapter that caught my attention was entitled 'Disciplinary technologies of sport performance'. In this chapter Shogan drew on the work of Foucault, particularly from his book *Discipline and Punish* to, among other things, highlight the use of micro or disciplinary technologies in sports coaching; problematize the perceived 'naturalness' of some technologies; and question why some technologies were considered ethical while others were not. One of the disciplinary technologies used by Shogan (2007) and Denison (2007) was technologies of docility, which focus on the technologies that control time, space and the modality of movement.

Upon reading the work of Shogan (2007) and Denison (2007) I considered it possible to use the discussion of disciplinary technologies in sports coaching to connect with the practical consciousness of the students while at the same time further exploring ethics. The lack of practical sessions associated with PHSE 330 meant there were limitations regarding how to recognize the students' practical consciousness. However, by providing sporting examples of the various disciplinary technologies and encouraging the students to talk and write about their experience of these technologies, arguably links were made to their practical consciousness and an emotional engagement with the topic subsequently encouraged.

In 2011, the content of the first half of the semester focused on performance enhancement and disciplinary technologies; specifically technologies of docility, normalization and 'subjectivation' (Foucault 1979; Denison 2007; Shogan 2007). For example, when introducing technologies of docility I illustrated how a coach's use of space could result in athletes being distributed in particular ways and being required to assume specific functions, which in turn could have implications for how they would be assessed and ranked. According to Shogan (2007), understanding how space (as well as other aspects of technologies of docility and other disciplinary technologies) operates on an athlete's body has implications for coaching ethically because it involves issues of welfare and fairness.

In the second half of the semester I once again introduced the students to the various ethical frameworks and the MED module. But this time, when introducing the module, I alerted them to the possible inconsistencies and tensions between the module and the CAC's Code of Ethics described above. In an attempt to reduce the inconsistencies I turned to Malloy *et al.* (2003) who undertook a more comprehensive approach to the decision-making process than described in the MED module. At each stage of their seven-stage model Malloy *et al.* required an analysis of the situation from three ethical perspectives, namely teleology (good), deontology (right) and existentialism (authentic). They suggest that by adopting a three-way ethical analysis the situation can be assessed more comprehensively than would be the case if only one perspective was utilized.

Reflecting on 'teaching' ethics

Disciplinary technologies and their application generated much interest amongst the students and some of the guest speakers (for the latter see Cassidy and Hessian 2011). Nonetheless, making links between disciplinary technologies and ethics is still a work in progress. In an attempt to strengthen the links I have returned to the literature, and in doing so have been encouraged to reflect on Foucault's shift in focus from disciplinary technologies to technologies of the self. By utilizing the technologies of the self Foucault said it enabled him to 'go back through what I was thinking, to think it differently, and see what I had done from a new vantage point and in a clearer light' (1985: 11). Moreover, technologies of the self provided Foucault with a framework to question 'the manner in which one ought to "conduct oneself" – that is, the manner in which one ought to form oneself as an ethical subject acting in reference to the prescriptive elements that make up the [moral] code' (1985: 26). In the context of sport, Markula and Pringle (2006: 153) suggest technologies of the self may assist coaches to reflect on their practices, and in doing so necessitate 'an ethical care of the self' and promote 'ethical practices that use power with the minimum of domination' (see also Chapter 13 by Fitzgerald in this volume).

Foucault (1985: 10) describes technologies of the self as 'those intentional and voluntary actions by which men [sic] not only set themselves rules of conduct, but also seek to transform themselves'. Thus, he became interested in how individuals respond to a particular moral code. But the question arose, how could technologies of the self assist me to 'teach' ethics without having a universal set of guidelines? Foucault (1985) suggests that one way to operationalize technologies of the self, and make links to ethics, is to attend to morality. I will return to this in the following section when I consider future directions.

When reflecting on the implementation of the adapted MED module, it was clear that tensions and confusions still existed. In 2011 new tensions surfaced when it came to evaluating the options or alternatives and selecting the best option or ideal solution, which is required in the MED module and seven-step decision-making model respectively. According to Malloy *et al.*:

when the alternatives are analyzed using three ethical perspectives, each is evaluated based on the extent to which it is good, right and authentic. ... The alternative that best satisfies these criteria in the most comprehensive manner is presumably the ideal alternative to select.

(2003: 111)

Yet, Malloy *et al.* recognize that 'unforeseen circumstances', beyond one's control, can influence the process of selecting the ideal solution. Therefore 'one's intent' becomes a strong 'determinant of ethical action' (2003: 111). While 'intent' has a history in discussions on ethics (for example, in the work of Kant and Aristotle) it has not been attended to in PHSE 330 and therefore warrants further attention.

Considerations for the future

In the introduction I highlighted two questions that were at the forefront of my mind as I attempted to negotiate what it meant to teach ethics to students enrolled in a university sports coaching unit. They were: (1) how do we problematize the stability of coaching knowledge? and (2) how do we teach sports ethics without taking the moral high ground? In the process of teaching and reflecting on teaching sport ethics over the past two years with these questions in mind I am now at a point where I need to explore the concept of morality and intent. My subsequent exploration and experimentation will draw on the work of Foucault, specifically in relation to how to problematize and individualize moral codes, and what, if any, links can be made to the notion of intent.

Aware that interpretations of morality are varied, Foucault proposes that morality be broadly understood as: 'a set of values and rules of action that are recommended to individuals through the intermediary of various prescriptive agencies such as the family (in one of its roles), educational [and sporting] institutions, churches, and so forth' (1985: 25). What is more, he considers morality to comprise two parts. These are a moral code and moral acts, with the moral code representing 'the prescriptions for "good" conduct' and moral acts denoting 'the way individuals actually behave based on the prescription (i.e., how carefully they follow the code)' (Markula and Pringle 2006: 140). Foucault (1983: 238) characterizes the moral code as having three aspects: those acts which are forbidden, those behaviours that have negative and positive value, and those actions that come about in the process of an individual constituting him/herself as a 'moral subject'. It is this third aspect that Foucault calls ethics and it is this aspect that I need to consider when redesigning and teaching PHSE 330 in 2012.

The MED module and the seven-step decision-making model can be considered to be examples of a moral code.[3] Students could be encouraged to consider how they and others in the coaching community respond to various moral codes. This can occur by focusing on how individuals problematize the codes of their particular sport and then 'identify what specific practices develop based on the initial problematization' (Markula and Pringle 2006: 140). This focus was reflected in a study conducted by Pringle and Hickey, in which they found that the participants 'produced selves, via the moral problematization of sporting pleasures and specific technologies of self, that rejected the values or moral codes of hypermasculinity in an attempt to create ethical masculinities' (2010: 115).

However, those who have worked within what has been called the 'critical project' know the difficulties associated with requiring students to problematize the status quo. For example, Tinning (2002: 224, 236) discusses the 'difficulties of "doing" critical pedagogy with postmodern students', concluding with a call for a 'modest pedagogy'. This call was, at least in part, due to the experience of having his pedagogical practices 'put under the spotlight' by, for example, being the researched and not the researcher, an experience he describes as 'not always (or even mostly) uplifting' (2002: 233). According to Tinning, those adopting modest pedagogies require some degree of circumspection 'in their claims to know' and would benefit from recognizing 'the limits of rationality as a catalyst for change' (2002: 236). Drawing on my work (Cassidy 2000), he notes that 'the use of rational discourse to problematize taken-for-granted practices will be insufficient to change those practices unless there is a corresponding level of emotional commitment to change' (2002: 236).

Individualizing the moral code may provide opportunities for students to develop an emotional connection with ethics. Foucault (1985) views the process of individualizing the moral code as comprising four aspects: ethical substance, mode of subjection, ethical work and telos. Markula and Pringle (2006) suggest that an understanding of these four aspects can assist us to operationalize the technologies of the self by providing a focus for our questions and reflections. For example, when reflecting on the *ethical substance* one can ask: 'What part of oneself should be subject to a work on the self?' (2006: 141). Once the ethical substance has been determined the next question (reflecting the *mode of subjection*) could be: 'why should I engage in ethical work?' followed by 'what is ethical work?' Foucault (1985: 27) describes *ethical work* as 'self-forming activities' that we perform on ourselves, not only to comply with a given rule, but in an attempt to 'transform oneself into the ethical subjects of one's behaviour'. At this point I have some reservations, and it relates back to Tinning's observations about the efficacy of the so-called critical project. According to Markula and Pringle, in undertaking ethical work there is an assumption that individuals have 'attitudes that facilitate continuous critical self-transformation' (2006: 141) and that they have the capabilities to adopt 'diverse practices' that enables an individual to 'engage in self-transformation' (2006: 142). Can we make this assumption of a class of 140 undergraduate students?

Finally, the fourth aspect of individualizing the moral code is *telos*, which refers to the goal of the ethical work. This raises the question; what sort of being do we aspire to be when we behave morally? While the process of individualizing the moral code appears to be a generative way to teach ethics without having a universal set of guidelines, I am still experimenting with how it will assist me to plan and teach an undergraduate unit on sports coaching. It definitely continues to be a work in progress.

Discussion Questions

If you desire to become a more ethical coach ask yourself the following questions:

1. What part of yourself as a coach do you wish to work on?
2. Why should you engage in this ethical work?
3. What 'self-forming activities' do you perform to:

   (a) comply with your sport's codes of conduct?
   (b) transform your behaviour so your coaching is more ethical?

4. What practices have you adopted that are innovative or different than your peers?
5. What sort of coach do you aspire to be when you behave morally and ethically?

Notes

1 This could equally be described as a degree in human movement, sport science or kinesiology.
2 SPARC is the government agency dedicated to fostering a sport and recreation environment.
3 Another example of a moral code is the Panathlon Declaration on Ethics in Youth Sport.

References

Amade-Escot, C. (2006) 'Student learning within the *didactique* tradition', in D. Kirk, D. Macdonald and M. O'Sullivan (eds) *The Handbook of Physical Education*. London: Sage, pp. 347–65.
Author unknown (2009) 'Bloodgate cover up attempt worse than crime', *The Times*, 26 August. Available at: www.timesonline.co.uk/tol/sport/rugby_union/article 6810037.ece (accessed 2010).
Author unknown (2010) 'Eric Devendorf dumped by Waikato Pistons', *Waikato Times*, 12 March. Available at: http://www.stuff.co.nz/sport/basketball/3573101/Eric-Devendorf (accessed 2010).
Author unknown (2011) 'Rugby coach convicted of assaulting son', *Otago Daily Times*, 28 July. Available at: http://www.odt.co.nz/regions/central-otago/171012/rugby-coach-convicted-asssaulting-son (accessed 2010).
Cassidy, T. (2000) 'Investigating the pedagogical process in physical education teacher education', unpublished thesis, Deakin University, Australia.
Cassidy, T. (2010) 'Understanding the change process: Valuing what it is that coaches do', *International Journal of Sports Science and Coaching*, 5(2): 143–7.
Cassidy, T. and Hessian, P. (2011) 'Is it more than a game? One coach's exploration of disciplinary technologies', paper presented at the Technologies in Sport: Performance, Bodies and Ethics symposium, Dunedin, 20–22 September.

Cassidy, T. and Kidman, L. (2010) 'Initiating a national coaching curriculum: A paradigmatic shift?', *Physical Education and Sport Pedagogy*, 15(3): 307–22.

Cassidy, T. and Tinning, R. (2004) '"Slippage" is not a dirty word: Considering the usefulness of Giddens' notion of knowledgeability in understanding the possibilities for teacher education', *Journal of Teacher Education*, 15: 175–88.

CAC (2011a) 'What is the NCCP?' Available at: http://www.coach.ca/what-is-the-nccp-s12507 (accessed 2 December 2011).

CAC (2011b) 'NCCP's Code of Ethics'. Available at: http://www.coach.ca/files/NCCP_Code_of_Ethics_2011_en.pdf (accessed 2 December 2011).

CAC (2011c) 'MED Workshop'. Available at: http://www.coach.ca/workshop-s14169 (accessed 2 December 2011).

Denison, J. (2007) 'Social theory for coaches: A Foucauldian reading of one athlete's poor performance', *International Journal of Sports Science & Coaching*, 2(4): 369–83.

Denison, J. (2010a) 'Planning, practice and performance: The discursive formation of coaches' knowledge', *Sport Education and Society*, 15: 461–78.

Denison, J. (2010b) '"Messy texts" or the unexplainable performance: Reading bodies' evidence', *International Review of Qualitative Research*, 3: 149–60.

Denison, J. and Avner, A. (2011) 'Positive coaching: Ethical practices for athlete development', *Quest*, 63: 209–27.

DeSensi, J. and Rosenberg, D. (2003) *Ethics in Sport Management*. Morgantown, WV: Fitness Information Technology.

Foucault, M. (1979) *Discipline and Punish: The Birth of the Prison*. New York: Vintage Books.

Foucault, M. (1983) 'The subject and power', in H. Dreyfus and P. Rabinow (eds) *Michel Foucault: Beyond Structuralism and Hermeneutics*, 2nd edn. Chicago, IL: University of Chicago Press, pp. 208–26.

Foucault, M. (1985) *The Use of Pleasure: The History of Sexuality*, vol. 2. London: Penguin.

Giddens, A. (1990) *The Consequences of Modernity*. Cambridge: Polity Press.

Giddens, A. (1991) *Modernity and Self-identity: Self and Society in the Late Modern Age*. Cambridge: Polity Press.

Hardman, A. and Jones, C. (eds) (2011) *The Ethics of Sports Coaching*. London: Routledge.

Hardman, A., Jones, C. and Jones, R. (2010) 'Sports coaching, virtue ethics and emulation', *Physical Education and Sport Pedagogy*, 15(4): 345–59.

Harvey, S., Kirk, D. and O'Donovan, T. (2011) 'Sport Education as a pedagogical application for ethical development in physical education and youth sport', *Sport, Education and Society,* iFirst Article: 1-23. DOI:10.1080/13573322.2011.610784.

Jones, C. (2008) 'Teaching virtue through physical education: Some comments and reflections', *Sport, Education and Society*, 13(3): 337–49.

Kelly, P. and Hickey, C. (2008) *The Struggle for the Body, Mind and Soul of AFL Footballers*. Melbourne: Australian Scholarly Publishing.

Malloy, D., Ross, S. and Zakus, D. (2000) *Sport Ethics: Concepts and Cases in Sport and Recreation*. Canada: Thompson Educational Publishing.

Malloy, D., Ross, S. and Zakus, D. (2003) *Sport Ethics: Concepts and Cases in Sport and Recreation*, 2nd edn. Canada: Thompson Educational Publishing.

Markula, P. and Pringle, R. (2006) *Foucault, Sport and Exercise: Power, Knowledge and Transforming the Self*. London: Routledge.

McNamee, M. (1998) 'Celebrating trust: Virtues and rules in the ethical conduct of sports coaches', in M. McNamee and J. Parry (eds) *Ethics and Sport*. London: E& fn Spon, pp. 148–68.

McNamee, M. (2008) *Sports, Virtues and Vices: Morality Plays*. Hoboken: Taylor and Francis.

Morgan, W. (2007) *Ethics in Sport*, 2nd edn. Champaign, IL: Human Kinetics.

Panathlon International (2004) Declaration on Ethics in Youth Sport. Available at: http://www.panathlon.net (accessed 7 December 2012).

Pringle, R. (2007) 'Social theory for coaches: A Foucauldian reading of one athlete's poor performance. A Commentary', *International Journal of Sports Science & Coaching*, 2(4): 385–93.

Pringle, R. and Hickey, C. (2010) 'Negotiating masculinities via the moral problematization of sport', *Sociology of Sport Journal*, 27(2): 115–38.

Shogan, D. (2007) *Sport Ethics in Context*. Toronto: Canadian Scholars' Press.

Stevenson, A. (2010). 'Salary cap breach no storm in a teacup', *Sydney Morning Herald*, 22 March. Available at: http://www.stuff.co.nz/sport/league/3613578/Storm-fans-shocked-saddened-by-scandal (accessed 22 April 2010).

Telfer, H. (2010) 'Coaching practice and practice ethics', in J. Lyle and C. Cushion (eds) *Sports Coaching: Professionalisation and Practice*. London: Elsevier, pp. 209–20.

Tinning, R. (2002) 'Toward a "modest pedagogy": Reflections on the problematics of critical pedagogy', *Quest*, 54: 224–40.

11 Examining morality in physical education and youth sport from a social constructionist perspective

Dean M. Barker, Natalie Barker-Ruchti and Uwe Pühse

Introduction[1]

In this chapter we show how ways of thinking about morality and behaviour are tied up with what we do as sport and physical education practitioners. We also introduce an alternative way of thinking that might help to develop ethical pedagogies. We begin by examining three 'interaction episodes' in three different physical education lessons at an inner city *Weiterbildungsschule*[2] in Basel, Switzerland. Two of the episodes came from the same class. The third episode was observed in a different class with a different teacher. After presenting a brief description of the three episodes, we introduce a social constructionist perspective as a way of thinking about morality. In the third part of the chapter, we apply this perspective to the episodes. In this section, we include a brief discussion of how constructionist understandings might inform ethics pedagogies in the future. The chapter finishes with a brief summary of the chapter's main arguments.

Episode one: Drago and Omer[3]

The lesson is just about to finish. Most of the boys are taking mats and balls back to the equipment room across the hallway. Seven boys have been asked to collect the bands that were used to designate teams and these boys have remained in the gym. Although some of the bands are still lying on the ground, the boys start to pick up their valuables from the tray on the ground. They think that it is time to go. Their teacher, Herr Hartmann, is standing perhaps 3 metres away attempting to watch the boys directly in front of him as well as those returning in the corridor. When he notices what the band boys are doing, he tells them that the lesson is not yet over. Typically for these boys, they follow his instructions without question and return their wallets and watches to the tray.

As this is happening, Drago, a tall, athletic boy with short-cropped hair, approaches Omer, a shorter, heavier boy with dark features. Having manoeuvred into a position behind Omer, Drago grips Omer's arm so that he is unable to turn. At the same time, he pushes Omer just behind the ear so that

Omer's head jolts slightly forward. It is not a violent gesture. For an observer, 'irritating' is probably a more apt descriptor. However, Drago does not let go and repeats the action three more times with increasing intensity. Omer shows displeasure and struggles to escape but he does not retaliate. The interaction is not finished. Drago lets go of Omer's arm but follows him several more steps until Omer has his side against the wall. Drago then continues pushing Omer's head five more times so that Omer's head almost hits the wall. No one else seems to be aware of what these two are doing. Standing approximately 4 metres away, Herr Hartmann has not noticed the interaction and calls the group to the middle circle. The boys start to move as a group. The interaction is still not finished. As they drift towards the centre of the gym, Drago drops his hands and his active stance, appearing to signal that the interaction is over. Omer turns his back and Drago instantly lunges, pushing Omer with much more force than previously. Omer staggers to keep his balance. This large movement captures the attention of another pupil, Abdullah, who reacts by pushing Drago forcefully. Drago turns his attention to Abdullah and a short, aggressive interaction between Drago and Abdullah begins. Omer pushes Drago from behind but Drago's attention is on Abdullah and he does not acknowledge Omer's action.

Episode two: Maurizio, Noa and Ali

Six boys and their teacher, Herr Dupont, are standing around the trampoline while a seventh attempts some introductory tasks in the two minutes of jumping time that he has been allocated. Herr Dupont has stressed the importance of safe spotting. Although not entirely vigilant, the boys standing on the trampoline's perimeter are taking their job seriously. They have their arms resting on the trampoline's spring covers and when the jumper looks as if he will lose control, they raise their arms. As the boy jumping finishes and begins to dismount, Herr Dupont indicates to Maurizio that it is his turn. There is a large range of body sizes and shapes in the class, but Maurizio is easily the smallest boy. He wears thick glasses, giving him an unsporty appearance even though he is as competent as many of the boys in the class. Maurizio is standing between two boys, Noa, one of the biggest boys in the class, who has only recently arrived in the class after having 'problems' at another school, and Ali, a boy who stands out in the class for two reasons: his inappropriate attire (black jeans and singlet) and his frequent and public questioning of Herr Dupont's authority.

Maurizio begins to climb onto the tramp. The springs are about the same height as his upper chest and he has to jump to get his upper body up on to the spring cover. It looks like a challenge for him, a point that is noted by his peers. Noa intervenes by grasping Maurizio at the top of his trousers and hauling him up. Ali sees what is happening and does the same from the other side, in effect, matching Noa's effort and balancing Maurizio. With the force of the two boys though, Maurizio is propelled up on to the tramp in an uncontrolled manner. Noa and Ali look at each other and laugh. Maurizio lifts himself to his feet and begins jumping, apparently unperturbed.

Episode three: Herr Dupont and Ali

The class is split into four teams. Two games of unihockey are taking place diagonally across the gym so that the games intersect. Rather than goals, the teams are playing with pins like those used for tenpin bowling. Each team has three pins, which they are trying to protect while at the same time upsetting those of the opposing team. Herr Dupont has made the rules regarding the pins clear: When placing your own team's pins, they cannot be spaced closer than 30 cm to one another, when knocking them down during the game, you can only hit one at a time and this must be done with the ball (not the hockey stick).

The pupils are not particularly fond of unihockey and are playing with only a moderate level of intensity and motivation. Herr Dupont is playing on one of the teams and the boys appear to try harder when playing with him. In the final rotation, Ali, the boy wearing the inappropriate clothes in the last example, knocks down all three pins. Although he has the ball in his possession, he uses his stick. He then returns to his own corner. Herr Dupont calls the games to a halt. Standing in the middle of the gym, he tells Ali to stand the pins up again. The rest of the boys have stopped as requested and are now waiting. Ali refuses, holding his ground at the opposite corner of the gym to the fallen pins. Herr Dupont tries again before walking over to Ali's corner and becoming more insistent. Eventually, the two of them make their way across the gym towards the fallen pins. Halfway across the gym, Ali sees a possible alternative and tells another pupil who is closer to the pins to right them. Herr Dupont immediately tells the pupil to leave the pins. A little more than 60 seconds after Herr Dupont first asked, Ali stands the pins. He places them together so that they are touching one another. At the end of the lesson, the pupils sit on the middle circle ring and listen to Herr Dupont provide a short summary of the lesson. He asserts that the lesson had gone well but that some people had ruined things by cheating and that 'a game won through cheating is not a game won'.

These episodes were observed during an ethnographic investigation. The investigation involved observations of teaching sequences (four 90-minute lessons and four 45-minute lessons) for three separate boys' classes. Alongside observations, two semi-structured interviews and numerous informal discussions were held with the three male teachers. At the end of the teaching sequences, between five and seven pupils were invited to take part in semi-structured interviews. Here, interview schedules based on observation notes and film clips were used to guide the conversations. The pupils that were interviewed were selected because they had been involved in the interactions during the lessons.

We found the three episodes interesting because in their own ways they encouraged an evaluation. They seemed to invite us to think about whether the behaviours involved were good or bad and, in this sense, they had a moral dimension (Loland 2006; Panathlon International 2004). Later in the chapter we will re-examine the episodes with some orientation from interview material. Before we do this though, we want to consider what is meant by moral behaviour. We are going to locate the idea within social constructionist thinking. Our approach to outlining what we mean by 'moral' will be done in two steps. First, we will take a brief look at social constructionism as a general mode of thought and examine some of its major principles. Second, we will look at what social constructionists have had to say about morality.

Social constructionism and ethics

The idea that 'things' like gender, race or ability are *socially constructed* is not new in the physical education and sport pedagogy literature (Kirk 1992; Chen and Rovegno 2000; Gorely *et al.* 2003; Wallian and Chang 2007; Barker and Rossi 2011). What is generally meant is that things (and our knowledge of these things) are productions of social processes. Potter expresses this notion eloquently, arguing that 'the world is not ready categorised by God or nature in ways that we are all forced to accept. It is *constituted* in one way or another as people talk it, write it and argue it' (1996: 98; emphasis in original).

Although the idea has a much longer history, the term 'social constructionism' was coined by Berger and Luckmann (1966) in the 1960s. Since then, it has given rise to a large range of projects in different disciplines. We want to focus on social constructionist thinking as it exists within a dialogical approach to social psychology. The focus of this approach is on how people interact with one another in everyday settings. John Shotter (1984, 1995a, 1995b) suggests that dialogical psychologists are interested in 'how people develop and sustain particular forms of relationships to one another through their talk and how from within these relational ways of talking, they make sense of their surroundings' (1995a: 160). Focusing on this kind of constructionism seems to makes sense given our primary task of understanding behaviours between pupils (and teachers) in physical education lessons.

In a dialogical approach, language is key. Talk is the means through which people construct their relationships to one another and is seen as 'active'. People talk to do things like influence other's behaviour and position people, including themselves (Edley 2001). Rather than being representative and past-oriented, talk is seen to constitute a social act that is future-oriented. For these reasons, social constructionists are particularly interested in elements of language like vocabulary and grammar (Shotter 1984).

To get at how language is important in human interactions, Shotter has introduced the notion of 'joint action' (Shotter 1995a). A joint action is a communicative event between two or more people. Joint action implies that events such as conversations do not belong to any one speaker but are communal. Participants cannot simply utter what they like because they have to consider how their fellow participants will react. The idea of community is tied to *meaning*. Meanings are seen as context specific (think about how football can assume different meanings in different countries) and dependent on agreement (see also Gergen 1995). Joint action also leaves open the possibility that what people intend to do with their talk and the actual outcomes of their comments can differ (think of any time that you have been misunderstood). This is because events are the sometimes-unexpected results of combinations. Finally, the idea of joint action grants speakers within situations the ability to influence the situation. Participants can, through the use of first-person statements, for example, open up a range of feasible responses from participants or close them down.

With its focus on language use and interaction, dialogical thinking is broadly concerned with human conduct. Interestingly though, a number of theorists have pointed out that the subjective nature of constructionism results in a relativist ethics where any action can be legitimated (Nightingale and Cromby 1999; Parker 1999; Liebrucks 2001). From the critic's point of view, the absence of universal meanings beyond social processes results in a world where 'anything goes'. Theft, for example, might be condemned by one person but justified by another. A social constructionist perspective – according to some theorists – does not offer a point from which to evaluate conduct.

Various constructionists have argued against this claim (Raskin 2001; Harré 2002). Edwards and his colleagues (1995) suggest that people have moral commitments and that a constructionist view does not demand that people give up these commitments. Similarly, Potter (1998) argues that particular constructions have consequences. He argues that 'for the relativist, what "goes" is at stake for the people; it is what is constructed and argued over. Different positions, cultures, and theories have different (any)things which go, don't go, or go a bit' (Potter 1998: 34).

Gergen (1994) raises three interesting points that are worth mentioning. He argues that a universal (or 'absolutist') ethics runs the risk of imperialism and discourages engaging one's opponent in dialogue. A social constructionist stance, in contrast, encourages collaborative searches for meaning and 'communal considerations of consequence' (Gergen 1994: 109). Second, Gergen suggests that social constructionists emphasize the importance of examining social settings as a way of understanding unethical behaviours. Instead of focusing on retribution when it comes to immoral behaviour, he suggests that we look at how social circumstances might be changed to prevent similar actions from recurring. Finally, Gergen suggests that, in reality, the learning of universal ethical principles has little to do with how people actually behave. For the social constructionist, behaviour developed in relationship with others is more important than principles.

In short, social constructionists maintain that they do have something to say about morality and ethics. In our view, Gergen and his colleagues' call for dialogue and negotiation around questions of behaviour points towards a tolerant and potentially generative ethical position. At the same time, we recognize that it is sometimes easier to describe something in abstract terms than apply an idea to concrete cases. It is the challenge of application and thinking in particular and tangible terms that we take up in the next section.

Reading episodes constructively

Before we return to the episodes introduced earlier, let us make a small note regarding sampling. We selected the episodes from slightly more than 1,600 minutes of film material in which literally thousands of interactions could be observed. To select three, we made decisions about what constituted an episode relevant to the notion of 'ethical behaviour'. These decisions were based on the theoretical premises of the investigation (see Gobo (2004) for a discussion of theoretical sampling). In this sense, the three episodes were already somewhat theory-laden when they were presented at the beginning of the chapter. What we are going to do below is not *apply* a theoretical framework to make sense of the episodes but rather *extend* it.

Drago and Omer

If we think of Drago and Omer's episode as joint action (Shotter 1995a), what stands out is not that one boy is hitting another in a way that causes physical discomfort or that he is doing something against the class rules. What stands out is that Drago is not considering Omer's point of view even though the interaction has 'consequences' for both of them. The event is being performed in an entirely one-sided manner – Drago is shaping the event for both participants. Indeed, there are dozens of aggressive acts in the film material from this class. Even in the same frame behind Drago and Omer, two boys are hitting each other. But the uni-dimensional nature of the interaction was rarely so clear. Omer did not initiate the interaction nor was he afforded the opportunity to end it. This is what makes the situation problematic from a social constructionist perspective.

Before we consider how we might deal with this as a teacher, let us think about what else a social constructionist might make of this situation. One area of interest is how the boys make sense of the situation. As mentioned, we explored the boys' own interpretations through post-observation interviews using film clips as prompts. Drago, Omer and several other boys were asked to explain what was happening in the clips they saw. Although offered independently of one another, the explanations for Drago and Omer's interaction were remarkably close. The boys all said that this kind of 'fun' goes on all the time, not just in physical education but in the breaks too. Further, it is not just Drago and Omer but all the boys in the class that partake in this kind of behaviour. In other words, it was normal.

We do not doubt that the boys see this kind of interaction as normal. Nor do we think that they were covering up what was 'really going on'. Even Omer's counter-intuitive response is logical if understood from a constructionist perspective. The convergence of answers is unsurprising because sense-making is communal and the boys in the class constitute a community. For Omer to question the meaning of a practice – a practice which is pervasive within the group and on which the community seems to have agreement – would be for him to question his own membership within the group. To adopt a different stance would be to position himself as outsider. In this way, the group's interactive practices and the meanings that they share hold them together in a two-way fashion (Shotter 1995a).

As a way forward for practitioners, we would make three suggestions. In line with a social constructionist approach (as well as the Panathlon Declaration on Ethics in Youth Sport [Panathlon International 2004]), the first is to emphasize the mutual nature of interactions. This could be done through discussion and reflection on activities that do and do not encourage joint participation. Most of the organized activities that take place in the name of physical education and youth sport *can* be undertaken in a uni-directional manner (where teachers or coaches make decisions on behalf of the participants) or a multi-directional manner (where participants contribute to decision-making processes). Both kinds of approaches could provide valuable 'talking points', and in this way, physical education and sport could provide forums in which to discuss issues that relate to reciprocity.

Second, we would point out that explanations of existing practices can be reconstructed. Teachers are by definition implicated in reconstructing meaning – this is part of teaching and learning (Gergen 1994). In this case, we could imagine describing uni-dimensional behaviour in ways that are unacceptable for the boys. This may require different ways of understanding behaviour, including hitting/fighting, but again, physical educators and sports pedagogues are in a position to provide these. To make one brief example, some martial arts afford constructions of actions like kicking or striking that entail reciprocity. From this perspective, it might be possible to re-frame Drago's behaviour as problematic in terms of ethos, rather than in terms of school rules.

Finally, it is important to emphasize that not every pupil at the school was engaged in uni-dimensional behaviour. Given that other pupils make up the larger 'school community', they could play an important role in co-constructing new meanings with Drago and his peers. We imagine it would be important for the boys to be exposed to, and perhaps immersed in, other classes and groups where uni-dimensional behaviour is not accepted. We would also suggest that it is important for the boys in this class to see themselves as part of the wider school community as well as a subgroup within it. Adopting different positions may provide space to reflect and perhaps opportunities to rethink the kind of 'one-way' interaction documented here.

Maurizio and his helpers

Initially, one might assign a degree of ambiguity to Maurizio's example. Were Noa and Ali trying to help Maurizio on to the trampoline or were they trying to ridicule him? This was, in fact, the first question that concerned us. During a conversation with the boys' teacher, Herr Dupont, one of us (Dean) noted the two boys' helping behaviour. This stood out because (1) instances of helping were seldom seen in any of the three classes, and (2) the two boys helping often broke classroom rules. Their behaviour seemed out of character. When the episode was floated as a possible example of desirable behaviour, Herr Dupont dismissed the suggestion. He felt that the two bigger boys had used the situation to humiliate the smaller boy. That the boys did it while attempting to look like they were helping actually made matters worse.

One reaction would be to ask Maurizio how he experienced the action. In this case, all three boys said that the act was well meant. While these constructions are consequential, let's stay with the ambiguous nature of the situation for a moment. For us, it was possible for pupils and teacher to read the situation differently because the situation was left 'unconstructed'. At no point did any of those involved say anything. We would propose that any of the participants in the situation had the opportunity to define the situation. Once on the tramp, Maurizio could have laughed and thanked the boys. Noa could have apologized for using too much force. Herr Dupont could have reprimanded the helpers for their actions. In each case, the other participants in the episode (and indeed the other boys who were observing) would have been invited to make sense of the event in a particular way. Interestingly, a reprimand would have encouraged a negative construction of the event while other utterances might not have. However, because the event was not talked through, its sense was left open.

If we think of what happened between Maurizio, Noa and Ali as a joint action, we can see it as immoral not because of how Maurizio might have felt but, once again, because it was one-sided. The event cannot be considered reciprocal because Maurizio did not have the opportunity to refuse help. It is not just the one-sidedness though. We can lift our 3-year-old on to the toilet seat so that he can brush his teeth. We do not have to ask him if this is tolerable. We can do this one-sided act because (1) we often help him, and (2) we (generally) agree that we can do things that he cannot. If we apply this logic to Maurizio's case, the fact that the boys were bigger and stronger and were showcasing this point through their actions *might* be problematic but not necessarily. More troublesome was the fact that this kind of interaction was not a part of Noa and Ali's routine practices – they did not usually help others; indeed, none of the pupils in this class did. In other words, helping in this manner was not part of the habitual practices of the group (Shotter 1995b). The meaning of 'assisting someone on to a trampoline' had not been agreed upon, which made it possible for it to be constructed as an act to induce embarrassment. In fact, this second construction was more aligned with the routine practices of the class and regardless of whether Noa and Ali meant well, this is how Herr Dupont interpreted their actions. This is why the relational aspect of reciprocity is important (Shotter 1995a) and why interactions can only be considered within the settings in which they take place.

This episode also has implications for practitioners. It encourages us to reflect on the conceptual frameworks that we use to make sense of our pupils and their behaviours. We should ask how these frameworks open up or close down behavioural possibilities and, regardless of how justified we believe our conclusions to be, we should leave some room for being surprised. In a related vein, the episode reminds us to use language actively and carefully. As this episode shows, silences can provide spaces in which misunderstandings not only occur but develop. Talking about how we behave can be a way to avoid confusion or conflict. In this respect, we would do well to acknowledge the forward-reaching consequences of 'feedback'.

Ali the 'cheat'

Finally, let's look at Ali, who, in contravention of the game's rules, knocked down three pins with his hockey stick and then refused to stand them back up again. What we want to draw attention to first is Gergen's idea of 'communal considerations of consequence' (Gergen 1994: 109). Let us explain. Once Herr Dupont had stopped the games, he and Ali began a discussion. This discussion in effect isolated them from the rest of the group. This may sound strange given that the other pupils were surrounding them; however, the other pupils were *watching*. They were not talking and they were not part of the action. This is important because it meant that the outcome of the interaction could only be decided upon by Ali and Herr Dupont.

This is a good example of where dialogue and communal consequences might have been particularly useful. The outcome of Herr Dupont and Ali's exchange affected all the members of the class. Further, it was already clear that there was disagreement. By involving the other boys Herr Dupont could have provided an opening for the community to agree on how the game should be played (and a chance to avoid public confrontation). It is possible that he was reluctant to adopt such a strategy. He might have feared that the boys would side with Ali, for example. We find this eventuality unlikely for two reasons. The first is that the boys had been playing by the rules, even if they were unmotivated. In other words, they had agreed on how to play the game. Ali's act went against the practices of the group. The second is that the rules have a certain sense of their own. They 'make' the game.

An important factor in this situation was that Herr Dupont was taking a universal view of cheating. This is evident in the comments he made at the end of the lesson and during the interview following the lesson. He stated simply that Ali was breaking the rules of the game, adding that, sooner or later, Ali needed to learn that it is not OK to break the rules. This sounds reasonable. At the same time it is hard to mistake the 'positioning' (Edley 2001) taking place in the statements. Ali is a 'cheat' who has not yet learned to obey rules. Indeed, this positioning was evident in Herr Dupont's pointed monologue at the end of the lesson. It is not our intention to side with Ali. It is, however, our intention to critique Herr Dupont's strategy and we do not think his appeal to universal rules was effective. This is because his appeal did not have the pedagogical result that Herr Dupont wanted it to have. Ali showed no sign of learning rules. Both during and after the lesson, Ali's main concern was denying that he was a cheat and the situation became a kind of stalemate. What if rather than ask: 'Was Ali's act right or wrong?', we ask: 'Why did Ali break the rules in this particular case?', 'Why Ali?', 'And why at this particular time and this particular lesson?' These are different questions that open up new considerations for pedagogues.

If we start with Ali we might find out that he has an 'us and them' view of pupils and teachers. He has had frequent contact with youth agencies and feels that he has been repeatedly and unfairly singled out for punishment in schools. We might discover that he does not particularly like living in Switzerland and is waiting till he is old enough to return to his country of origin. In many respects, and not just at school, he feels that he is trying to play by rules created by 'others' that disadvantage him. If we then look at the episode we can note that the game was unpopular and the boys were not taking it seriously. This lack of authenticity was reinforced by the fact that the result did not count and that there were two games occurring through one another. Further, for these boys, expressing dissatisfaction with the lesson content through low-level disruption was not untypical. In one respect, Ali's action could be considered as an expression of boredom rather than as a rule violation. We would also point to the types of interactions that had been occurring between Ali and Herr Dupont in previous lessons. 'Public confrontations' were common both before and after the described episode.

As we have hinted, all of these factors could be used to construct the episode differently post hoc. The real value of these considerations, however, lies not in their ability to re-frame the past but in their potential to generate alternative actions for the future.

Rather than concluding that some children just cheat and that these children need to learn to follow rules, we might consider the ways in which they become (or do not become) members of the class and how they develop commitments to the practices of the community. In the classroom we might use group discussions as a method for settling disputes rather than simply citing fairplay, which is assumed to be universal (see Harvey and his colleagues' discussion of sports panels within Sports Education in Chapter 7 of this volume). We might also look at the way that games are introduced and how rules of games are experienced by players. A deep understanding of game rules appears to be intimately linked with an understanding of games per se and yet, in our experience, rules are not examined in great detail in physical education lessons. We might also consider the cultural significance of games and how rules are constructed, negotiated and sometimes broken in other areas of society. Let us be clear: these are not new ideas. We would argue, though, that it is the combination of these ideas with a different set of assumptions that could have unconventional and potentially productive results for practitioners.

Concluding thoughts

We began this chapter by describing three interaction episodes. These episodes provided the practical points of reference for our discussion of a social constructionist ethics. The specific aims of the chapter were to show the features of behaviour that a social constructionist interpretation brings to the fore and propose some implications for physical educators and sport pedagogues alike. Here, the general thrusts of our argument were that practitioners should be cautious of universal understandings of ethics and the ways they position pupils; consider pupils as members of communities that are held together by shared practices; and, finally, reflect on situational and contextual factors when making sense of pupils' actions.

Importantly, we did not set out to produce a set of guidelines prescribing how practitioners should deal with ethical problems. This kind of project would run counter to constructionist thinking, where every setting should be treated on its merit. Rather, our aim was to sketch out an approach that could provide orientation for dealing with typical problems or challenges relating to morality. We believe that concepts like 'joint action' and 'reciprocity' are useful, not because they tell us what to do in general but because they help us to think of appropriate solutions in our own circumstances. This is essential in sport pedagogy where the number of possible interactions between pupils and teachers/players and coaches that occur within different class/team and school/sports club environments is, if not infinite, then at least very high.

Discussion Questions

1. How does elite sport in general support a universal understanding of ethical behaviour? How does it support a relativist understanding? What implications do these understandings have for sport practitioners working with children and youths?
2. A social constructionist take on morality emphasizes dialogue and community agreement. If we accept that community agreement is important, what are the implications for teachers or coaches and how they interact with their charges?
3. Considering what you have read, think of an interactive episode that had an ethical dimension to it. Try to identify some of the contextual factors that contributed to the episode. How could these factors have been changed or re-defined?

Notes

1 This chapter is based on Barker, D., Barker-Ruchti, N. and Pühse, U. (2011) 'Constructive readings of interactive episodes: Examining ethics in physical education from a social constructionist perspective', *Sport, Education and Society. iFirst*: 1–16, DOI:10.1080/13573322.2011.601290.

2 In the eighth school year, pupils in Basel enter either a *Weiterbildungschule*, which lasts for two years and which serves as preparation for a trade apprenticeship, or a *Gymnasium*, which lasts for five years and prepares pupils for tertiary study.
3 All names given are pseudonyms.

References

Barker, D. and Rossi, T. (2011) 'Understanding teachers: The potential and possibility of discourse analysis', *Sport, Education and Society*, 16(2): 139–58.

Berger, P. L. and Luckmann, T. (1966) *The Social Construction of Reality: A Treatise in the Sociology of Knowledge*. Baltimore, MD: Penguin.

Chen, W. and Rovegno, I. (2000) 'Examination of expert and novice teachers' constructivist-orientated teaching practices using a movement approach to elementary physical education', *Research Quarterly for Exercise and Sport*, 71: 357–72.

Edley, N. (2001) 'Interpretive repertoires, ideological dilemmas and subject positions', in M. Wetherall, S. Taylor and S. Yates (eds) *Discourse as Data: A Guide for Analysis*. London: Sage, pp. 189–228.

Edwards, D., Ashmore, M. and Potter, J. (1995) 'Death and furniture: The rhetoric, politics and theology of bottom line arguments against relativism', *History of the Human Sciences*, 8: 25–49.

Gergen, K. (1994) *Realities and Relationships*. Cambridge, MA: Harvard University Press.

Gergen, K. (1995) 'Social construction and the education process', in L. P. Steffe and J. Gale (eds) *Constructivism in Education*. Hillsdale, NJ: Lawrence Erlbaum Associates, pp. 17–40.

Gobo, G. (2004) 'Sampling, representativeness and generalizability', in C. Seale, G. Gobo, J. Gubrium and D. Silverman (eds) *Qualitative Research Practice*. London: Sage, pp. 405–26.

Gorely, T., Holroyd, R. and Kirk, D. (2003) 'Muscularity, the habitus and the social construction of gender: Towards a gender-relevant physical education', *British Journal of Sociology of Education*, 24(4): 429–48.

Harré, R. (2002) 'Public sources of the personal mind: Social constructionism in context', *Theory and Psychology*, 12(5): 611–23.

Kirk, D. (1992) *Defining Physical Education: The Social Construction of a School Subject in Postwar Britain*. London: Falmer Press.

Liebrucks, A. (2001) 'The concept of social construction', *Theory & Psychology*, 11(3): 363–91.

Loland, S. (2006) 'Morality, medicine, and meaning: Toward an integrated justification of physical education', *Quest*, 58(1): 60–71.

Nightingale, D. and Cromby, J. (1999) *Social Constructionist Psychology: A Critical Analysis of Theory and Practice*. Buckingham: Open University Press.

Panathlon International (2004) Declaration on Ethics in Youth Sport. Available at: http://www.panathlon.net (accessed 23 July 2011).

Parker, I. (1999) 'Against relativism in psychology', *History of the Human Sciences*, 12: 61–78.

Potter, J. (1996) *Representing Reality: Discourse, Rhetoric and Social Construction*. London: Sage.

Potter, J. (1998) 'Fragments in the realization of relativism', in I. Parker (ed.) *Social Constructionism, Discourse and Realism*. London: Sage, pp. 27–45.

Raskin, J. (2001) 'On relativism in constructivist psychology', *Journal of Constructivist Psychology*, 14: 285–313.

Shotter, J. (1984) *Social Accountability and Selfhood*. Oxford: Blackwell.

Shotter, J. (1995a) 'Dialogical psychology', in J. Smith, R. Harré and L. Van Langenhove (eds) *Rethinking Psychology*. London: Sage, pp. 160–78.

Shotter, J. (1995b) 'In dialogue: Social constructionism and radical constructivism', in L. Steffe and J. Gale (eds) *Constructivism in Education*. Hillsdale, NJ: Lawrence Erlbaum Associates, pp. 41–56.

Wallian, N. and Chang, C. (2007) 'Language, thinking and action: Towards a semio-contructivist approach in physical education', *Physical Education and Sport Pedagogy*, 12(3): 289–311.

12 Doing moral philosophy with youth in urban programs

Strategies from the Teaching Personal and Social Responsibility model and the Philosophy for Children Movement

Paul M. Wright, Michael D. Burroughs and Deborah P. Tollefsen

Introduction

Numerous scholars have contributed to our understanding of the role moral philosophy can and should play in youth sport and physical education (e.g. Shields and Bredemeier 1995; Hsu 2004; Morgan 2006). While this literature has implications for community-based youth sport, extra-curricular sport, physical education, and the ongoing structure and organization of all three, it has failed to determine whether the broader context of these programs in terms of their location (i.e. urban, suburban, or rural settings) has impacted on the policies and pedagogies around ethics in sport. From an absolutist position, some may argue that context should not matter, but we believe an effective pedagogy is one that is responsive to the learners as well as the context in which it is being delivered. For instance, consider large urban cities that are densely populated with inhabitants who are diverse in terms of race, culture, language, education, as well as socioeconomic levels against many rural locations that are sparsely populated and very similar in terms of the factors previously outlined. While the fundamental processes and skills involved in moral decision-making may be the same in both of these locations, as well as many of the ethical dilemmas faced by today's youth, those growing up in large urban environments often face these issues earlier, more frequently, and with potentially more dire consequences.

Depending on their neighborhood, family, and immediate social environments, youth who are more likely to engage in behaviors that place themselves or others at risk are often less likely to see positive role models or participate in programs that address moral decision-making (Miller *et al.* 1997). For these reasons, our chapter focuses on pedagogical strategies for working with youth in physical activity and sport programs within urban environments. Although we come from different academic disciplines (Deborah and Michael from philosophy and Paul from physical education and sport pedagogy), our approaches are similar in that we all work directly with youth, designing and delivering programs that focus on their holistic development. Paul's programs focus on promoting personal and social responsibility through physical activity, whereas Deborah's and Michael's focus on philosophical discussion and critical thinking. The pedagogical strategies shared in this chapter have proven effective in our work with urban youth in Memphis, Tennessee, USA.

Designing and delivering physical activity and sport programs that effectively engage youth in urban settings presents unique challenges. Youth growing up in more impoverished urban areas are at greater risk of being disengaged at school and less likely to participate in structured extra-curricular programs including organized sport (Ennis 1999; Sandford *et al.* 2006). We are primarily interested in helping youth develop as people with an ethical and social awareness, capable of contributing positively to their own community. Therefore, we focus more on teaching them applied ethics and helping them develop transferable life skills rather than promoting specific aspects of sport culture or teaching them rules and definitions related to ethics. For this reason, most of the strategies we discuss in this chapter are not tied to the traditional youth sport context, but can also be applied in settings such as physical education, after-school programs, or summer camps. More-over, our approach relies much less on traditional didactic instruction and more on empowering youth to engage in moral decision-making processes that support moral action. In the following section of this chapter, we discuss the conceptual framework underpinning our approach. We then go on to describe specific program features and share pedagogical strategies that have been field-tested in our work based in the Teaching Personal and Social Responsibility (TPSR) model and the Philosophy for Children movement.

Conceptual framework

Moral philosophy

Ethics (or better, moral philosophy) deals with fundamental questions con-cerning the nature of good and evil, right and wrong, how one ought to live his or her life, what sort of person one should be, and what considerations are relevant when trying to resolve a moral dilemma. A variety of historical and contemporary theories attempt to answer these questions: utilitarianism, deontology, Confucianism, virtue theory, and natural law to name just a few. Regardless of how one answers these questions, the approach to them is the same – one of careful, rational consideration. Ethical theories are developed by appeals to reason and defended by rational argumentation. And although the content of ethical theories may differ, philosophers generally agree that ethical reasoning, like practical reasoning in general, requires the exercise of rationality rather than mere emotion (though moral emotions such as empathy certainly have their role to play). Moral decision-making requires self-reflection, critical evaluation, and a willingness to take different perspectives into consideration. Teaching ethics to youth, through sport or any other ped-agogical means, is not a matter of passing on ethical principles or specific ethical rules for them to follow. Such principles and rules will no doubt differ from community to community. Nor is it a matter of teaching them the the-ories offered by philosophers past and present. Rather, it involves exercising their rational capacities to develop the critical thinking skills they need to make judgements about how to live well and how to treat themselves and others with respect (Hsu 2004).

As made clear in the Panathlon Declaration on Ethics in Youth Sport (Panathlon International 2004), virtues such as fairness play a crucial role in sport. Being able to think clearly, critically, and carefully about the concept of fairness provides young adults and children with resources to identify fairness or unfairness in everyday contexts. It provides them with a rational explana-tion for behaving fairly rather than simply telling them it is a rule they must follow. In this respect, the attempt to get youth to think critically about con-cepts like fairness is an attempt to move them from a mere follower of rules to someone who understands, takes ownership of, and, in some cases challenges the norms within their own community. It aims to provide them with the resources to think abstractly and transfer concepts from one context to another, from sport to family relations, from friendship to political contexts. Because social injustice and disparity abound in harsh urban environments, the sorts of critical thinking and agency discussed here are essential for indi-viduals and communities to break free of such patterns (McLaughlin *et al.* 1994; Miller *et al.* 1997).

Philosophy for Children

Because the teaching of ethics to youth is not a matter of providing them with facts or information to store and restate on a test, because it is less a matter of content than a matter of method or skill, and because it aims to instill a sort of rational autonomy in the child, it requires a unique pedagogical approach. In *Pedagogy of the Oppressed*, Paulo Freire (2003) provides a useful distinction between two fundamentally different approaches to education. First, the 'banking concept of education' involves approaching the child-student as a passive receptacle for information to be 'filled' by the teacher (Freire 2003: 72). In this traditional approach to education, the child-student's pri-mary tasks are to listen to the teacher, memorize necessary information, and demonstrate mastery of a predetermined lesson. In the case of moral education, the banking concept of education would involve the student mastering those elements of ethical theory deemed significant by the teacher and, in turn, demonstration of this mastery for the teacher.

Second, the 'dialogical' or 'problem-posing' method involves a radically different approach to education and the pedagogical relation between teacher and student, one of direct importance for our pedagogical approach in this chapter. Here the child-student is engaged by the teacher as a fellow critical thinker, as a 'critical co-investigator in dialogue with the teacher' (Freire 2003: 81). In this pedagogical relation – a paradigm critical pedagogical relation – the student and teacher are viewed as partners in the learning process. The intended result is for the student, along with the teacher, to take ownership of the lesson, to question and apply the intellectual content of, say, a discussion of ethics to her daily life. Thus, in the study of moral philosophy the student's own questions, experiences, and insights are not tertiary to the lesson, but rather are significant elements of the learning process itself. This approach increases the relevance of the lessons, which is often a key to connecting with disengaged students (Cothran and Ennis 1999; Ennis 1999).

The problem-posing method has (tacitly or explicitly) been adopted by the Philosophy for Children movement in the US. Although Philosophy for Children is composed of diverse movements, it can be characterized broadly as an educational movement that rethinks both the pedagogical relationship between student and teacher and the intellectual capabilities of young students. Doing philosophy with children requires teachers and students to engage in dialogue and collective critical thinking (akin to Freire's problem-posing approach). It further entails a belief in young students as capable of contributing positively to philosophical discussion, as possessed of valuable insights, and as capable of taking ownership of their own education. Thus, practitioners of the Philosophy for Children movement engage the student as a fellow philosopher in a discussion of ethics and incorporate those ethical questions of import to the student into a given lesson or discussion.

Teaching Personal and Social Responsibility

Hellison's (2010) TPSR model is an instructional model that uses sport and physical activity as a vehicle for teaching life skills. This model aligns with the empowerment-based approach of the Philosophy for Children movement and has been developed primarily in programs for underserved youth in urban environments over the past four decades (Hellison and Martinek 2006). In TPSR programs, personal (how we conduct ourselves) and social (how we treat others) responsibility are integrated into the physical activity experience and discussed directly. A number of pedagogical strategies are used to allow students to practice life skills such as leadership, conflict resolution, and decision-making in the program, but the ultimate aim of the model is that students will apply these skills in other parts of their life and in the future. For example, instead of just telling students that it is good to be a leader, we actually give them opportunities to lead and be in charge of others. Within the context of our program, we let students lead exercises or be in charge of their peers while running an activity station. We let students know our expectations before letting them take on leadership roles, we debrief with them afterward, and we discuss ways they could take on leadership roles in other settings. For other examples of specific pedagogical strategies used in TPSR, see Hellison (2010).

Research has demonstrated that TPSR can be effective in creating a positive, student-centered learning environment in which urban youth take on more active and responsible roles than usual (DeBusk and Hellison 1989; Cutforth and Puckett 1999; Wright and Burton 2008). Several studies also indicate that the emphasis on reflection and life skill transfer increases relevance for youth in urban environments and supports positive changes in attitude and behavior 'outside the gym' (Martinek *et al.* 2001; Walsh *et al.* 2010; Wright *et al.* 2010) as well as helping them envision alternative possible futures (Walsh 2008). These findings provide insights as to how and why the pedagogical approaches described here appear effective in engaging youth, even in challenging urban environments.

Our setting

Memphis, the city where we have done most of our work in the past several years, is like many other large cities in the US insofar as it contains 'inner-city' neighborhoods with high rates of poverty, unemployment, crime, teen pregnancy, academic failure, and drug activity. Much of our work has been conducted in these neighborhoods and/or served youth who live in them. Certainly, not every child growing up in a large city is exposed to the extreme conditions seen in some inner-city neighborhoods. However, national datasets routinely show that children growing up in large urban centers are more likely to be exposed to negative influences and risky behaviors related to illicit drugs, violence, crime, and gangs than their counterparts in suburban or rural settings (US Government 2012).

Sadly, in Memphis, as in many other large cities in the US, patterns of poverty, poor education, health disparities, and high crime rates are repeated generation after generation. Public school systems in US cities where such negative influences abound often reflect racial and economic disparities and a legacy of social injustice (Bond and Sherman 2003; Rushing 2009). For instance, the majority of the 103,593 students in the Memphis City School system are African American (85 per cent) and 87.2 per cent of the student population is classified as economically disadvantaged. Only 37.4 per cent of the 46,284 students in the Shelby County school system, which serves the surrounding suburbs, are African American and 33.2 per cent of the student population is classified as economically disadvantaged. Academic achievement in the city of Memphis routinely lags behind state and national averages and in 2009 the high school graduation rate was only 62.1 per cent compared to 96.3 per cent in the Shelby County system, the wider system within which Memphis is located (State of Tennessee 2012).

While the profile of Memphis as a city will not match all others, it certainly does represent many of the issues and challenges often associated with large urban environments. For instance, according to the US Federal Bureau of

Investigation (2010) crime statistics, Memphis had the sixth highest violent crime rate of all cities in the US. Data from the 2009 Youth Risk Behavior Survey (YRBS) administered to high school students in Memphis by the US Centers for Disease Control and Prevention (2012) indicate that 61.6 per cent reported having sexual intercourse, 37.8 per cent reported being in a fight one or more times during the 12 months before the survey, and 39.5 per cent reported using marijuana one or more times during their life.

In such a context, the idea of promoting moral decision-making and moral action takes on a special significance. Every obstacle and negative influence presents youth in these environments with a choice. Some of the decisions they make have strong moral implications and influence their own well-being as well as the lives of those around them. Unfortunately, many of the same social conditions that make moral decision-making and moral action so important for these youth make it less likely that they will be trained in or offered opportunities to practice them. This insight is one that has been offered to us by many of our students and discussion group participants. Given our experience in this context and what we have learned with and from our students, we believe it is important to consider these factors when designing sport and physical activity programs for youth in urban environments.

It should be noted that approximately half (48.2 per cent) of the Memphis City Schools' high school students in the YRBS survey described above reported that they did not play on sports teams run by their school or community groups during the 12 months before the survey. Youth in urban environments who could benefit the most from positive youth sport experiences are quite often the least likely to have the access, support, and resources necessary to participate in them. This is all the more reason why we take a broader view in this chapter to include strategies that might be applied not only to community-based and extra-curricular sport programs, but also to physical education and physical activity in general.

Our programs

Philosophical horizons

Deborah and Michael have applied the principles of the Philosophy for Children movement in Philosophical Horizons, a community outreach program of the Department of Philosophy at the University of Memphis. Founded in 2008, Philosophical Horizons primarily works with urban youth in Memphis City Schools, grade levels ranging from sixth to twelfth. Philosophical Horizons projects in the Memphis community take multiple forms, ranging from philosophy discussion groups with middle school students to introductory philosophy courses for high school students to philosophical teaching workshops for local teachers, graduate students, and undergraduate students.

In their work with young students Deborah and Michael are guided by two fundamental aims: first, they help students develop critical thinking and analytical reasoning skills that are crucial to success in school and, further, in any career or discipline they choose to pursue. Second, and most importantly, they work to help students gain confidence in their ability to speak and be heard as valuable contributors to discussion, as philosophers. Many urban youth in Memphis struggle with a lack of educational resources and the problems surrounding socioeconomic disadvantage. These students, for the most part, have had little opportunity to engage in equal, participatory dialogue in the classroom. Focusing on providing these youth with a different educational experience, Philosophical Horizons works to create an intellectual 'safe space' for young students to cultivate a confident, philosophical voice.

TPSR physical activity programs

Paul has primarily offered physical activity programs that are based on Hellison's (2010) TPSR model. For several years, he taught martial arts and fitness lessons that were integrated into the required Lifetime Wellness course of the Memphis City Schools physical education curriculum for high school students in one of the most impoverished neighborhoods in Memphis. For the next several years, he taught similar content in an after-school program for students in grades four through eight who had been identified as being at risk of academic failure due, in large part, to behavior issues. In both of these settings, Paul was working with many students who were disengaged, struggling with impulse control, and/or frequently being disruptive and disrespectful to others. These are challenges commonly cited in the literature on urban physical education (Cothran and Ennis 1999; Ennis 1999; Ennis *et al.* 1999; Wright and Burton 2008). With groups and individuals that required more development in these areas, Paul would focus on responsibility goals that are fundamental to creating a safe, positive, and functional learning environment such as respecting the rights and feelings of others, participating, trying new things, and giving good effort. While these are basic skills, many of the students coming from troubled backgrounds needed direct coaching and feedback on them before taking on other responsibilities.

As groups and individuals progressed with these foundational responsibility goals, Paul's commitment was always to increase the level of empowerment and responsibility he shared with them. For example, as students appeared ready he would increasingly give them opportunities to make group or individual decisions, share their opinions, work independently, set goals, and take on leadership roles. Some individual students got farther than others, but integrating these elements consistently and over time proved an effective means of creating a more student-centered, engaging, and functional environment for learning and personal growth. To the extent possible, usually with brief discussions at the end of class, Paul would emphasize the importance of the life skills and responsibilities the students were working on in the program, and invite the youth to share thoughts and experiences regarding the transfer of these life skills to other parts of their lives. See Hellison (2010) for a more detailed description of the typical TPSR lesson format and teaching strategies.

In our collaborative work, we (Paul, Michael, and Deborah) have visited each other's programs, discussed our different approaches, and conducted some lessons/activities jointly. Through this process, we found that our objectives and pedagogical approaches were very compatible and that we had complementary strengths and opportunities to learn from one another. For instance, while Paul was committed to promoting reflection and the transfer of life skills from the physical activity setting, he saw from observing the Philosophical Horizon programs how much farther he could take these discussions with his students, especially regarding broader issues such as social justice. Conversely, Deborah and Michael saw in Paul's TPSR programs the opportunities sport and physical activity offer to link potentially abstract conversations about topics such as fairness and honesty to concrete situations and experiences. It also drew their attention to the benefits of integrating kinesthetic learning into their existing programs, especially as a way of connecting with students who were less engaged by discussion alone. In the next section of this chapter, we share specific strategies and examples that we have drawn from our collective experience and this collaborative project.

Recommended practices

Creating an appropriate climate

Regardless of the program type (youth sport, physical education, etc.), it is the responsibility of adult program leader, teacher, or coach to establish clear and explicit expectations for the ways individuals conduct themselves and treat each other. In developing these expectations, we suggest that responsible adults involve students or team members in the decision-making process, thereby providing group accountability for conduct and goals. Through what they say, reinforce, and ignore, program adults convey messages and establish a tone regarding what is acceptable in a program. Therefore, before focusing on the lessons or topics related to ethics/moral philosophy, we urge program leaders to create an appropriate climate, a subculture if you will, for the sort of reflection and dialogue essential for promoting moral decision-making and moral action. Specifically, for youth to feel comfortable reflecting, sharing their thoughts, and engaging in discussion about real-life issues, they must all feel included, accepted, and safe. Programs in which social exclusion, disrespect, aggression, and intimidation are unchecked will not present fertile ground for the type of pedagogy we espouse.

While this would hold true in any context, it is especially important in urban settings where the culture of schools is less likely to promote reflection, open dialogue, student empowerment, and a democratic learning environment (Schilling *et al.* 2007; Wright and Burton 2008; Lee and Martinek 2009). It is important to note that creating a subculture, especially one that runs counter to the norm, takes time, persistence, and patience. However, for program leaders who wish to go beyond the 'banking' concept of education (Freire 2003), it is absolutely necessary.

Planning activities to prompt discussion

For coaches in youth sport programs, actual competitions can provide ample reference points for subsequent discussion of ethical dilemmas and virtues such as honesty and fairness. In addition to debriefing after a game or match on technical matters and strategy, one could also select an incident or event that poses an ethical problem and facilitate a youth discussion around it (see Chapter 7 by Harvey, Kirk and O'Donovan). Remember, if this is a lecture, led by an adult, with a 'right answer' predetermined from the start, prior to dialogic engagement with the students/team members, then the youth are not being given an opportunity to develop the critical thinking and reflective skills that are hallmarks of the dialogical approach to education.

Physical education teachers and program leaders in other settings may not automatically have the concrete and authentic examples presented in competitive sport programs, but they can integrate games and activities that could be used in the same way. Even for those working with younger children, specific age-appropriate activities can be designed to prompt discussion around specific virtues. For example, in Paul's after-school program, he held an impromptu push-up contest one day as part of the fitness portion of the lesson. All students (most aged 8 through 11) were reminded of the proper form and cadence to perform a push-up and told to do as many as they could before they reached fatigue and/or could not maintain the proper form. Each student kept their own count and no one, including Paul, was to police, monitor, or coach anyone else. After the time had expired everyone reported their number, which ranged from as low as 3 to as high as 87. There were some immediate heated reactions (even the simplest competition can bring this out) to the veracity of some reported figures. However, instead of entertaining these disputes, everyone's report was taken at face value and the discussion was shifted to the virtue of honesty. What if someone had been dishonest, why would that matter? Why might they make that choice? What would be the harm if they did? Why is honesty important? When might the issue of honesty come up at school?

Another example comes from a lesson we jointly delivered to a group of third graders (mostly 8 or 9 years old). This group participated in the Philosophical Horizons program, having weekly discussions in the classroom. On this particular occasion, we met them in their physical education class and structured a simple footrace. All students were paired up and raced against the same partner two times across the gym (more accurately, a multi-purpose room). The first race was very traditional, but before the second, we added a twist. We told them that all students who had been winners the first time could only run (hop) on one foot in the second race. Once again, the reactions to this change were immediate and strong. However, we followed through with the plan and sat in a circle to discuss the varied thoughts and feelings this had inspired immediately afterward. One of the most interesting themes that emerged from students' discussion (facilitated by us) was the notion of what is a fair vs. an unfair advantage. We discussed this in terms of the race they had just run but it was also applied to other sport experiences and eventually other areas of life, for example, when two people are competing for the same job, what constitutes a fair vs. an unfair advantage? Although the conversation did not go as far as broader social justice issues this particular day with this group of students, this example clearly shows how such planned activities and subsequent dialogue could lead to that type of discussion.

Introducing philosophy dialogues

While the examples above capitalize on the experiential nature of physical activity and competition to spark authentic reactions, there is also value in examining hypothetical scenarios and dilemmas. Depending on the type of program and age of the youth participants, program leaders may consider facilitating discussions using scripted philosophy dialogues. In the book *Dialogues with Children*, Gareth Matthews (1984) illustrates the advantages of using dialogues for fostering group discussions with young philosophers. Like Matthews, Philosophical Horizons staff often craft 'philosophy dialogues' to begin elementary, middle school, and high school philosophy discussion group sessions.

The use of these dialogues is advantageous for the following reasons: first, philosophy dialogues concretize potentially abstract philosophical concepts and questions for young philosophers. Dialogues contain two or three main characters, each participating in a scripted discussion on a given philosophical concept (truth, justice, fairness, etc.). These characters are generally of the same age as discussion group participants and voice their positions in (relatively) common vernacular as opposed to philosophical jargon, thereby providing for an open and accessible discussion for all involved. Second, discussion group participants read the dialogue aloud, assuming the position of a given character in the dialogue. In doing so, group members are engaged with the philosophical topic on hand at the start of a session, giving voice to the contrasting positions that all group members will come to evaluate. Third, following the reading of the dialogue, focused discussion on the philosophical positions represented in the dialogue can begin, as opposed to a focus on the positions of individual discussion group members. Thus, students can begin to critique and explore philosophical positions without feeling that they are being intellectually aggressive toward their classmates (a common worry in students unfamiliar with philosophical group discussion). Ideally, a dialogue concludes with a philosophical question for the group to consider and continue to discuss rather than a defined answer. Following an initial discussion of the dialogue staff members can draw out the essential themes of group interest and offer follow-up questions to refine and continue the philosophical discussion of most import to discussion group members (see the Appendix at the end of this chapter for a sample dialogue on the topic of fairness).

Organizing a youth summit

The strategies and practices we have recommended thus far require different levels of planning and structure, but they can all be integrated into lessons or practices led by an individual teacher or coach. Sometimes individuals do this work in isolation and represent a 'drop in the bucket' in terms of the impact their message might have on youth. This may be especially true in harsh inner-city environments where this message might be counter to the dominant culture. However, for individuals fortunate enough to have committed colleagues and organizational support, the opportunity for synergy between groups and programs can strengthen this alternative set of norms and present more large-scale opportunities for engaging youth. For instance, a youth summit, like the one described in more detail below (see also 'sports panels' in Chapter 7 by Harvey, Kirk and O'Donovan), could be integrated into a community sport league, intramurals, school- , district- , or event state-wide athletics programs, as well as throughout a physical education department.

At the conclusion of each academic year, Philosophical Horizons staff organize a culminating experience for young philosophers participating in the program. Our most recent culminating experience, the Philosophical Horizons Youth Summit on Children's Rights, was attended by middle and high school students from Memphis City Schools (approximately 45 students). The structure of the youth summit was derived from the general educational approach of our program. Philosophical Horizons sessions focus on philosophical issues of import to young students and a premium is always placed on students gaining the confidence to actively participate in and eventually lead discussion. For the youth summit students were brought together to participate in an intergenerational dialogue on issues of direct import to their own lives: children's rights, the adult–child distinction, and the place of the child and student in the political realm. Further, the event allowed students to discuss and begin to develop a list of those rights most fundamental for a flourishing human life (with the ultimate aim of creating a student-authored Philosophical Horizons Bill of Children's Rights). As with our group discussions throughout the year, students were encouraged to take leadership in the discussion and develop their own reasoned positions to share with all in attendance.

A similar structure could be adopted within a variety of youth sport and physical activity contexts, providing for a student-led discussion of ethics and, further, the adoption of a student-authored set of team or league rules. As with the youth summit, a general philosophical discussion topic can be raised for a youth sport group such as 'fairness' or 'sportspersonship'. Once the topic is introduced the adult's role is that of discussion facilitator, posing questions or clarifying remarks when necessary (remember that it is key here to avoid Freire's banking concept of education). To begin, the most important element of such a discussion will be the experiences and insights of team members. Discussion can begin with, for example, team members providing starting points on what it means to be fair or a 'good sport'. From concrete observations or examples a move can be made – potentially introduced by the adult facilitator depending on the age of the group and the momentum of the discussion – to ask the team what rules or guidelines they would set in order to create a fair environment on the playing field. As with the youth summit, a space is created here for youth to engage in a philosophical discussion, and, if they so choose, to create a student-developed code of ethics or set of team rules.

Conclusion

In bringing this chapter to a close, we want to re-emphasize some of the key elements of our approach and share our final thoughts. Regarding our work with youth, we believe understanding the context and life experiences of individual learners is essential to relevant and effective pedagogy. This is especially true in harsh urban environments where not all but many more youth may feel disenfranchised, disengaged, and disconnected. For youth growing up in these environments, life lessons regarding ethics and moral reasoning that come through sport and physical activity programs can and should, in our opinion, not just be a means to an end (i.e. fewer problems in competition because everyone knows and follows the rules), but be considered valuable in and of themselves as they contribute to the holistic development and life trajectories of individual youth. We focus on developing the skills youth need, such as reflection and critical thinking, to make moral decisions and act morally, not just in sport but in all aspects of their lives. We strive to promote independent thinking, student voice, and empowered thinking aligned with Freire's dialogical view of education. However, our approach may stand in stark contrast to the culture and dominant views on education seen in many urban schools and sport programs which embody the banking concept of education.

To put these ideas into practice and develop recommendations for others, we have drawn on our extensive work with youth in urban environments. Deborah's and Michael's work with Philosophical Horizons and Paul's work with the TPSR model have been instrumental in shaping our recommendations, but we do not believe practitioners or policy-makers reading this chapter need worry about replicating these programs per se. Instead, we would encourage them to consider ways they might apply or adapt the commitments, strategies, and structures from our work that seem relevant and feasible. For those who may need to make a case for adopting some of these ideas, it should be noted that this approach is consistent with the Panathlon Declaration on Ethics in Youth Sport (Panathlon International

2004) and its effectiveness in urban environments is supported in the academic literature.

Our closing thoughts have to do with avoiding stereotypical thinking when working in urban environments (Harrison 2001; Harrison and Worthy 2001). We have highlighted the importance of context and the need to understand the unique struggles and challenges faced by many youth in large cities. However, it is central to our approach to also see the unique strengths, abilities, and potential of these individuals. While they may be more likely to see negative role models, do not assume that positive, loving, and supportive influences cannot also be found in their homes, schools, and communities. It is also important to understand that not all students and schools in urban settings are low achieving. Regarding individual students – in our experience low academic achievement often does not reflect limited intellectual ability. Our encouragement here is not to set or lower expectations for individuals based on their family, neighborhood, school, or academic record. Strive to understand these things as a way of understanding and reaching the individual, but do not use these elements of a given student's life to label them. We have seen on many occasions that students who were typically viewed as disengaged and/or problematic were extremely bright and had a lot (in terms of thoughts, abilities, and personality) to share. The challenge in these cases is less a lack of intellectual ability on the part of students, and more of finding the way to connect with students and draw out their gifts and talents. While we do not have a perfect record of success or a panacea to offer, we have seen in our own experience that success in these cases almost always hinges on changing the teacher–student relationship.

As explained earlier, some groups and individuals need to develop basic social skills before taking on more responsibility and participating in more democratic processes, but to the extent each can be involved in these, they should. In closing, sport and physical activity programs in urban settings provide valuable experiences for developing life skills that can be applied in so many other ways for the betterment of individuals and communities. Of course, most good teachers, coaches, and program leaders are already skilled at meeting youth where they are developmentally and facilitating their progress to the next stage with regard to various content and skill areas. We encourage them to take the same approach to teaching life skills that support moral decision-making and moral action.

Discussion Questions

1. We endorse considering context, cultural differences, and student perspectives in our approach to doing moral philosophy with children and youth. However, we do not subscribe to moral relativism; what is the difference?
2. What are some of the obstacles one might encounter trying to employ a dialogic approach to education in a traditional youth sport program situated in an urban environment?

3. How could current coaches, teachers, and youth workers who tend to operate from the banking concept of education be introduced to and trained in using the dialogic approach in ways that would make it clear enough and compelling enough that they might adopt it and change their practice accordingly?

Appendix

A dialogue on fairness

Scene: The conclusion of a soccer game
Characters: Derrick, Elicia, Andre
Keywords: advantage, cheating, fair, unfair (in italics)

DERRICK: Hey Elicia! Great game!

ELICIA: Yeah, I'm not so sure about that.

DERRICK: Why? What's wrong?

ELICIA: Well, the winning goal I scored shouldn't have counted. I used my hand to knock the ball across the goal line. So, we won but we had a clear *advantage* with that play not being seen by the referee.

ANDRE: Well, didn't the other team have an *advantage* over your team too?

ELICIA: What do you mean?

ANDRE: Think of it this way. The team you were playing was older than your team and bigger too. That was definitely an *advantage* for them. So, I say both teams had *advantages* and they cancel each other out.

ELICIA: But the issue isn't just about having an *advantage*. My *advantage* was *unfair*. After all, they weren't *cheating*. It's not always against the rules for a team to be older or bigger than another team. But it's always against the rules to use your hands to score a goal in soccer.

DERRICK: That's true. But I still don't see why that makes their *advantage* (being older and bigger) *fair*, while your *advantage* (the handball goal) is *unfair*. It seems to me we need to figure out what kinds of *advantages* are *fair* and what kinds of *advantages* are *unfair*.

ANDRE: How about this: an *advantage* is *fair* when the majority of the group believes it to be *fair*, *unfair* when the majority of the group believes it to be *unfair*.

ELICIA: That seems like it could cause a lot of problems though.

ANDRE: Why?

DERRICK: Well, with that idea of *fairness* can't anything end up being *fair*?

ANDRE: Sure. Whatever the majority thinks is *fair* just is *fair*.

ELICIA: What if the majority of the players on the field think that tackling other players during the game or using their hands is *fair*? We wouldn't even be playing soccer anymore. And, besides, is what is *fair* really just a matter of majority opinion?

DERRICK: Yeah. Elicia has a point. I think that certain things are *fair* and certain things are *unfair* whether the majority of people think so or not.

ANDRE: OK. Like what?

DERRICK: Well, I'm not sure. I need to think about it some more. But I still think that there is a lot more to something being *fair* or *unfair* than majority opinion.

References

Bond, B. and Sherman, J. (2003) *Memphis in Black and White*. Mount Pleasant, SC: Arcadia Publishing.

Cothran, D. J. and Ennis, C. D. (1999) 'Alone in a crowd: Meeting students' needs for relevance and connection in urban high school physical education', *Journal of Teaching in Physical Education*, 18: 234–47.

Cutforth, N. and Puckett, K. (1999) 'An investigation into the organization, challenges, and impact of an urban apprentice teacher program', *The Urban Review*, 31: 153–72.

DeBusk, M. and Hellison, D. (1989) 'Implementing a physical education self responsibility model for delinquency prone youth', *Journal of Teaching in Physical Education*, 8: 104–12.

Ennis, C. D. (1999) 'Communicating the value of active, healthy lifestyles to urban students', *Quest*, 51: 164–69.

Ennis, C. D., Solmon, M. A., Satina, B., Loftus, S. J., Mensch, J. and McCauley, M. T. (1999) 'Creating a sense of family in urban schools using the "sport for peace" curriculum', *Research Quarterly for Exercise and Sport*, 70: 273–85.

Freire, P. (2003) *Pedagogy of the Oppressed*. New York: Continuum.

Harrison, L. (2001) 'Understanding the influence of stereotypes: Implications for the African American in sport and physical activity', *Quest*, 53: 97–114.

Harrison, L. and Worthy, T. (2001) 'Just like all the rest: Developing awareness of stereotypical thinking in the physical education classroom', *Journal of Physical Education, Recreation, and Dance*, 72: 20–24.

Hellison, D. (2010) *Teaching Responsibility Through Physical Activity* (3rd edn). Champaign, IL: Human Kinetics.

Hellison, D. and Martinek, T. (2006) 'Social and individual responsibility programs', in D. Kirk, D. Macdonald and M. O'Sullivan (eds) *The Handbook of Physical Education*. Thousand Oaks, CA: Sage, pp. 610–26.

Hsu, L. (2004) 'Moral thinking, sports rules and education', *Sport, Education and Society*, 14: 339–52.

Lee, O. and Martinek, T. (2009) 'Navigating two cultures: An investigation of cultures of a responsibility-based physical activity program and school', *Research Quarterly for Exercise and Sport*, 80: 230–40.

Martinek, T., Schilling, T. and Johnson, D. (2001) 'Evaluation of a sport and mentoring program designed to foster personal and social responsibility in underserved youth', *The Urban Review*, 33: 29–45.

Matthews, G. B. (1984) *Dialogues with Children*. Cambridge, MA: Harvard University Press.

McLaughlin, M. W., Irby, M. A. and Langman, J. (1994) *Urban Sanctuaries: Neighborhood Organizations in the Lives and Futures of Inner City Youth*. San Francisco, CA: Jossey-Bass.

Miller, S. C., Bredemeier, B. J. L. and Shields, D. L. L. (1997) 'Sociomoral education through physical education with at-risk children', *Quest*, 49: 114–29.

Morgan, W. J. (2006) 'Philosophy and physical education', in D. Kirk, D. Macdonald and M. O'Sullivan (eds) *The Handbook of Physical Education*. Thousand Oaks, CA: Sage, pp. 97–108.

Panathlon International (2004) Panathlon Declaration on Ethics in Youth Sport. Available at: http://www.paralympic.org/export/sites/default/IPC/IPC_Handbook/Section_2/Panathlonx20Declarationx20English.pdf (accessed 30 January 2012).

Rushing, W. (2009) *Memphis and the Paradox of Place: Globalization in the American South*, Chapel Hill, NC: University of North Carolina Press.

Sandford, R. A., Armour, K. M. and Warmington, P. C. (2006) 'Re-engaging disaffected youth through physical activity programmes', *British Educational Research Journal*, 32: 251–71.

Schilling, T. A., Martinek, T. and Carson, S. (2007) 'Youth leaders' perceptions of commitment to a responsibility-based physical activity program', *Research Quarterly for Exercise and Sport*, 78: 48–60.

Shields, D. L. L. and Bredemeier, B. J. L. (1995) *Character Development and Physical Activity*. Champaign, IL: Human Kinetics.

State of Tennessee (2012) Tennessee Department of Education Report Card on Tennessee Schools. Available at: http://www.tn.gov/education/reportcard (accessed 29 January 2012).

US Centers for Disease Control and Prevention (2012) Youth online: high school youth risk behaviour survey, Memphis, TN 2009 and United States 2009 results. Available at: http://apps.nccd.cdc.gov/youthonline/App/Results.aspx (accessed 29 January 2012).

US Federal Bureau of Investigation (2010) *Uniform Crime Reports*. Available at: http://www.fbi.gov/about-us/cjis/ucr/ucr (accessed 29 January 2012).

US Government (2012) *Healthy People 2020 – Improving the Health of Americans*. Available at: http://www.healthypeople.gov/2020 (accessed 29 January 2012).

Walsh, D. (2008) 'Helping youth in underserved communities envision possible futures: An extension of the Teaching Personal and Social Responsibility model', *Research Quarterly for Exercise and Sport*, 79: 209–21.

Walsh, D., Ozaeta, J. and Wright, P. M. (2010) 'Transference of responsibility model goals to the school environment: Exploring the impact of a coaching club program', *Physical Education and Sport Pedagogy*, 15: 15–28.

Wright, P. M. and Burton, S. (2008) 'Examining the implementation and immediate outcomes of a personal-social responsibility model program for urban high school students', *Journal of Teaching in Physical Education*, 27: 138–54.

Wright, P. M., Li, W., Ding, S. and Pickering, M. (2010) 'Integrating a personal-social responsibility program into a lifetime wellness course for urban high school students: Assessing implementation and educational outcomes', *Sport, Education, and Society*, 15: 277–98.

13 Rethinking inclusion through the lens of ethical education

Hayley Fitzgerald

Introduction: the heterogeneous gym

For some time educators have been aware of the diversity of pupils in their classes. The account quoted below, from Hellison and Templin (1991: 27), reflects multiplicity and I am sure if you consider your own teaching or coaching experiences other kinds of differences will also come to mind.

> Billy wants to be there, Mary doesn't. Suzi is an exceptionally skilled athlete, Joey has difficulty with any physical activity. Danny is back in school after two suspensions, Karen has a perfect attendance record. Pam is epileptic, Larry is learning disabled, and Dave has a congenital heart defect. Tom constantly complains, and Don brings the teacher an apple every day. Andrew is a 4-foot, 5-inch ninth grader, and Jack is a 6-foot, 5-inch ninth grader. Kay's father is the CEO of one of the country's largest companies, and they live in the suburbs; Sue lives with her divorced mother in the inner city, and they are on welfare.

Internationally, with an increasing acknowledgement of diversity in schools and other community contexts has come greater recognition for the need to work towards inclusive practice (Peters 2007; Gabel and Danforth 2008). Inclusion has become 'the mantra of education systems worldwide' (Rioux and Pinto 2010: 622). Indeed, it has steadily permeated physical education and youth sport, and we continue to be bombarded with an assortment of messages reminding us to be inclusive. This includes the *inclusion talk* in the school staff room, the featured articles in professional journals, or (yet) another new education or sports policy making inclusion central. Some of you may have even studied a programme or participated in professional development that focuses on inclusive practice. *Inclusion* is a term that seems increasingly to slip off the tongue of practitioners, academics and politicians. Within physical education and youth sport it is the mantra of the moment and implicitly recognized within the Panathlon Declaration on Ethics in Youth Sport (Panathlon International 2004). Inclusion seems to be the 'right thing' to incorporate in our professional vocabulary – the extent to which it is embedded into professional practice is of course a very different matter.

This chapter interrogates the mantra of inclusion by focusing on issues concerning disability. In doing this I take up Ware's call to include issues concerning disability within education. Ware argues: '[D]isability is a long overdue conversation among critical theorists, pedagogues, and educationalists who fail to recognize disability as a cultural signifier; nor do they include disability as a meaningful category of oppression' (2001: 112). The recent special edition of the *British Journal of the Sociology of Education*, entitled 'Sociology of disability and education', perhaps signals the positive developments that have occurred since Ware's observations. However, the kind of thinking found in this special edition has yet to be embraced within physical education and youth sport scholarship and thinking. This chapter first of all provides a brief reminder of the ways in which disabled people[1] have historically been treated and understood within society. After this, I offer a number of short interview extracts generated from young disabled people that focus on their reflections of physical education and youth sport. By drawing on the ten criteria of ethical education outlined by Fernández-Balboa (2011), I reflect on these extracts and discuss the utility of rethinking inclusion through this lens. I argue that this alternative vantage point offers greater possibilities for educators, researchers and policy developers to think inclusively. My concluding remarks serve as a reminder of the importance of considering the person first and foremost, rather than being overly concerned with defining or describing their disability. I contend that practising in ways that promote an ethical education will enable practitioners, researchers and policy developers to work in a more meaningful way with (disabled) pupils in order that they can experience positive and fulfilling youth sport.

Disabled people, inclusion and youth sport

We only have to look back at recent history to get a sense of the way in which disabled people have been treated and understood in life generally and in youth sport. For example, in 1972 Miller and Gwynne published *A Life Apart: A Pilot Study of Residential Institutions for the Physically Handicapped and the Young Chronic Sick*. This book explores the day-to-day experiences of staff and residents at a number of institutions in the United Kingdom (UK). Of the residents it was observed that:

> To lack any actual or potential role that confers a positive social status in the wider society is tantamount to being socially dead. To be admitted to one of these institutions is to enter a kind of limbo in which one has been written off as a member of society but is not yet physically dead. In these terms, the task that society assigns – behaviourally though never verbally – to these institutions is to cater for the socially dead during the interval between social death and physical death.
>
> (Miller and Gwynne 1972: 80)

Similarly, the narratives found in *Stigma: The Experience of Disability* (Hunt 1966) provide a unique understanding of the lived experiences of 12 disabled people. In the 'Foreword', Townsend describes what was to follow as 'an uncomfortable book' because:

> it reveals how inadequate are the existing services for the disabled in Britain. ... It shows that these inadequacies are not just unwitting gaps in the outer fabric of the Welfare State which would be filled if called to public attention. They reflect a much deeper problem of a distortion of the structure and of the value-system of society itself. ... Incapacity, unproductiveness, slowness and old age are implicitly if not explicitly deplored.
>
> (in Hunt 1966: vi)

This extract from Paul Hunt's narrative emphasizes the kinds of reactions he has encountered to his disability:

> Those we meet cannot fail to notice our disablement even if they turn away quickly and avoid thinking about us afterwards. An impaired and deformed body is a 'difference' that hits every-one hard at first. Inevitably it produces an instinctive revulsion, has a disturbing effect.
>
> (Hunt 1966: 150)

Margaret Gill's narrative provides a perspective of those living in 'mainstream' society and offers a glimpse into physical education:

> The 'I wants' of childhood become 'I want to be normal'; 'I want to run in the races, play football, netball, tennis, like the others'. The reply from his classmates is invariably the hard truth: 'We don't want you; you are too slow; we shall never win if *you* are with us'; and when it is time to 'pick teams' the disabled child is always left until the last.
>
> (in Hunt 1966: 100)

All these accounts serve as powerful reminders of the ways in which disabled people have historically been marginalized and 'othered' within society (Shakespeare 1994). I am sure most readers hope that these accounts are a thing of the past and not reflective of understandings in today's society. Of course a major shift in the UK and internationally since the publication of *A Life Apart* and *Stigma: The Experience of Disability* has been deinstitutionalization, the development of anti-discriminatory legislation and the implementation of policies that seek to redress inequalities experienced by disabled people (Goodley 2011; Slee 2011). For example, the UK Equity Act (2010) requires public bodies to develop an equality scheme and action plan in order to demonstrate how people will be protected from discrimination and how equality and diversity will be promoted across the key equality strands, including disability. Internationally, within a sporting context, there is growing recognition that disabled people have a 'right' to sport. The United Nations Convention on the Rights of Persons with Disabilities (United Nations 2006) explicitly expresses this right, as do a number of international sporting organizations (International Council for Sport Science and Physical Education 2003; International Disability in Sport Working Group 2007). Coupled with this kind of recognition there have also been specific policy developments in sport (Thomas and Smith 2009) and education (Peters 2007; Gabel and Danforth 2008) that seek to promote inclusion.

While the rationale for supporting the inclusion of disabled people in education and sport has been advocated through human rights, legislation, policy, programmes and curricula, there continues to be confusion about what constitutes inclusion and how practitioners can best work towards it (Morley *et al.* 2005; Jerlinder *et al.* 2009; Stevenson 2009; Vickerman and Coates 2009; Haycock and Smith 2010, 2011). For example, Haycock and Smith (2010) found that teachers claimed to be working towards inclusion using practices that could also be viewed as promoting exclusion. Such practices included separating disabled pupils from the main class, engagement in easily adaptable activities and using non-physical education staff to support disabled pupils. Slee and Allan (2001: 181) contend that 'we are still citing inclusion as our goal; still waiting to include, yet speaking as if we are already inclusive'. That is, the mantra of inclusion is all around us but its tangibility is less self-evident. Within physical education and youth sport I would argue that there has been little desire to make tangible understandings of inclusive practice. If there was such an appetite we would already know (or at least be grappling with) the answers to these critical questions: 'What do we *mean* when we talk of including? What *happens*? *Whose* interests are being served? And most of all, into *what* do we seek to include?' (Graham and Slee 2008: 95). One way of shedding light on some of these questions is to consider the views of disabled young people and their accounts of physical education and youth sport. As I have argued elsewhere, it is important to listen to the voices of young disabled people in order that we can critically reflect on how to better support positive physical education and youth sport experiences (Fitzgerald *et al.* 2003; Fitzgerald 2009). With this in mind, I next offer a number of short interview extracts generated from young disabled people that focus on their reflections of physical education and youth sport. The interviews used in this chapter are taken from a larger research project involving 35 mainstream ('regular') schools in the Midlands of England (data from this research are reported elsewhere; see, for example, Fitzgerald 2005 and Fitzgerald and Kirk 2009).

Reflections of (inclusive) physical education

Schools and universities are contexts in which one can oppress or liberate, care for others or mistreat them, foster dignity or frustrate it, awaken private and social awareness, or promote mediocrity and passivity. Whether educators do one thing or another depends on having or lacking ethical principles.

(Fernández-Balboa 2011: 44)

I'm in the problem pile – Jane

I used to do PE, like when the others did, you know every week. I'd be with the class and we'd do stuff like dance and rounders and games. Rounders was the best. I liked PE, I knew I could do what Mrs Jones told me. One time she got me to show the rest of 'em this dance move. She said my style was good. Look like this [demonstrates the dance move], see. Yeah, it was the one thing I told me Mum about and I could tell Mum was pleased and then I had to show Nan. Once on Sports Day I got third for the running, the short not long [race]. ... Like I say, that was in primary school. It's changed now, now I'm at the high school. PE's changed, big changes, I miss primary for that, it's like my PE time has stopped. Just for me and I don't know why. Mum doesn't get it and has seen Mr Robinson [form tutor]. The [physical education] teacher doesn't like me and I get asked all the time, 'do you want to sit out'. I feel like if I do it [take part in physical education] I'm getting in the way. I say I'm not bothered and the teacher tells me to go to the computers. It's not bad really, getting homework done at school. What I feel like is, it's like the teacher sorts problems out all in one go, no kit, wrong kit, misbehaving and me. Can you see I'm on the problem pile? PE is over for me.

Mr Morgan is the best – Paul

In a word I say PE is brill. It's not my favourite but it's up there with ICT and Science. I have Mr Morgan and he is the best one [physical education teacher] here and it's not just me saying it, you ask the others over there. ... He is bothered about me and how I get on. He'll check stuff and it helps him to know I'll get on OK. Like the other week we started basketball and he wanted to know if I'd be able to dribble using my crutch. I knew I could, I've done it before. I showed him. But 'cause of my crutch I can't dribble with one and then the other, you know, for getting round people. 'Cause Mr Morgan knows I can't he set up two skills and we had to pick one. That's good 'cause then I do the practice like everyone. You know, you need to practise to get better. ... He's [Mr Morgan] got this thing about changing partners, like I'll be with three or four people. To start with it was a big pain, and I know, I could tell, people didn't want to be with me. What it is, it's them looking at me funny 'cause of my crutches? I know my leg's a bit different but I can pretty much do most stuff. Well, balancing isn't my thing, hate beams, my arms go all over the place. Brian Smith is the worst partner 'cause he kicks my crutches, on purpose like, and shouts if I'm slow. But, well, the rest are good and get on OK. I like working with Jim, Steve, Mark the best. They aren't bothered 'bout my crutches and just know what to do like Mark, he'll say 'lets' do it like this' and Mr Morgan will tell us we're doing a good job and been creative. I reckon they'll make good PE teachers, just like me.

I'm not a PE person – Dave

I'm not a PE person. I hate PE. Why do they make me do PE? It is a waste of time, the worst thing. PE is for them, you know the ones. The sporty boys, the tough guys, the ones that have loads of mates, the ones the girls like, 'cause they're fit and fast, with muscles that'll get bigger and better. Yeah, that's what they are, winners. The worst time for me is when they pick teams, no one wants to be with me. God, I hate that part of PE. I just stand there, I can't look up, it's the worst thing. I am always last and then well the teacher [Mr Browne] makes it worse, 'And who's last? It's Dave. You'll have to go there.' He doesn't like me, I can tell. He never has a good word to say and doesn't bother 'bout me. I get 'Dave you sit out for this' and I'm like thinking this isn't PE, PE is about doing, moving, activity not sitting. When I'm told, I just sit out. ... Yeah, I've seen, it's Jack, Matthew, Stephen who he's with all the time. Why's he helping the good ones? Whereas me, he keeps away. For just one time I'd like all that to be different, yeah for it to be fun for everyone and not just them good ones. You know, I'd say I try really hard but that doesn't get me nowhere and no one notices. ... I wish the [physical education] teacher was me, like the film, have you seen it, when people swap, get to be the other. Then he'd see it's hard to do PE, how they all, all of them stare, he'd see how miserable it is.

Going to the Ability Sports Club – James

When I go to Ability [a sports club] you get all kinds there. Like, on a good night there'll be six, seven frames and two or three wheelchairs. We're all the same like in a chair, frame and that's fair like we're all the same. ... It's different than PE, well, like in the big class mostly able-bodied kids, like a couple of wheelchairs. So mostly I stick out in PE and it's hard, the teacher doesn't help me. Ability [Sports Club] is different, we are all the same. Geoff, the coach, has his hands full, he knows we all want to do well and get better. ... [At the club] it's a lot more competitive, even like practising we all want to get better and like we'll work. Like if you don't, you're not going to get better for games and that. I know Geoff wants us all to do well. We get a goal each week. Like the other week it was 'better passing'. Geoff reckons I hold onto the ball too much. I can see what he's saying but sometimes I get carried away, and panic, and just hold on. Geoff told us as well that if we're in a team we need to use the team. He yells, 'use your team, use your team, your team can help you'. Now, I can see I'm thinking more about passing and he's right it opens the game up and everyone is part of the game.

Rethinking inclusion through the lens of ethical education

It is important to recognize that each of us will read these short extracts in different ways. When you read them were any of these stories familiar to you? Did you feel any empathy towards Jane, Paul, Dave or James? In what ways will these reflections help you to begin to consider the questions posed by Graham and Slee (2008) around the meaning and interests served in these 'inclusive' contexts? When I read Dave's and Jane's accounts I was struck by the piecemeal attempts that seem to have been made to work towards inclusive practice. In fact, Dave's account portrays his physical education teacher as someone who is positively promoting exclusion rather than inclusion. In this era of inclusion, Dave's and Jane's reflections also reminded me of other research that reveals far from positive physical education and youth sport experiences (for a review see Vickerman and Coates 2008). Indeed, disabled pupils can feel marginalized when teachers allocate different activities, structure participation in different places, give prominence to other 'bodies' perceived as more able and grant exemptions from part or all of a physical education lesson (Fitzgerald 2005). Individually, each of these practices may not be considered as exclusionary but if pupils are continually exposed to a combination of these it is easy to see how physical education can become an isolating and negative experience for many young people. Some commentators have argued that the continued replication of such practices will ultimately threaten the broader legitimacy of physical education: 'School physical education and sport may be in crisis, at least in part because they represent a series of modernist bodily practices concerned with normalizing and regulating children's bodies through methods and strategies which are perhaps already culturally obsolete' (Kirk 2004: 63). With this broader evidence in mind, I am left wondering if, after nearly 20 years of promoting a mantra of inclusion, we should perhaps reconsider how we can support practitioners such as (community) sports coaches and those engaged in physical education teacher education (PETE) to think inclusively in ways that move beyond the superficiality currently evident.

In part this could be achieved by refocusing on what Westcombe-Down (2009: 20) calls a pedagogically fit teacher. That is a teacher who 'establishes and maintains a positive, inclusive and safe learning environment'. Such a teacher may, for example, recognize that 'one size' does not fit all and in this way work to support personalized learning. In this environment you might reasonably expect pupil confidence, skills and values to be positively nurtured. Qualities less evident from my reading of Dave's and Jane's interview extracts. A pedagogically fit teacher would also be attentive to the need to promote an ethical education. Of course, this is not a new approach to conceptualizing the work of educators. For example, Fernández-Balboa (2011) outlines ten criteria, and associated questions, that should be considered in relation to an ethical education. These are:

1. Direct evidence – 'Can educators affirm with evidence that the education they provide is desirable, beneficial, and dignifying to students and society?'
2. Transcendence – 'Is what educators do absolutely necessary and transcendent for students and society?'
3. Coherence – 'Can educators show that their pedagogy (including principles, purposes, contents, and methods) is consistent with the principles of Universal Dignity?'
4. Consequences – 'What are the consequences, concerning individual and social benefits, of what educators do and teach in the classroom? Who are the beneficiaries and who loses out?'
5. Progress – 'Do educators take the lives of their students to higher levels regarding Dignity, self-esteem, compassion, and so on?'
6. Conservation – 'In what ways and by what means do educators teach *pick-ack nefesh* (life/soul preservation) and *tikkum olam* (world reparation)?'
7. Acknowledgement – 'Do educators acknowledge students' Dignity as an intrinsic value? Is Dignity recognized in explicit form in curricula, methods and classroom relations?'
8. Reciprocity – 'Do educators realize that what they give is what they could directly or indirectly receive? Do they know that their action has an effect in the world that, eventually, will affect them and their descendants?'
9. Fallibility – 'In their ideas and deeds *in* and on *education* (and life in general), do educators accept that they may be mistaken? Do they consider and accept alternative viewpoints?'
10. Humility – 'Are educators sufficiently humble to accept their own limitations and admit that many of their actions and beliefs may lack essence, congruence, and significance?'

(Fernández-Balboa 2011: 50–1)

Educators can use these criteria to reflect on their pedagogical performance. Although it should be acknowledged that this process can be challenging for some practitioners who may not relish the prospect of such self-reflection. According to Fernández-Balboa (2009: 149): 'I may be scared of facing parts of ourselves and experiences associated with pain, guilt, danger, insecurity, etc. Not everyone is prepared to do so.' A useful way of beginning to bridge this kind of self-reflective impasse is to encourage reflection through the experiences of others. So, next, I will briefly take the extracts from Jane, Paul, Dave and James and reflect on what these tell me about how their physical education teachers and coach are practising in relation to the criteria for ethical education.

From my reading of Jane's reflection of physical education at her primary school, Paul's account and James's, I gleaned a sense they were benefiting in a positive manner from their physical education and youth sport experiences. The *direct evidence* is reflected in the ways they mention their physical education teachers and coach as recognizing their achievements (Jane), respecting and listening to their views (Paul) and expressing a desire to do well (James). Paul's extract also highlights two other important features of his teacher's practice. First, he explains that his physical education teacher adopted a strategy of regularly alternating practice partners. In doing this Paul is exposed to different classmates and the *reciprocity* in the longer term, for pupils like Jim, Steve and Mark, may be a better understanding and appreciation of other disabled people in society. Second, Paul's extract draws attention to the way his physical education teacher offers a number of alternative practice activities. For Paul, the short-term *consequence* is skill *progression* that can be utilized in game play situations. Similarly, the extract from James illustrates *consequences* associated with the development of specific passing skills and *progress* regarding a greater awareness of working with other team members. By adopting a pedagogy that offers Paul and James this possibility, these practitioners are providing the 'colourful threads' that promote *Universal Dignity* (Fernández-Balboa 2011: 45).

What is interesting about James's extract is the contrast in experience between physical education and community sport (Ability Sports Club). He describes physical education as a place where he 'sticks out' and 'the teacher doesn't help'. However, his account of the Ability Sports Club offers the possibilities for far more positive *consequences* and *progress*. In light of these different experiences, I am left wondering why, in spite of negative reflections of physical education, James has been motivated to engage in community sport. Moreover, what is it that the community coach is doing to promote a positive outlook towards sport? These would seem to be questions that an inclusive practitioner should also want to explore in order to promote positive experiences within physical education and youth sport.

Jane, like Dave, seems to get little *transcendence* (inspiration) from their high school physical education experiences. The *consequences* for them may be feelings of continued alienation towards physical education. Jane is at least extracted from her physical education environment but in this way her self-esteem and *dignity* through physical education will not *progress* to higher levels. Dave, however, has to continue to endure physical education and this remains a negative experience. Interestingly, Dave is able to maturely reflect on his experiences and makes the astute suggestion that his physical education teacher should try to be him in order to better understand his experiences of physical education. There seemed to be little *humility* and *conservation*; instead *fallibility* is evident in Jane's and Dave's reflections of their teachers' (in)actions. In Fernández-Balboa's (2009) terms one might liken the actions of these teachers to a 'poisonous pedagogy'. Of course the *consequences* and implications of Jane's and Dave's physical education experiences reach far beyond their time at school and could impact on their lifetime outlook towards community sport. To this end their teachers are not *acknowledging dignity* as an intrinsic value, and instead disregard the possibility that their practices may impact on the pupils in the longer term.

Closing remarks

When I have shared the interview extracts from Jane, Paul, Dave and James with my undergraduates I always ask if there are any questions they want to ask about these pupils that will help them with their reflections of the ethical practices of the physical education teachers. Do you have a question? I can guarantee at least half of the class want to know about the pupils' disabilities. I purposefully do not state this, nor do I answer this question. My reason for this response is because, more than anything, an ethical (and inclusive) educator should focus on *who* their pupil is rather than concerning themselves with medically defined labels. Do not obscure your views of the disabled pupils you will teach by immediately seeking out the answer to this question. They are so much more than their disability and an ethical educator will be attentive to the whole person. Here I am not suggesting that disability does not matter but rather that it is a question to be considered once you know your pupil(s). According to Fernández-Balboa (2011: 51), 'walking the talk of ethics in the practice of education' is not an easy task, it is one though, that all educators should be working towards if they are truly concerned with including *all* young people in (physical) education and youth sport.

If inclusion was working in our schools and sports clubs there would not be a need for this chapter. As already indicated, I am inclined to conclude that inclusion is not working, although by saying this I am not suggesting I know exactly what inclusion is, what it feels or looks like. I am merely observing that while the material experiences of disabled young people in physical education and youth sport contexts do not improve, then inclusion cannot be working. Educators should be preoccupied and concerned as to why this is the case. This may be a 'scary' (Fernández-Balboa 2009) and 'uncomfortable' (Townsend in Hunt 1966) proposition to contemplate but it is one that requires serious attention. In this chapter I have offered one way of moving such discussions forward by rethinking inclusion through the lens of ethical education. I hope this provides a starting point for your self-reflection and ongoing critical dialogue.

Discussion Questions

1. Westcombe-Down (2009) suggests a pedagogically fit teacher 'establishes and maintains a positive, inclusive and safe learning environment'. Outline a recent teaching/coaching experience where you felt you were achieving these outcomes. In relation to an ethical education, what 'direct evidence' (criterion 1) do you have to support what you say?
2. If you were providing professional development to Jane's and Dave's physical education teachers how would you go about supporting them to reflect upon the ten criteria relating to an ethical education?
3. Some scholars claim that inclusive physical education will not be possible without radical reform of the subject. Discuss how physical education needs to change in order to become more inclusive.

Read the four short interview extracts from Jane, Paul, Dave or James and consider how you would work to change their experiences of physical education and youth sport.

Note

1 I acknowledge that the international audience of this chapter will have different expectations regarding the way in which disability and disabled people are understood. Given that this chapter has been influenced by literature from British Disability Studies I believe it is important to adopt the understanding of disability found within this field. This includes referring to 'disabled people' rather than 'people with disabilities'. See, for example, Barnes *et al.* (1999: 7): 'We will avoid the phrase "people with disabilities" because it implies that the impairment defines the identity of the individual, blurs the crucial conceptual distinction between impairment and disability and avoids the question of causality.' This understanding of disability is also accepted and used by the British Council for Disabled People (BCDP) and the Disabled Peoples' International (DPI).

References

Barnes, C., Mercer, G. and Shakespeare, T. (1999) *Exploring Disability: A Sociological Introduction*. Cambridge: Polity Press.

Fernández-Balboa, J. (2009) 'Bio-pedagogical self-reflection in PETE: Reawakening the ethical conscience and purpose in pedagogy and research', *Sport, Education and Society*, 14(2): 147–63.

Fernández-Balboa, J. (2011) 'Sailing towards "Happycity": Ethics plus education', in J. A. Kentel (ed.) *Educating the Young: The Ethics of Care*. Oxford: Peter Lang, pp. 39–60.

Fitzgerald, H. (2005) 'Still feeling like a spare piece of luggage? Embodied experiences of (dis)ability in physical education and school sport', *Physical Education and Sport Pedagogy*, 10(1): 41–59.

Fitzgerald, H. (2009) 'Are you a "parasite researcher"? Researching with young disabled people', in H. Fitzgerald (ed.) *Disability and Youth Sport*. London: Routledge, pp. 145–59.

Fitzgerald, H. and Kirk, D. (2009) 'Identity work: Young disabled people, family and sport', *Leisure Studies*, 28(4): 469–88.

Fitzgerald, H., Jobling, A. and Kirk, D. (2003) 'Valuing the voices of young disabled people: Exploring experiences of physical education and sport', *Physical Education and Sport Pedagogy*, 8(1): 175–201.

Gabel, S. L. and Danforth, S. (2008) 'Disability and the international politics of education', in S. L. Gabel and S. Danforth (eds) *Disability and the Politics of Education: An International Reader*. Oxford: Peter Lang, pp. 1–13.

Goodley, D. (2011) *Disability Studies: An Interdisciplinary Introduction*. London: Sage.

Graham, L. J. and Slee, R. (2008) 'Inclusion?', in S. L. Gabel and S. Danforth (eds) *Disability and the Politics of Education: An International Reader*. Oxford: Peter Lang, pp. 81–99.

Haycock, D. and Smith, A. (2010) 'Inclusive physical education? A study of the management of national curriculum physical education and unplanned outcomes in England', *British Journal of Sociology of Education*, 31(3): 291–305.

Haycock, D. and Smith, A. (2011) 'Still "more of the same for the more able?" Including young disabled people and pupils with special educational needs in extra-curricular physical education', *Sport Education and Society*, 16(4): 507–26.

Hellison, D. R. and Templin, T. J. (1991) *A Reflective Approach to Teaching Physical Education*. Champaign, IL: Human Kinetics.

Hunt, P. (ed.) (1966) *Stigma: The Experience of Disability*. London: Geoffrey Chapman.

International Council for Sport Science and Physical Education (2003) *Young People with Disabilities in Physical Education/Physical Activity/Sport In and Out of Schools: Technical Report for the World Health Organization*. Geneva: World Health Organization.

International Disability in Sport Working Group (2007) *Sport in the United Nations Convention on the Rights of Persons with Disabilities*. Boston, MA: International Disability in Sport Working Group/United Nations Office of the Special Advisor to the Secretary-General on Sport for Development and Peace.

Jerlinder, K., Danermark, B. and Gill, P. (2009) 'Normative approaches to justice in physical education for pupils with physical disabilities – dilemmas of recognition and redistribution', *Disability and Society*, 24(3): 331–42.

Kirk, D. (2004) 'Corporal power and school practice', in J. Evans, B. Davies and J. Wright (eds) *Body Knowledge and Social Control Studies in the Sociology of Physical Education and Health*. London: Routledge.

Miller, E. J. and Gwynne, G. V. (1972) *A Life Apart: A Pilot Study of Residential Institutions for the Physically Handicapped and the Young Chronic Sick*. London: Tavistock.

Morley, D., Bailey, R., Tan, J. and Cooke, B. (2005) 'Inclusive physical education: Teachers' views of including pupils with special educational needs and/or disabilities in physical education', *European Physical Education Review*, 11(1): 84–107.

Panathlon International (2004) Declaration on Ethics in Youth Sport. Available at: http://www.panathlon.net (accessed 23 January 2012).

Peters, S. (2007) '"Education for all"? A historical analysis of international inclusive education policy and individuals with disabilities', *Journal of Disability Policy Studies*, 18(1): 98–108.

Rioux, M. H. and Pinto, P. C. (2010) 'A time for the universal right to education: Back to basics', *British Journal of Sociology of Education*, 35(5): 621–42.

Shakespeare, T. (1994) 'Cultural representation of disabled people: Dustbins for disavowal?', *Disability and Society*, 9(3): 283–99.

Slee, R. (2011) *The Irregular School: Exclusion, Schooling and Inclusive Education*. London: Routledge.

Slee, R. and Allan, J. (2001) 'Excluding the included: A recognition of inclusive education', *International Studies in Sociology of Education*, 11(2): 173–91.

Stevenson, P. (2009) 'The pedagogy of inclusive youth sport: Working towards real solutions', in H. Fitzgerald (ed.) *Disability and Youth Sport*. London: Routledge, pp. 119–31.

Thomas, N. and Smith, A. (2009) *Disability, Sport and Society: An Introduction*. London: Routledge.

United Nations (2006) Convention on the Rights of Persons with Disabilities. Available at: http://www.un.org/disabilities/convention/conventionfull.shtml (accessed 9 January 2009).

Vickerman, P. and Coates, J. (2008) 'Let the children have their say: Children with special educational needs and their experiences of physical education – a review', *Support for Learning*, 23(4): 168–75.

Vickerman, P. and Coates, J. (2009) 'Trainee and recently qualified physical education teachers' perspectives on including children with special educational needs', *Physical Education and Sport Pedagogy*, 14(2): 137–53.

Ware, L. (2001) 'Writing, identity, and the other: Dare we do Disability Studies?', *Journal of Teacher Education*, 52(2): 107–23.

Westcombe-Down, D. (2009) 'Pedagogical fitness, teacher quality', *Professional Educator*, 8(1): 18–21.

Conclusions

Stephen Harvey and Richard L. Light

The chapters in this volume are written on a range of topics related to the ethical practice of youth sport from different perspectives, and by authors from different cultural settings, but there are some clear common themes that emerge from them. They all suggest that sport has great potential as a medium for fostering children's positive social, moral and ethical development, but confirm previous warnings that this development is not automatically achieved by mere engagement in sport (Siedentop *et al.* 2004). Many chapters in this book remind us of the countless recurrences of negative issues in youth sport, such as cheating, negative coaching, physical, sexual and emotional abuse, and player/spectator violence. These practices present a constant threat to the ethical practice of youth sport and we must acknowledge that, in part, these may be attributable to an adult-centric version of youth sport with an overemphasis on winning, particularly by over-zealous adults such as coaches and parents.

While the chapters in this book emphasize these threats to youth sport, they also provide positive and practical suggestions for responding to them. Perhaps the strongest message to come through is that, for sport to realize its potential as a medium for positive social, moral and ethical learning, these must be intentionally taught, since they are not necessarily 'caught' in the sense that they are born out of experience (Twietmeyer 2007). For children to receive an ethical education through sport there are still many challenges at the macro (policy and strategy), meso (professional and institutional) and micro (personal and social) levels of youth sport. We therefore conclude by offering some thoughts at these three levels in terms of: (1) policy, (2) the structures of youth sport, and (3) the pedagogies employed by those teachers and coaches involved in physical education and youth sport (while recognizing that pedagogy is deeply embedded in and shaped by larger social and cultural fields). We look at these challenges separately below, but appreciate their inherent interconnectedness.

Policy

In several chapters in this book the authors have argued that the ongoing and future development of sport as an ethical practice is dependent upon youth sport practitioners possessing a sound awareness of child development (see Kerr and Stirling, Chapter 2) as well as a consciousness of, and adherence to, codes of ethical practice such as the Panathlon Declaration on Ethics in Youth Sport (Panathlon International 2004). This, in turn, requires clear, well-articulated policies that can be implemented in ways that will actually have an effect upon practice, avoiding what Maesschalck and Vanden Auweele refer to as the 'implementation deficit' in Chapter 1. The need for appropriate preventive policies and safeguards for coaches, parents and performers within youth sport education programmes is a point made abundantly clear by Van Veldhoven in Chapter 8. These policies and safeguards are necessary in order to create laws that bind professional practice but also to ensure accountability.

At the 'Janus conference', held 3–5 March 2000, ten prominent scholars in physical education discussed its future in the twenty-first century. In responding to an article written by Judith Rink, Patt Dodds elaborated on notions of accountability. Drawing on Doyle's (1986) theory of classroom ecology, Dodds (2001) identified primary and secondary learning vectors. The primary learning vector she outlined was associated with creating 'learner and learning centered school-based physical education programs for all students' (2001: 167), which, she highlighted, was to be driven by key stakeholders that included policy makers as well as teachers. Below this, secondary learning vectors operated 'on the physical education system, most notably contributing to the marginality of physical education in the school system' (2001: 167).

Dodds argued that accountability must change in order to support all children's rights to learn via physical education and sport. This accountability was first driven by the need to produce more robust data on the effect of our physical activity and sport programmes. This, she argued, was currently hampered by the fact that there are still a number of incompetently delivered programmes. This may have been a result of the second and third accountability vectors, knowledge obsolescence and self-destructive behaviours. In Chapter 4 De Martelaer and colleagues outlined this knowledge obsolescence by drawing on the work of Livingston, noting that there is limited formal training in ethics in teacher and coach education and, consequently, a limited knowledge base among those who are central to fostering ethical practice in physical education and youth sport. Similarly, teachers' and coaches' destructive practices, such as the win-at-all-costs approach, have also served to sour the profession of teaching and coaching in youth sport settings.

While we understand these accountability vectors were pointed very much at physical education, they also resonate in youth sport, and if it were not for these issues of accountability this book would possibly not be needed. We therefore see the need for appropriate legislation that can safeguard children and which requires appropriate qualifications for those who would like to be engaged in youth sport. We also agree that there needs to be a sense of accountability to a set of standards for those involved in youth sport. Harm can be caused to young people not just simply by physical acts, but also socially and emotionally via direct and indirect forms of discrimination, as defined by the UK Equality Act (2010). For example, in Chapter 5 Cobley *et al.* reported that sport-based relative age effects (RAEs) offered an indirect form of discrimination while in Chapter 3 on the Youth Olympic Games Parry and Lucidarme also raised issues of exploitation of athletes, age and fairness, talent identification and early specialization. While we appreciate that some of these issues may be dealt with by policy, some, as we have also noted in this book, necessitate changes to the structures of youth sport, which will be dealt with in the next section.

Structure of youth sport

Siedentop (2001) argued that physical education (and sport) should respond to two agendas: (1) the public health agenda, and (2) the child and youth development agenda. He contended that youth sport has a significant part to play contributing to both these agendas through the development of social capital via youth sports programmes that are inclusive, allow children to make healthy choices, and reinforce responsible behaviour that defines *who* they are and *how* they should live. To specifically meet the needs of the youth development agenda highlighted above, Siedentop suggests that a 'community infrastructure for physically active sports and recreation' (PASR; Siedentop 2001: 193) is needed where 'there is a seamless movement between school, community and private sector providers' (2001: 195). Siedentop went on to report that times of high youth delinquency in the USA, such as the times after school hours, can be times in which communities can focus on using sport as a vehicle for the acquiring of internal goods (such as knowledge of how to act, behave and respond to situations appropriately) with a context-specific pedagogy focused on developing these goods, a point made abundantly clear in Chapter 12 by Wright *et al.*

The suggestions by Siedentop (2001) echo the sentiments of Twietmeyer (2007) who, drawing on the work of Timothy Fort, stated that mediating institutions or communities were ones where internal goods were promoted via interactions from *both* within and outside the specific community. This permits the development of connections between an individual's self-interest to the goods of others, thus promoting social, moral and ethical development, and mediating between smaller communities (such as a school physical education lesson) and the larger world (of global professional sport).

Notwithstanding the sociological and economic challenges of Siedentop's suggested PASR model, a chapter in the *Sport Education: Research-based Practice* text by Penney and Clarke (2005) presented an account of Lister's groundbreaking work in Australia where teachers collaborated with development officers to foster strong school–community links. The young cricketers involved stated that they would like to take up roles other than performer, such as officiating, coaching, administrative duties and publicity roles. What is more, many rejected the notions of full-sided games in preference for modified smaller-sided versions of the game such as those used in Teaching Games for Understanding and in Game Sense (see Chapter 6). Parry and Lucidarme's chapter on the Youth Olympic Games gave us very specific example of FIBA33, a modified three-on-three form of basketball played on a half-court with one basket and 5-minute play periods, which drew spectators to its intense and dramatic format and was certainly a more developmentally appropriate game form than the full version of basketball.

Moreover, the observations by Lister bring to the fore the critical reflection needed on current institutionalized practices in youth sport. Given the more contemporary view of children in society, children should be treated as *active agents* and feel empowered to have a voice and role in shaping youth sport in ways that go beyond tokenistic involvement (Alexander 2001), and where their voices and presence are *embedded in* the culture and development of youth sport. Listening to young people's voices and involving them in decision-making is therefore crucial not only to the sustainable practice of sport but also to the social, moral and ethical development of children (see a recent text on *Young People's Voices in Physical Education and Youth Sport* by O'Sullivan and MacPhail 2010).

In this way, we may see some of the developments in community youth sport that pedagogical models such as Sport Education have brought to physical education, some of which were outlined by Harvey *et al.* and reiterated in other chapters such as Chapter 5 by Cobley *et al.* These suggestions included: bonus points for players' rotations so as to encourage equal playing time, sports panels for youth leagues being comprised of players (possibly alongside adults), negotiations of modified playing rules before contests, bonus points and awards for incidents of fair play, young officials and coaches, secondary school sports panels running events in local elementary 'feeder schools' along the lines of 'Step-Into-Sport' (a UK-based programme; Quill and Clarke 2005), etc. As Cobley *et al.* highlighted, children could gain much from these experiences in terms of developing self-confidence and self-determination compared to adult forms of the game, which additionally over-emphasize winning. The ideas suggested above and by many authors in this book will seek to challenge the current 'status quo' of youth sport and aid in the development of participation and elite performance, a concern which was additionally raised in the chapter by Cobley *et al.*

A very pressing concern for those in youth sport is, therefore, how to enact this change in culture and the current structure of sport, one that is principally predetermined by adults, in order to develop this inclusive culture. Certainly, formal education needs to play its part. What is more, listening to the wants and needs of young people is required, as are clear and articulate policies laid out by governing bodies of sport, with the associated accountability of those involved within these governing bodies to enact these planned changes. Research will also play its part in allowing these young people a voice in how specifically structures may change to ensure that youth sport remains inclusive. The judicious use of awards, in particular those based on the Olympic movement and Pierre de Coubertin's original notions of sports-personship, can offer inclusive experiences of sport to young people (see Chapter 7 by Harvey *et al.*) and are part of those involved in youth sport rethinking their pedagogical approach and broadening their definition of pedagogy, to which we now turn.

Pedagogy and pedagogical approaches

This book has shown the value of youth sport practitioners focusing on elements of ethical development through their pedagogical approach. This necessitates that this pedagogical approach is focused on a broader definition of pedagogy that includes social, moral and ethical development (see Tinning 2008). For example, we have seen from Light (and others such as De Martelaer *et al.*, and Kerr and Stirling in Chapters 4 and 2, respectively) that humanistic athlete-centred pedagogical approaches, such as Game Sense, afford the opportunity to reposition the coach as a facilitator of learning. In doing so, they not only structure the environment for learning technical and tactical skills, but for the players to learn about expression, experimentation and creativity. They also make coaching a more ethical practice by providing equality of opportunity for learning and enjoyment while redressing unequal power relations between coach and players.

We have also seen how teachers/coaches may construct a learning environment that is autonomy supportive (see Chapter 4 by De Martelaer *et al.*), so that young people can actively take responsibility for their own behaviours rather than having to rely on a teacher/coach. These authors also showed how providing a high degree of choice and freedom (high autonomy-support) without communicating any clear guidelines or expectations for behaviour (low behaviour control) may allow practitioners to enhance children's cognitive and emotional growth within sport as they learn for themselves (with support of the teacher/coach/leader) how to recognize and respond to a wide variety of complex situations.

This collection has also demonstrated that those involved in teaching/coaching youth sport need to possess a sound understanding of children and child development so that they understand *who* they are coaching as well as *how* to coach them and *what* content to use (Fernández-Balboa 2011). Teacher and coach education programmes therefore need to focus on producing what Westcombe-Down (2009: 20), as cited by Fitzgerald in Chapter 13, refers to as a 'pedagogically fit' teacher, one who 'establishes and maintains a positive, inclusive and safe learning environment', recognizes that one size does not fit all and would also be attentive to the need to promote an ethical education for those who they teach/coach. As Fitzgerald reminded us, by using the work of Fernández-Balboa, teachers and coaches can then reflect on their pedagogical performance using his criteria (Fernández-Balboa 2011: 51) to see if they are 'walking the talk of ethics in the practice of education', a task which is not easy, but is one that 'all educators should be working towards if they are truly concerned with including *all* young people in (physical) education and youth sport' (Fitzgerald, Chapter 13).

A further result in developing a broader definition of pedagogy that includes social, moral and ethical development is that those involved in youth sport can engage young people in dialogue in order to deconstruct critical issues through the identification of 'teachable moments', a point most clearly articulated by both Barker *et al.* and Kentel in Chapters 11 and 9, respectively. Using a social constructionist lens on ethics Barker *et al.* showed us how teachers and coaches could avoid a universal understanding of ethics and begin to understand how context shapes ethical behaviour. The focus of the 'teachable moment' using this theoretical lens was the dialogue and debate that ensued when deconstructing and reconstructing the event in order to understand how circumstances may be changed to prevent a recurrence of a particular incident. Similarly, in citing the work of Freire (1998) and Heidegger (1962), Kentel (Chapter 9) outlined how engaging youth in dialogue was critical for getting them to address the complex issues and power structures facing them and others in order to uncover the truth. Wright *et al.* (Chapter 12) noted that promoting personal and social responsibility through physical activity, and focusing on philosophical discussion and critical thinking were strategies for engaging urban youth in their own holistic development. They sum up what they feel teaching ethics to young people should entail:

> Teaching ethics to youth, through sport or any other pedagogical means, is not a matter of passing on ethical principles or specific ethical rules for them to follow. Such principles and rules will no doubt differ from community to community. Nor is it a matter of teaching them the theories offered by philosophers past and present. Rather, it involves exercising their rational capacities to develop the critical thinking skills they need to make judgements about how to live well and how to treat themselves and others with respect.
>
> (Wright *et al.*)

Summary

In Chapter 8 Van Veldhoven quite clearly articulates the need for policies to be supported by appropriate sport structures and pedagogies that are employed by those who have leadership roles in the youth sport domain. We have seen in this book, for example, how redressing an *indirect* form of discrimination within the bounds of the UK Equality Act (2010), such as sport-based RAEs, could generate substantial social, health and economic dimensions in the long term for many young people. Certainly, it is not simply the sole responsibility of those involved at the micro levels of youth sport (for example, teachers and coaches) to generate a call to action from the macro (such as the government) and meso (for example, national and/or international governing bodies of sport) levels or vice versa. It is a collective responsibility of all these levels to generate both bottom-up and top-down approaches to help sustain sport as a practice. For example, youth sports practitioners need to be 'walking the talk of ethics in the practice of education' (Fernández-Balboa 2011: 51) and engage youth in critical thinking so they can live well and treat others with integrity, dignity and respect. Meanwhile, national and/or international governing bodies of sport need to investigate ways to develop and implement community-based sport projects which provide opportunities for young people to gain both internal and external goods, and which adhere to an ethical framework such as the Panathlon Declaration of Ethics in Youth Sport (Panathlon International 2004) and prevent indirect discrimination, such as sport-based RAEs. Finally, government legislators need to ensure that appropriate policies are in place to safeguard and protect children as they engage in sport so that they are not subjected to abuse and other direct forms of discrimination to guarantee that youth sport plays a positive part in the physical, social, moral and ethical growth of young people across the globe.

References

Alexander, T. (2001) *Citizenship in Schools: A Practical Guide to Education for Citizenship and Personal Development*. London: Campaign for Learning.

Dodds, P. (2001) 'Accountability and politics linked through assessment: Negotiating a place at the tables of power for physical education in the 21st century', in P. Ward and P. Doubtis (eds) *Physical Education in the 21st Century*. Nebraska: University of Nebraska-Lincoln, pp. 166–75.

Doyle, W. (1986) 'Classroom organization and management', in M. C. Whitrock (ed.) *Handbook of Research on Teaching*. New York: Macmillan, pp. 392–431.

Fernández-Balboa, J. (2011) 'Sailing towards "Happycity": Ethics plus education', in J. A. Kentel (ed.) *Educating the Young: The Ethics of Care*. Oxford: Peter Lang, pp. 39–60.

Freire, P. (1998) *Pedagogy of Freedom: Ethics, Democracy, and Civic Courage*. Lanham, MD: Rowman and Littlefield.

Heidegger, M. (1962) *Being and Time*, trans. J. Macquarie and E. Robinson. New York: Harper and Row.

O'Sullivan, M. and MacPhail, A. (eds) (2010) *Young People's Voices in Physical Education and Youth Sport*. London: Routledge.

Panathlon International (2004) Declaration on Ethics in Youth Sport. Available at: http://www.panathlon.net (accessed 23 July 2011).

Penney, D. and Clarke, G. (2005) 'Sport Education and lifelong learning', in D. Penney, G. Clarke, M. Quill and G. Kinchin (eds) *Sport Education: Research-based Practice*. London: Routledge, pp. 99–108.

Quill, M. and Clarke, G. (2005) 'Sport Education in Year 8 games', in D. Penney, G. Clarke, M. Quill and G. Kinchin (eds) *Sport Education: Research-based Practice*. London: Routledge, pp. 140–64.

Siedentop, D. (2001) 'To inform their discretion', in P. Ward and P. Doubtis (eds) *Physical Education in the 21st Century*. Nebraska: University of Nebraska-Lincoln, pp. 187–98.

Siedentop, D., Hastie, P. A. and van der Mars, H. (2004) *Complete Guide to Sport Education*. Champaign, IL: Human Kinetics.

Tinning, R. (2008) 'Pedagogy, sport pedagogy, and the field of kinesiology', *Quest*, 60: 405–24.

Twietmeyer, G. (2007) 'Suffering play: Can the time spent on play and games be justified in a suffering world?', *Quest*, 59: 201–11.

UK Equality Act (2010) Available at: http://www.legislation.gov.uk/ukpga/2010/15/contents (accessed 30 January 2012).

Westcombe-Down, D. (2009) 'Pedagogical fitness, teacher quality', *Professional Educator*, 8(1): 18–21.

Index